Kidnapped

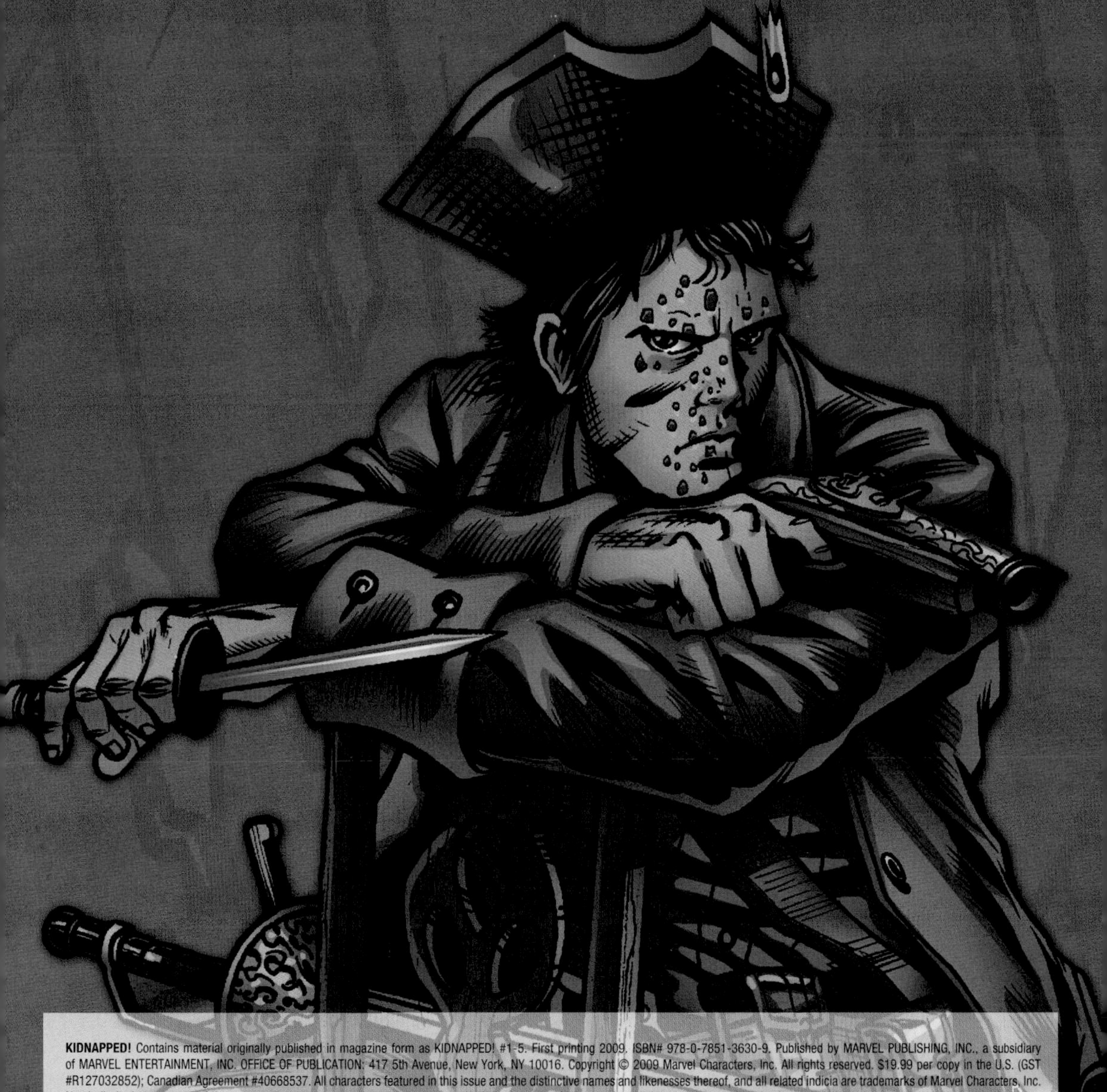

KIDNAPPED! Contains material originally published in magazine form as KIDNAPPED! #1-5. First printing 2009. ISBN# 978-0-7851-3630-9. Published by MARVEL PUBLISHING, INC., a subsidiary of MARVEL ENTERTAINMENT, INC. OFFICE OF PUBLICATION: 417 5th Avenue, New York, NY 10016. $19.99 per copy in the U.S. (GST #R127032852); Canadian Agreement #40668537. **Printed in the U.S.A.** ALAN FINE, CEO Marvel Publishing Division and EVP & CMO Marvel Characters B.V.; DAN BUCKLEY, President of Publishing - Print & Digital Media; JIM SOKOLOWSKI, Chief Operating Officer; DAVID GABRIEL, SVP of Publishing Sales & Circulation; DAVID BOGART, SVP of Business Affairs & Talent Management; MICHAEL PASCIULLO, VP Merchandising & Communications; JIM O'KEEFE, VP of Operations & Logistics; DAN CARR, Executive Director of Publishing Technology; JUSTIN F. GABRIE, Director of Publishing & Editorial Operations; SUSAN CRESPI, Editorial Operations Manager; ALEX MORALES, Publishing Operations Manager; STAN LEE, Chairman Emeritus. For information regarding advertising in Marvel Comics or on Marvel.com, please contact Mitch Dane, Advertising Director, at mdane@marvel.com. For Marvel subscription inquiries, please call 800-217-9158.

10 9 8 7 6 5 4 3 2 1

Kidnapped

Adapted from the novel by
ROBERT LOUIS STEVENSON

Cover Artists: GERALD PAREL & DENNIS CALERO

Assistant Editors: NATHAN COSBY, LAUREN SANKOVITCH
& LAUREN HENRY

Editor: RALPH MACCHIO

SPECIAL THANKS TO CHRIS ALLO, JEFF SUTER, JIM NAUSEDAS & RICH GINTER

Collection Editor: MARK D. BEAZLEY
Assistant Editors: JOHN DENNING & CORY LEVINE
Editor, Special Projects: JENNIFER GRÜNWALD
Senior Editor, Special Projects: JEFF YOUNGQUIST
Senior Vice President of Marketing & Sales: DAVID GABRIEL
Book Designer: SPRING HOTELING

Editor in Chief: JOE QUESADA
Publisher: DAN BUCKLEY
Executive Producer: ALAN FINE

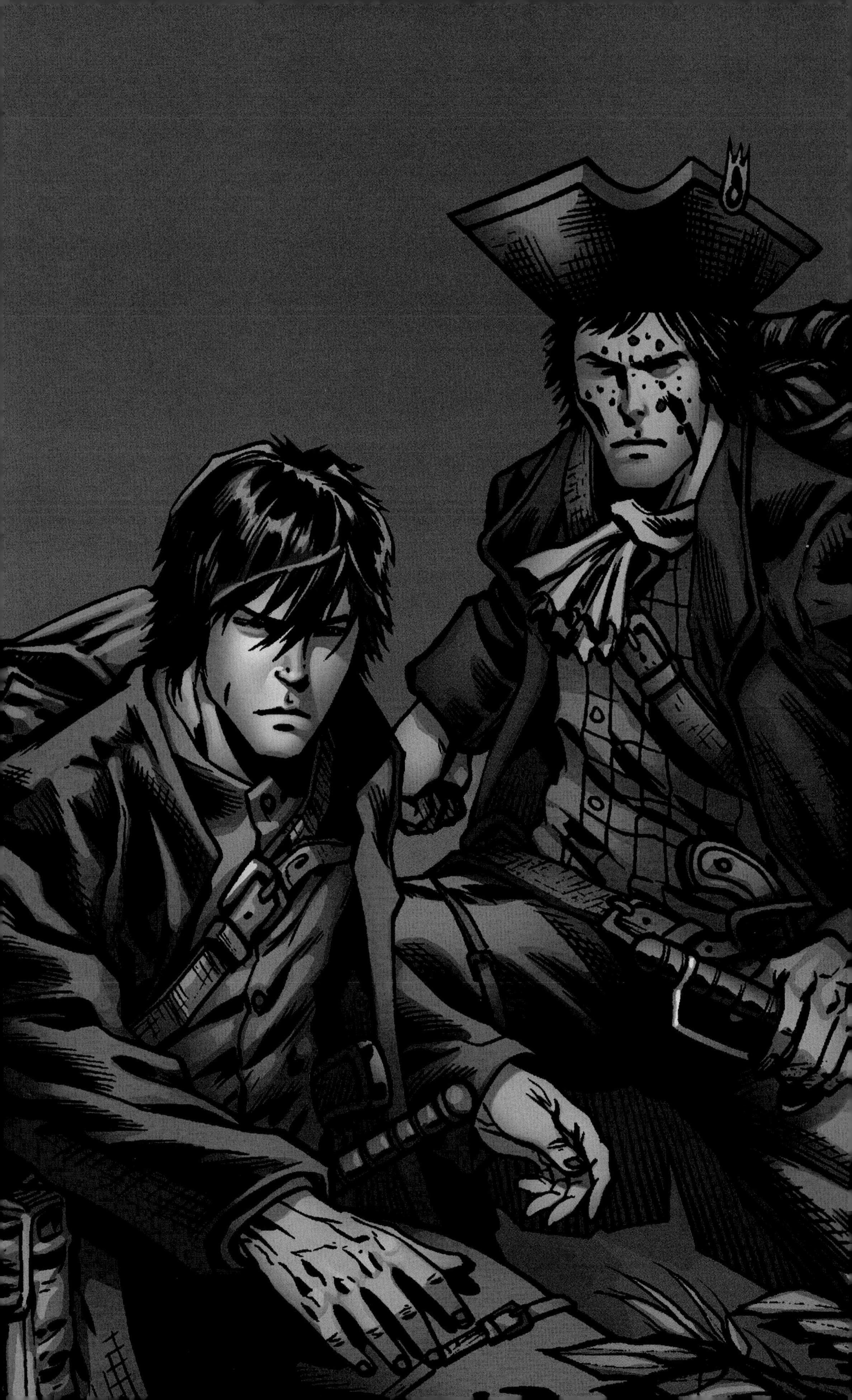

Kidnapped

A Personal Introduction
by Roy Thomas

1887.

That's a long time ago for a novel to have been written, yet still be appreciated today, more than 120 years later. Appreciated not just by literature professors and high school teachers and librarians, either, but by readers young and old, male and female, in whom it has inspired adaptations in other fields, such as films and graphic novel adaptations.

Yet that's precisely what Robert Louis Stevenson's *Kidnapped* has achieved.

In some ways, this tale has a lot in common with his even more famous *Treasure Island,* which I was pleased to adapt for the *Marvel Illustrated* series with artist Mario Gully, who's also drawn this graphic novel. Again there's a young boy as the hero… a rousing adventure both at sea and traipsing over hill and dale… a dastardly villain or two.

This time, though, Stevenson chose perhaps to adhere a bit more to that old adage (which I presume was known even in the late 19th century) of "Write what you know." So, rather than whisk David Balfour away to a non-existent Treasure Island, as he had Jim Hawkins and his associates, the author sent this (slightly older) lad on an exciting voyage from Scotland to… Scotland.

David's adventures begin soon after he leaves his small hometown of Essendean, going on foot to seek out a relative upon the death of his father. Soon he is at sea, quite literally—and kidnapped, as the title goes, in the bargain—winding up on a different wild Scottish coast and trying to make his way back to Queensferry, where he was (as we would say) "shanghaied." Ah, but it's what happens along the way that makes the story.

This time, as opposed to the fanciful total fiction of *Treasure Island,* Stevenson shoehorned a considerable amount of true history into his storytelling. And, because truth and fiction are so inextricably intermingled in *Kidnapped,* it may help to know some facts with which Stevenson and his English and Scottish readers in 1887 would have been far more familiar than would be most readers today.

In the 18th century, there was a fierce dispute in the British Isles over who should be king. Many Scots remembered the not-so-long-ago day when Scotland had been a separate country, before it was conquered by England and absorbed into a greater kingdom. They wanted to seat James Edward, a Scotsman (of the "house" called Stuart), on the throne, in place of King George, whose father had been German. This led to a rebellion in 1715, which was bloodily suppressed. Then, in 1745, came a second revolt, the so-called "Jacobite uprising – "Jacobus" being the Latin form of the name "James." The Jacobite forces whose candidate for kingship was James' grandson "Bonnie Prince Charlie," was put down violently by the English. Many Scottish clan leaders were killed, imprisoned, or fled to exile in France.

Along with this background, which underpins the events of this novel (which occur in the year 1752), the colorful rogue named Alan Breck Stewart is also a very real historical personage.

As related in the course of the story by Alan (who bore the marks of a youthful bout of smallpox on his face), he had enlisted in the British Army in 1745 and had taken part in the Battle of Prestonpans, amid the Jacobite uprising, Afterwards, he'd changed sides and become an intense Jacobite. After the revolt was put down, he joined a Scottish force that was part of the army of France (which was always, in those days, a deadly enemy of England

and all things English)… and he secretly sailed back to Scotland from time to time to collect "rents" for the defeated Highlands leaders now living in France. Even exiles living abroad need money to get on, after all.

It's during one such mission that Alan's boat is rammed by the *Covenant,* the very ship onto which young David Balfour has been abducted. It's at this point that history and fiction become enmeshed.

For the English want money ("rent") from the Scots, too. The most famous episode in Alan Breck Stewart's life is the murder of Colin Roy Campbell—the so-called "Red Fox"— who was the Royal agent in charge of collecting that money from the Ardshiel Stewarts, clan leaders who were blood-kin of Alan's. Based on circumstantial evidence, Alan was sought for the crime; soon afterward, he was even given a trial *in absentia,* declared guilty, and sentenced to death. (As in Stevenson's novel, his kinsman James of the Glen was executed as an alleged accessory to the murder.)

What happened to Alan Breck Stewart after he took it on the lam under sentence of death is unknown. Did he return to France and live out his life there? According to one account, he fought against the English in America during what the Colonies called the French and Indian War. But this cannot be proved, so Robert Louis Stevenson was free to weave his own tapestry of Alan's life following the so-called "Appin Murder."

And weave it he did, as Alan—with David, of course—wanders over much of the Highlands, evading capture and meeting such colorful characters as Robin Oig, a son of the another historical Scottish rebel, the famous Rob Roy. Stevenson naturally involves Alan in the final resolution of young David's difficulties with his uncle Ebenezer and—well, read the following 110 pages to see how it all comes out.

For, like the old saying goes, "Getting there is half the fun."

Or, in the case of Stevenson's classic novel, considerably *more* than half of it.

For myself, the main problem in working on this adaptation with editors Ralph Macchio, Lauren Sankovitch, and Lauren Henry and artists Mario Gully and Jason Martin was to try to keep the story flowing and not get bogged down relating backstory. At the same time, without some knowledge of the factual background, the tale would be nothing but a lot of running around, from here to there and back again, for no real reason. So we tried to embed bits of the information in the narration (just as Stevenson had done), without getting in the way of the excitement and the adventure.

Because, make no mistake about it, this story *is* an exciting adventure.

120 years of satisfied readers can't be wrong!

Roy

Roy Thomas has been a writer and often editor in the comic book field since 1965, when he became "staff writer" and editorial assistant to Stan Lee early in the Marvel Age of Comics. He served as Marvel's editor-in-chief from 1972-74, and has written over the years for Marvel, DC, and other companies—but above all for Marvel, where he is best known for his work on such titles as The Avengers, The X-Men, Conan the Barbarian, The Invaders, *et al. Besides currently adapting some of the classics in the* Marvel Illustrated *series, he also edits the comics-history magazine* Alter Ego.

Kidnapped

PREFACE

The so-called Jacobite Revolution in Scotland was an attempt by northern clans to restore a Scottish ruler—a member of the Stuart family—to the throne of Great Britain after three decades of rule by other houses. They felt that King George I, born in Hanover (Germany), had no legitimate claim to the crown. Their revolt in 1714-15 had failed. In 1745 they rebelled again, this time to make their own "Bonnie Prince Charlie" the monarch of the British Isles, but their uprising was harshly put down.

Half a dozen years later, the fires of resentment still smoldered in the Highlands… the hatred of being ruled by a second King George, from far-off London, had not been abated by time… and a sixteen-year-old Scottish lad was about to be swept into the maelstrom of violent events, as related by Robert Louis Stevenson, author of the immortal *Treasure Island*…

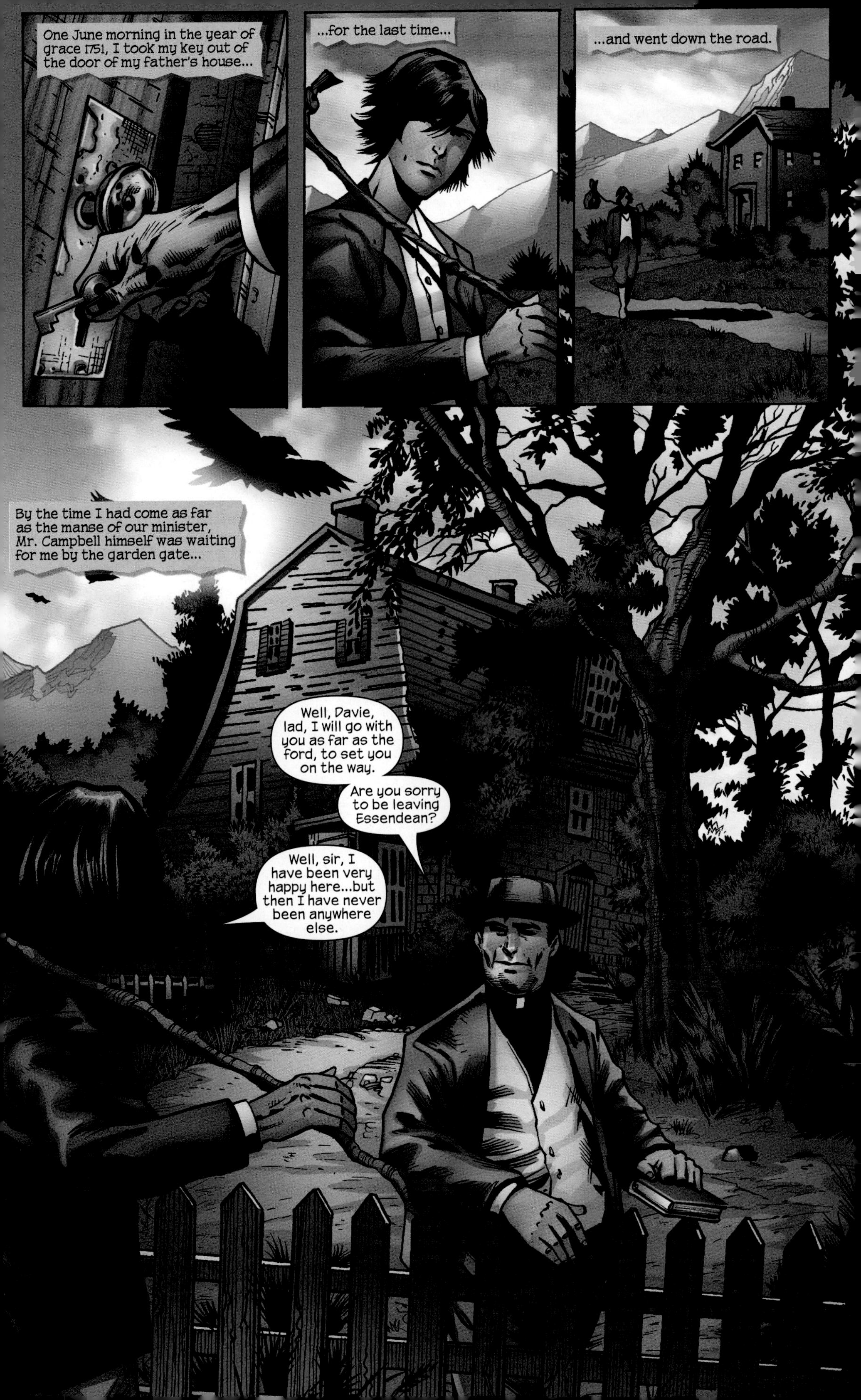
One June morning in the year of grace 1751, I took my key out of the door of my father's house...
...for the last time...
...and went down the road.
By the time I had come as far as the manse of our minister, Mr. Campbell himself was waiting for me by the garden gate...
Well, Davie, lad, I will go with you as far as the ford, to set you on the way.
Are you sorry to be leaving Essendean?
Well, sir, I have been very happy here...but then I have never been anywhere else.

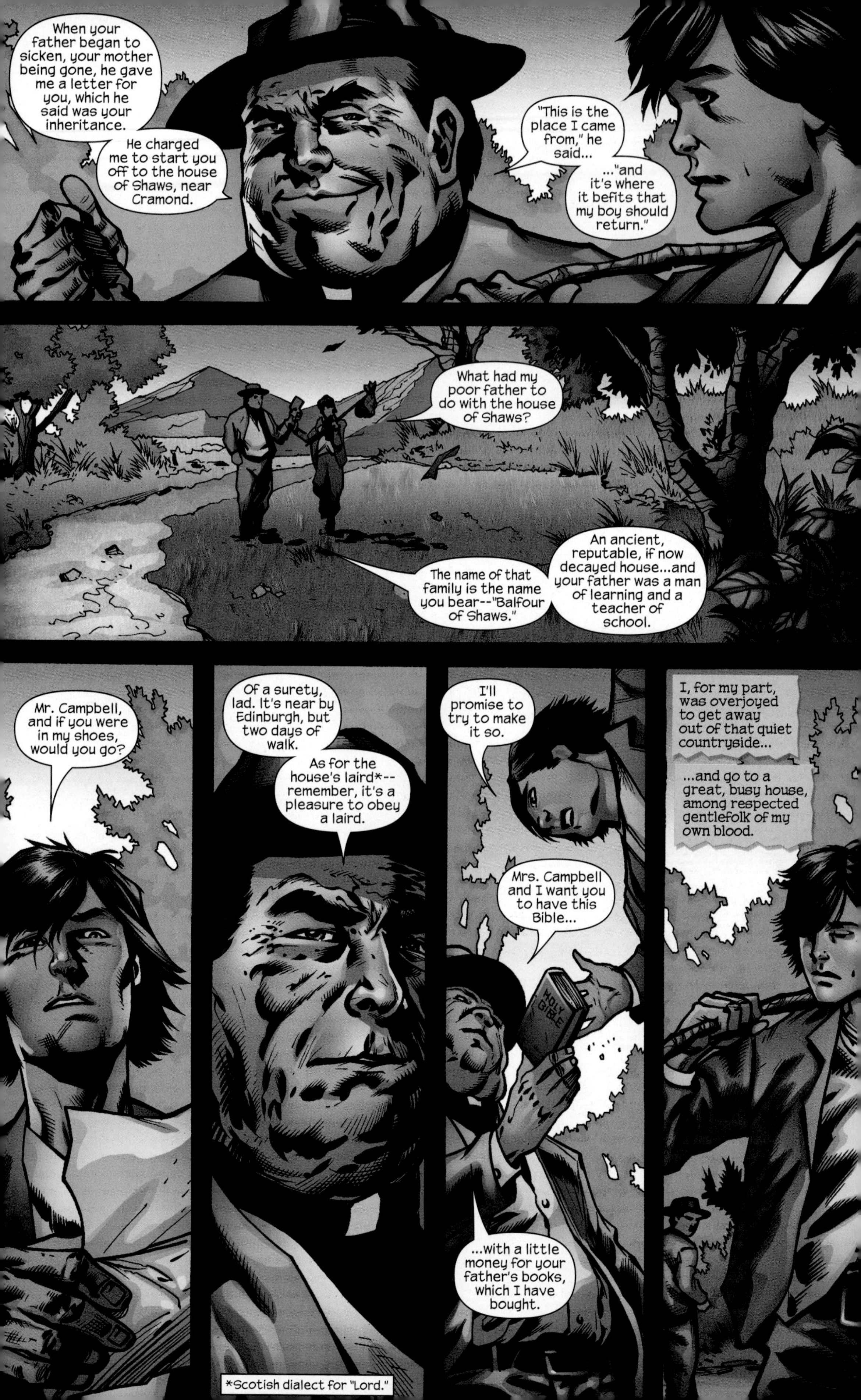
When your father began to sicken, your mother being gone, he gave me a letter for you, which he said was your inheritance.
He charged me to start you off to the house of Shaws, near Cramond.
"This is the place I came from," he said...
..."and it's where it befits that my boy should return."
What had my poor father to do with the house of Shaws?
The name of that family is the name you bear--"Balfour of Shaws."
An ancient, reputable, if now decayed house...and your father was a man of learning and a teacher of school.
Mr. Campbell, and if you were in my shoes, would you go?
Of a surety, lad. It's near by Edinburgh, but two days of walk.
As for the house's laird*--remember, it's a pleasure to obey a laird.
I'll promise to try to make it so.
Mrs. Campbell and I want you to have this Bible...
HOLY BIBLE
...with a little money for your father's books, which I have bought.
I, for my part, was overjoyed to get away out of that quiet countryside...
...and go to a great, busy house, among respected gentlefolk of my own blood.
*Scotish dialect for "Lord."

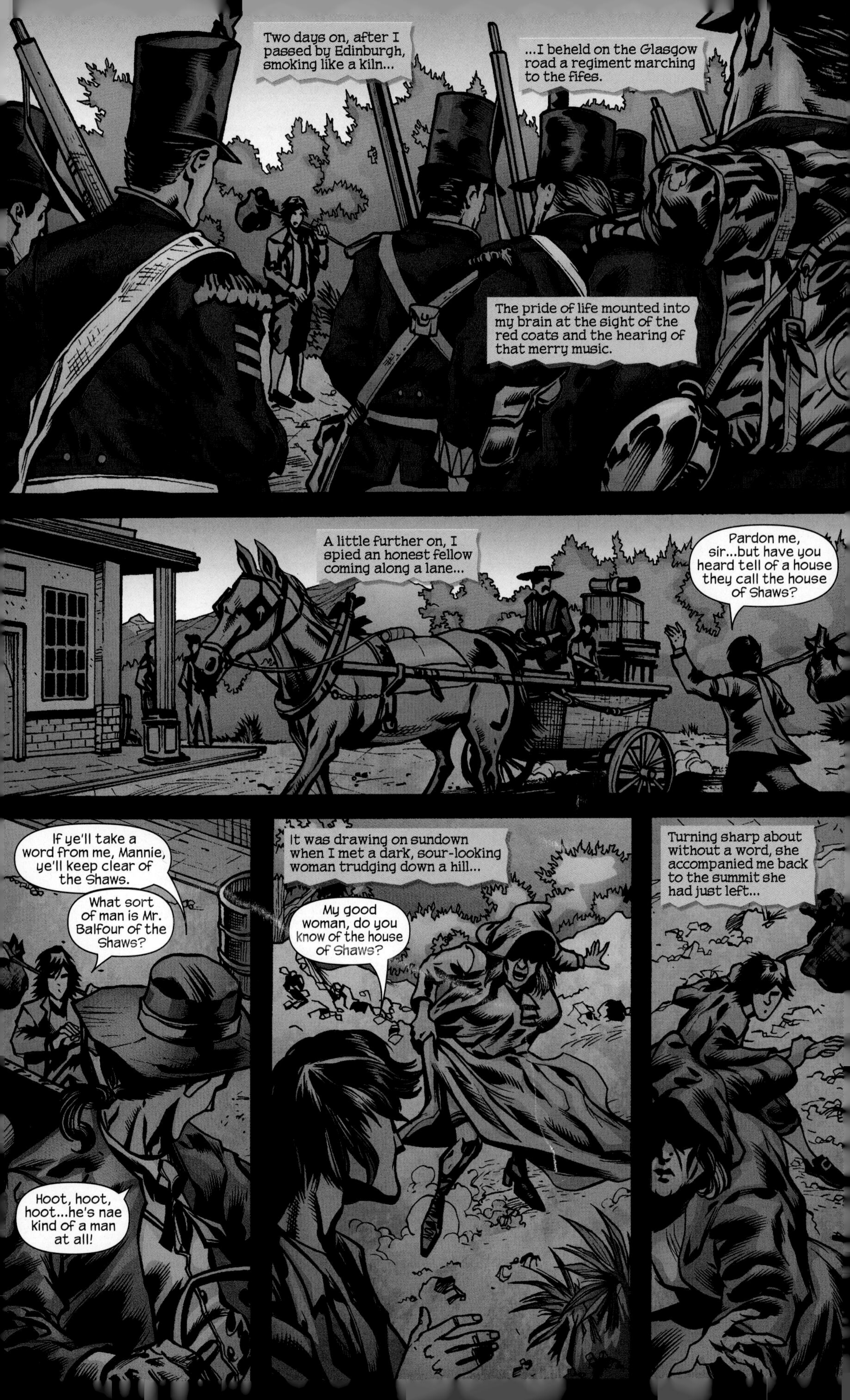
Two days on, after I passed by Edinburgh, smoking like a kiln...
...I beheld on the Glasgow road a regiment marching to the fifes.
The pride of life mounted into my brain at the sight of the red coats and the hearing of that merry music.
A little further on, I spied an honest fellow coming along a lane...
Pardon me, sir...but have you heard tell of a house they call the house of Shaws?
If ye'll take a word from me, Mannie, ye'll keep clear of the Shaws.
What sort of man is Mr. Balfour of the Shaws?
Hoot, hoot, hoot...he's nae kind of a man at all!
It was drawing on sundown when I met a dark, sour-looking woman trudging down a hill...
My good woman, do you know of the house of Shaws?
Turning sharp about without a word, she accompanied me back to the summit she had just left...

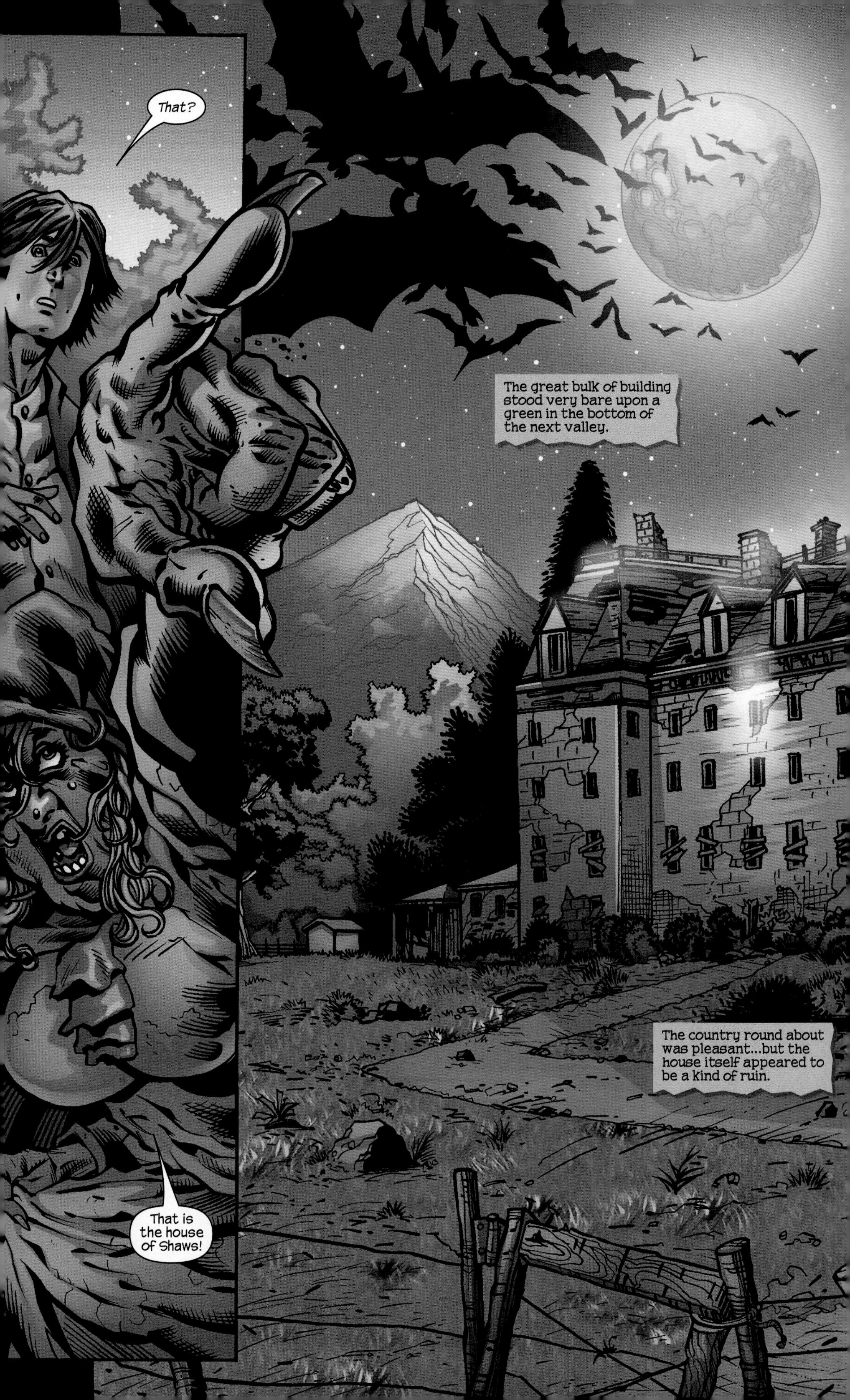
That?
The great bulk of building stood very bare upon a green in the bottom of the next valley.
The country round about was pleasant...but the house itself appeared to be a kind of ruin.
That is the house of Shaws!

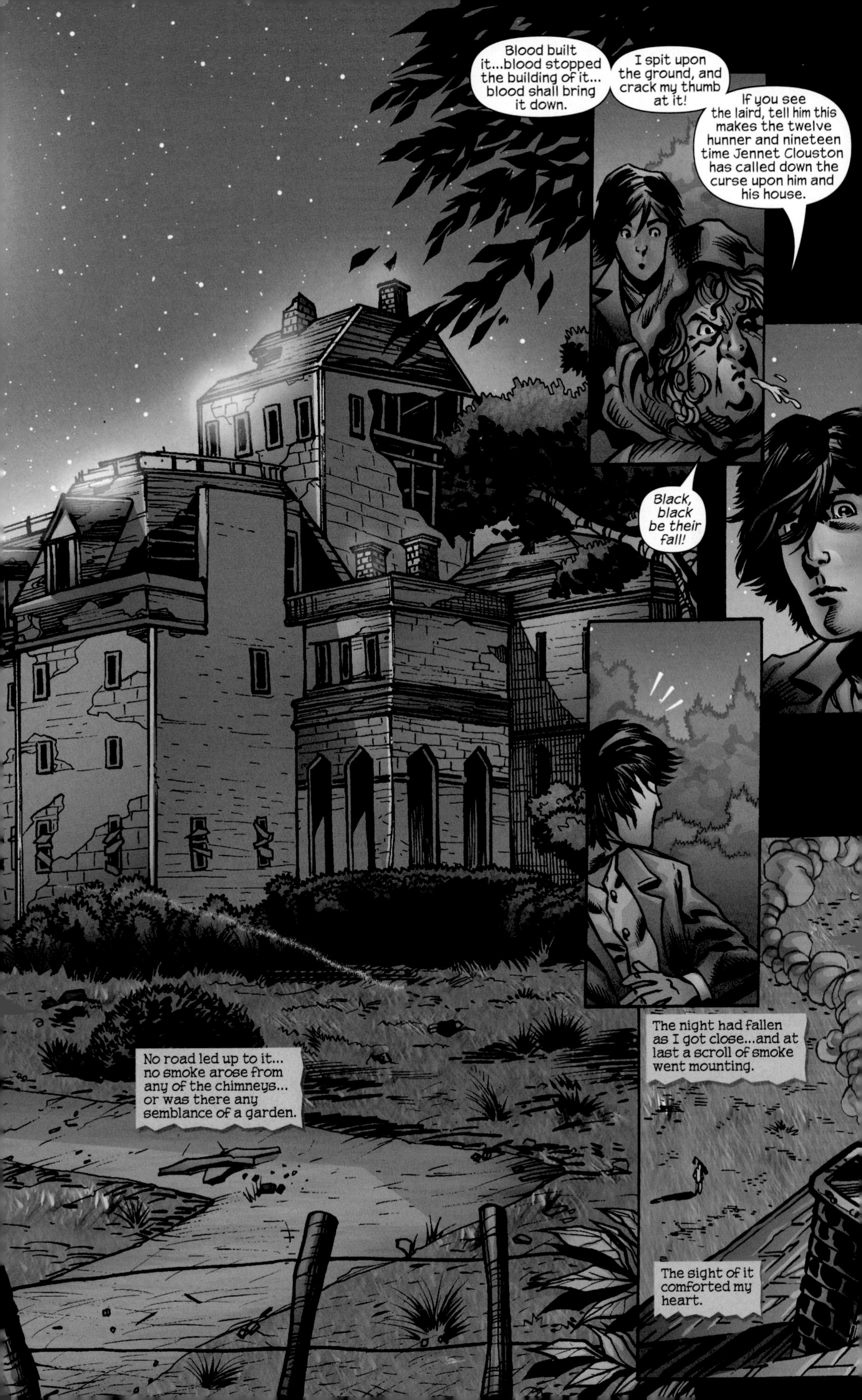
Blood built it...blood stopped the building of it... blood shall bring it down.
I spit upon the ground, and crack my thumb at it!
If you see the laird, tell him this makes the twelve hunner and nineteen time Jennet Clouston has called down the curse upon him and his house.
Black, black be their fall!
No road led up to it... no smoke arose from any of the chimneys... or was there any semblance of a garden.
The night had fallen as I got close...and at last a scroll of smoke went mounting.
The sight of it comforted my heart.

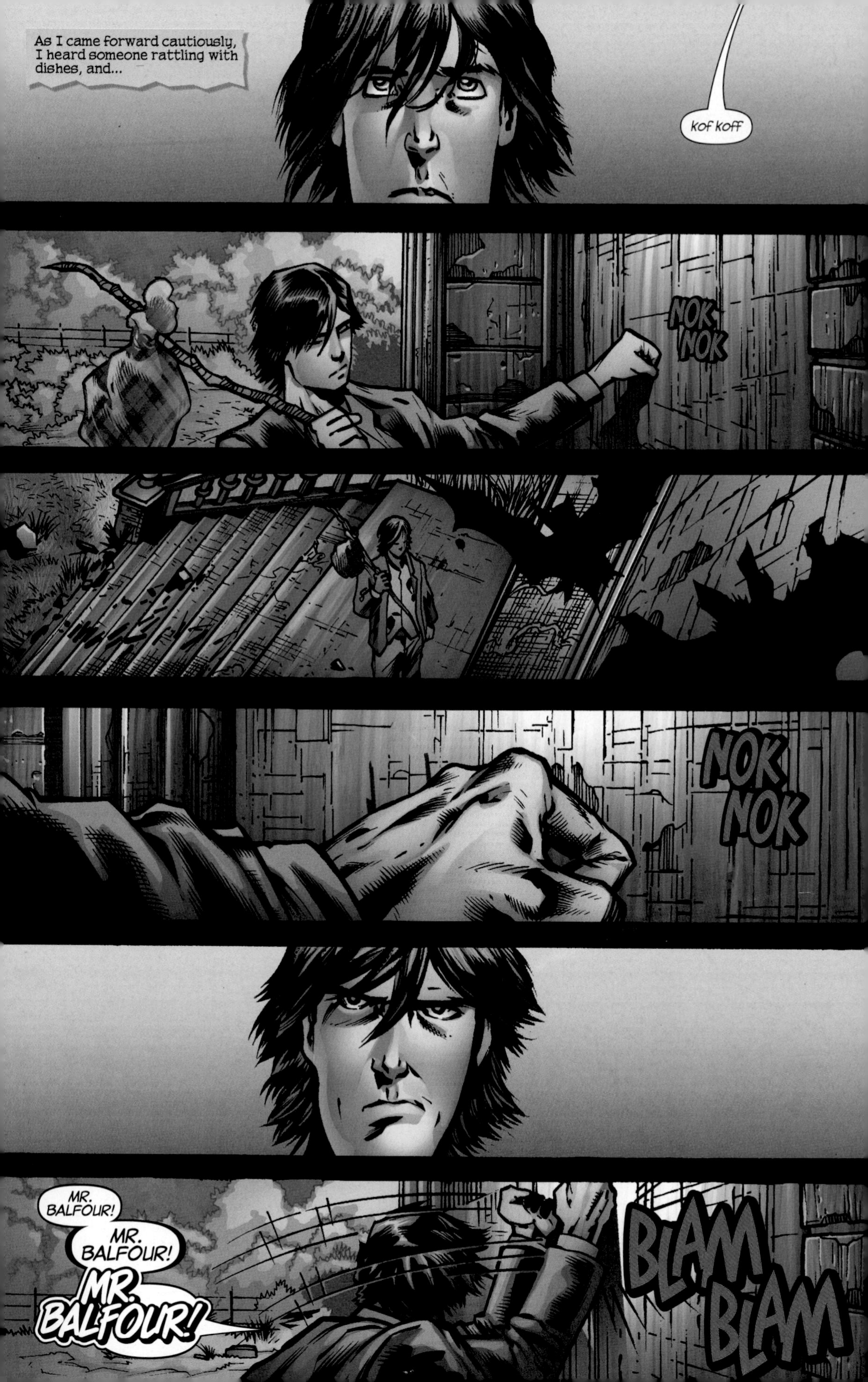

As I came forward cautiously, I heard someone rattling with dishes, and...
kof koff
NOK NOK
NOK NOK
MR. BALFOUR!
MR. BALFOUR!
MR. BALFOUR!
BLAM BLAM

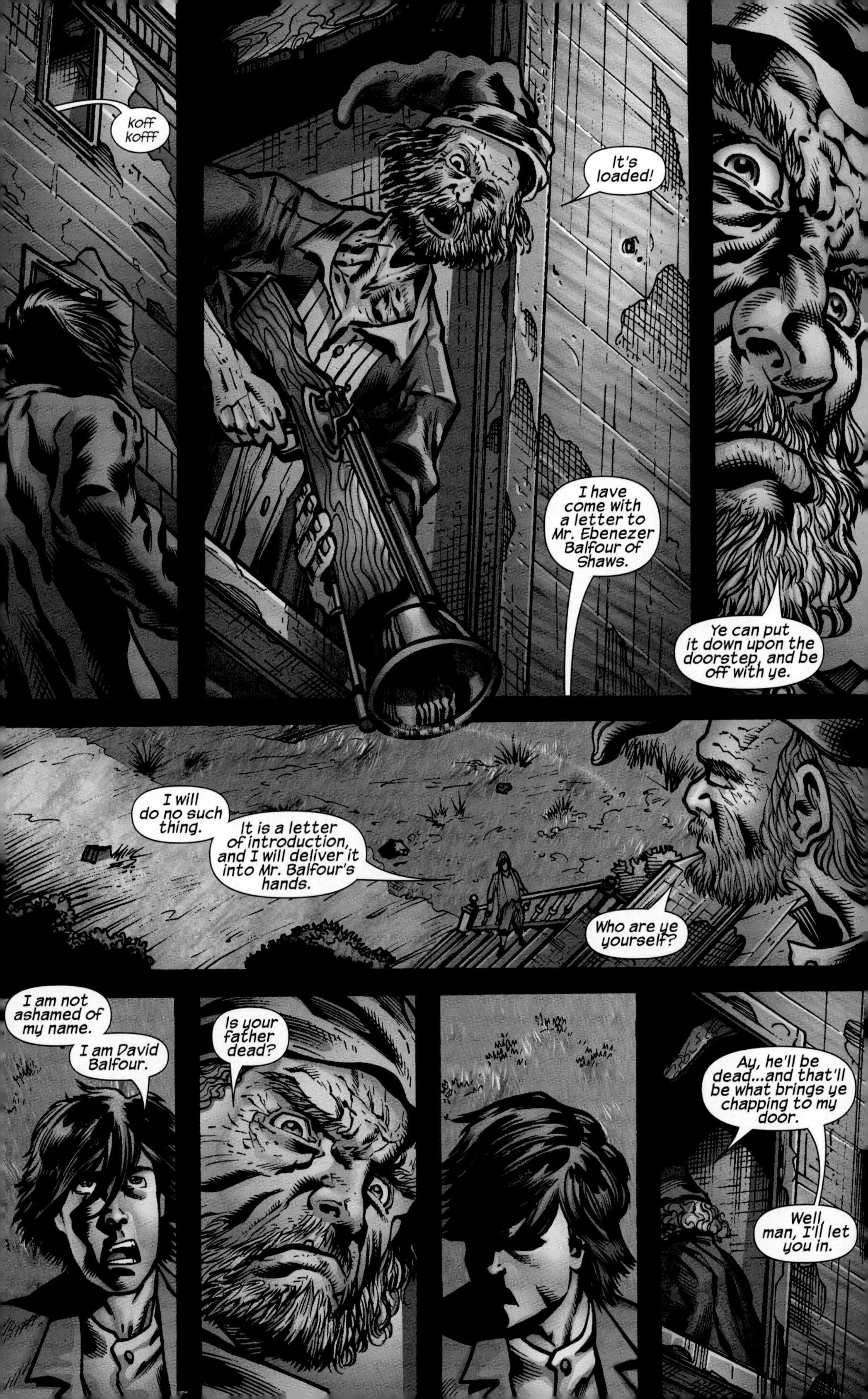
KOFF KOFFF
It's loaded!
I have come with a letter to Mr. Ebenezer Balfour of Shaws.
Ye can put it down upon the doorstep, and be off with ye.
I will do no such thing.
It is a letter of introduction, and I will deliver it into Mr. Balfour's hands.
Who are ye yourself?
I am not ashamed of my name.
I am David Balfour.
Is your father dead?
Ay, he'll be dead...and that'll be what brings ye chapping to my door.
Well, man, I'll let you in.

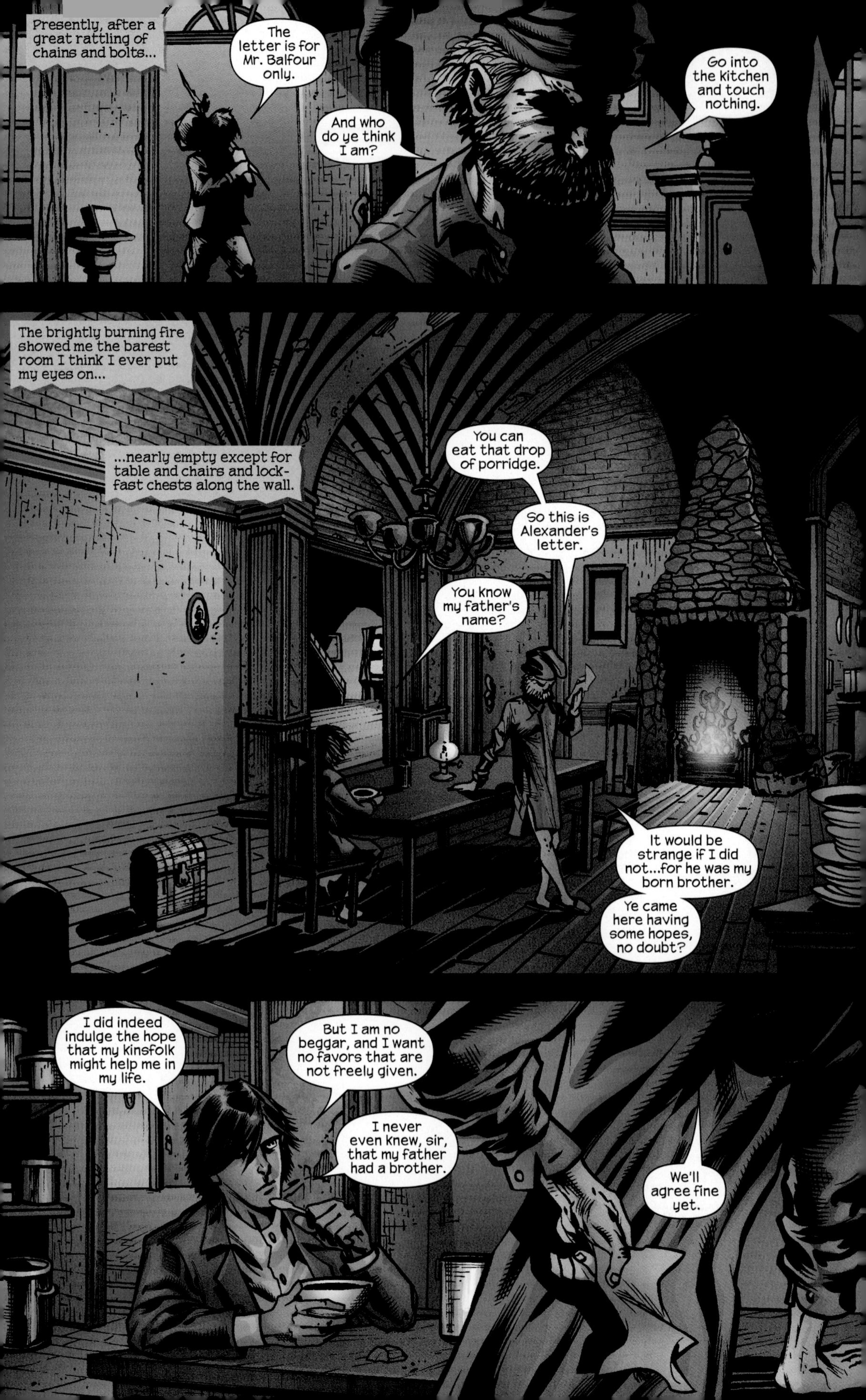
Presently, after a great rattling of chains and bolts...
The letter is for Mr. Balfour only.
And who do ye think I am?
Go into the kitchen and touch nothing.
The brightly burning fire showed me the barest room I think I ever put my eyes on...
...nearly empty except for table and chairs and lock-fast chests along the wall.
You can eat that drop of porridge.
So this is Alexander's letter.
You know my father's name?
It would be strange if I did not...for he was my born brother.
Ye came here having some hopes, no doubt?
I did indeed indulge the hope that my kinsfolk might help me in my life.
But I am no beggar, and I want no favors that are not freely given.
I never even knew, sir, that my father had a brother.
We'll agree fine yet.

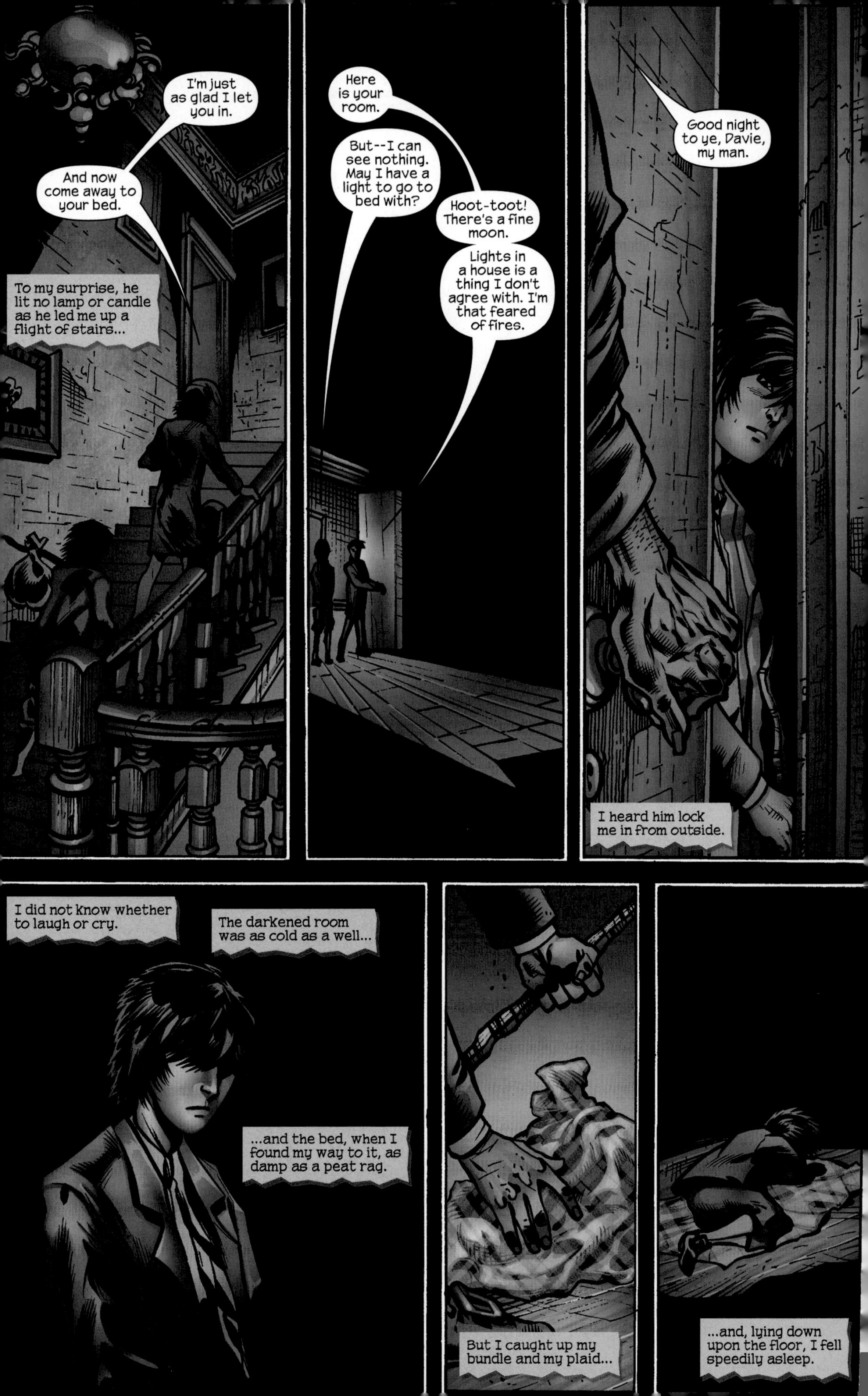
I'm just as glad I let you in.
And now come away to your bed.
To my surprise, he lit no lamp or candle as he led me up a flight of stairs...
Here is your room.
But--I can see nothing. May I have a light to go to bed with?
Hoot-toot! There's a fine moon.
Lights in a house is a thing I don't agree with. I'm that feared of fires.
Good night to ye, Davie, my man.
I heard him lock me in from outside.
I did not know whether to laugh or cry.
The darkened room was as cold as a well...
...and the bed, when I found my way to it, as damp as a peat rag.
But I caught up my bundle and my plaid...
...and, lying down upon the floor, I fell speedily asleep.

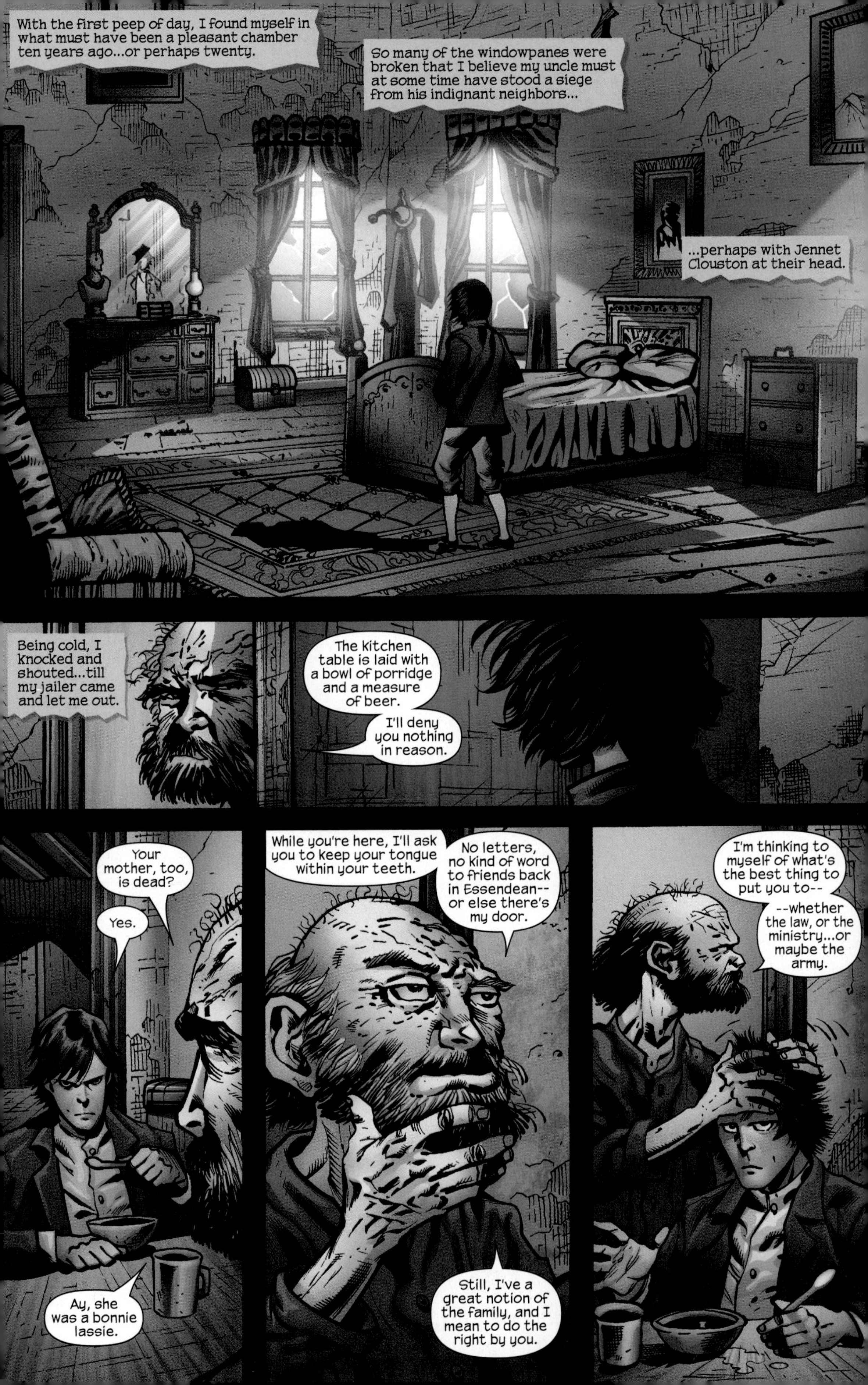
With the first peep of day, I found myself in what must have been a pleasant chamber ten years ago...or perhaps twenty.
So many of the windowpanes were broken that I believe my uncle must at some time have stood a siege from his indignant neighbors...
...perhaps with Jennet Clouston at their head.
Being cold, I knocked and shouted...till my jailer came and let me out.
The kitchen table is laid with a bowl of porridge and a measure of beer.
I'll deny you nothing in reason.
Your mother, too, is dead?
Yes.
Ay, she was a bonnie lassie.
While you're here, I'll ask you to keep your tongue within your teeth.
No letters, no kind of word to friends back in Essendean--or else there's my door.
Still, I've a great notion of the family, and I mean to do the right by you.
I'm thinking to myself of what's the best thing to put you to--
--whether the law, or the ministry...or maybe the army.

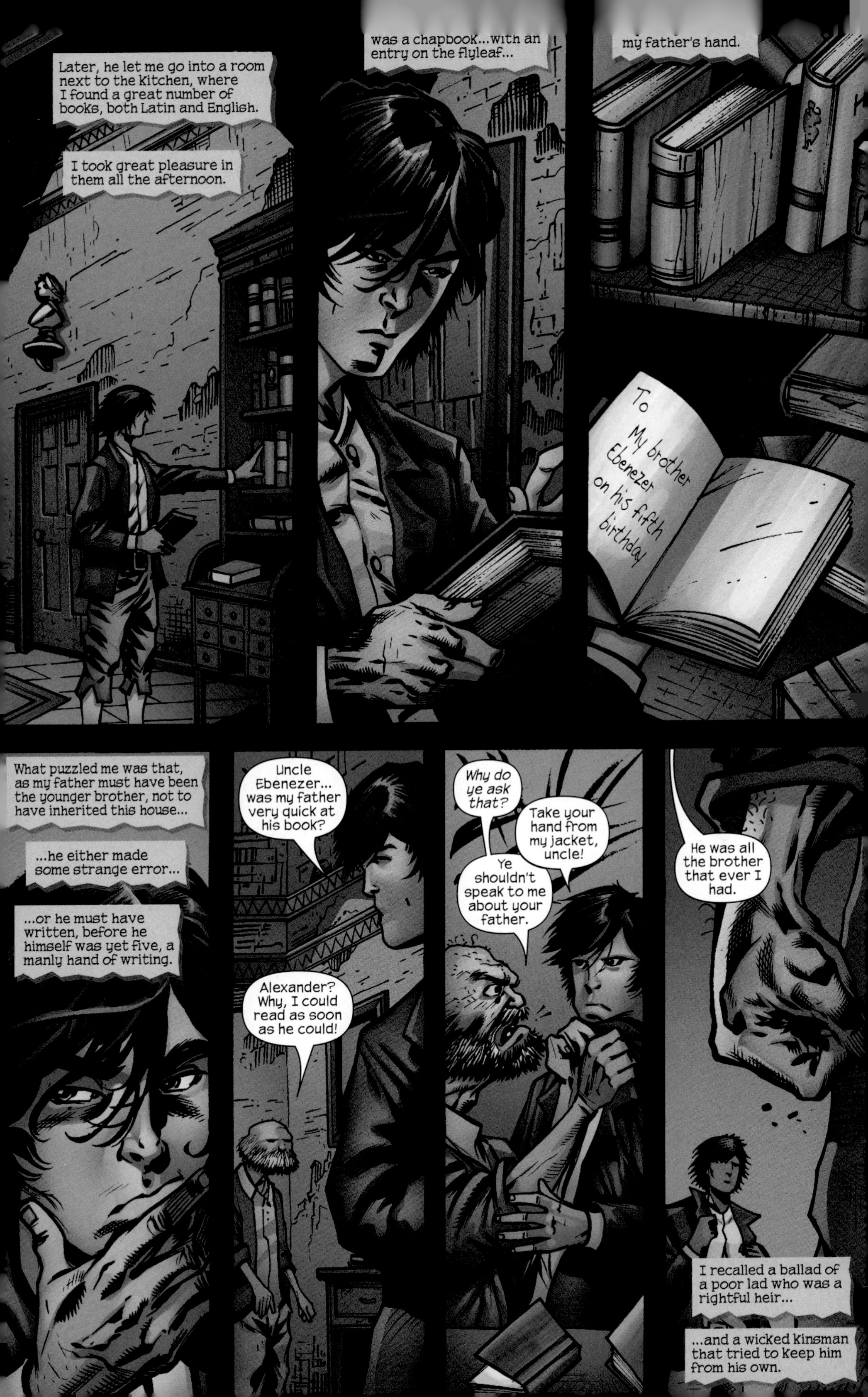

Later, he let me go into a room next to the kitchen, where I found a great number of books, both Latin and English.
I took great pleasure in them all the afternoon.
was a chapbook...with an entry on the flyleaf...
my father's hand.
To My brother Ebenezer on his fifth birthday
What puzzled me was that, as my father must have been the younger brother, not to have inherited this house...
...he either made some strange error...
...or he must have written, before he himself was yet five, a manly hand of writing.
Uncle Ebenezer... was my father very quick at his book?
Alexander? Why, I could read as soon as he could!
Why do ye ask that?
Take your hand from my jacket, uncle!
Ye shouldn't speak to me about your father.
He was all the brother that ever I had.
I recalled a ballad of a poor lad who was a rightful heir...
...and a wicked kinsman that tried to keep him from his own.

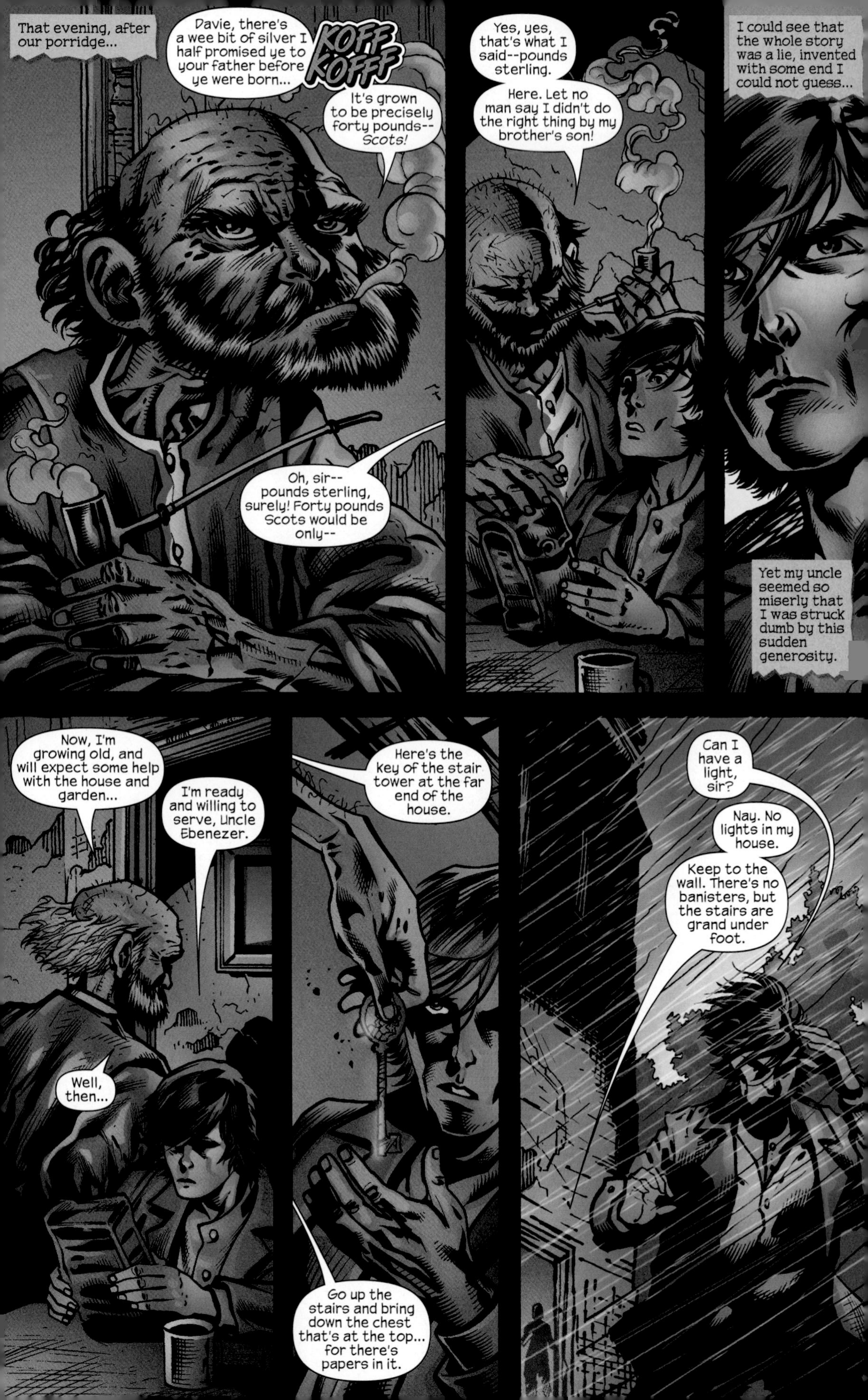

That evening, after our porridge...
Davie, there's a wee bit of silver I half promised ye to your father before ye were born...
KOFF KOFFF
It's grown to be precisely forty pounds-- Scots!
Oh, sir-- pounds sterling, surely! Forty pounds Scots would be only--
Yes, yes, that's what I said--pounds sterling.
Here. Let no man say I didn't do the right thing by my brother's son!
I could see that the whole story was a lie, invented with some end I could not guess...
Yet my uncle seemed so miserly that I was struck dumb by this sudden generosity.
Now, I'm growing old, and will expect some help with the house and garden...
I'm ready and willing to serve, Uncle Ebenezer.
Well, then...
Here's the key of the stair tower at the far end of the house.
Go up the stairs and bring down the chest that's at the top... for there's papers in it.
Can I have a light, sir?
Nay. No lights in my house.
Keep to the wall. There's no banisters, but the stairs are grand under foot.

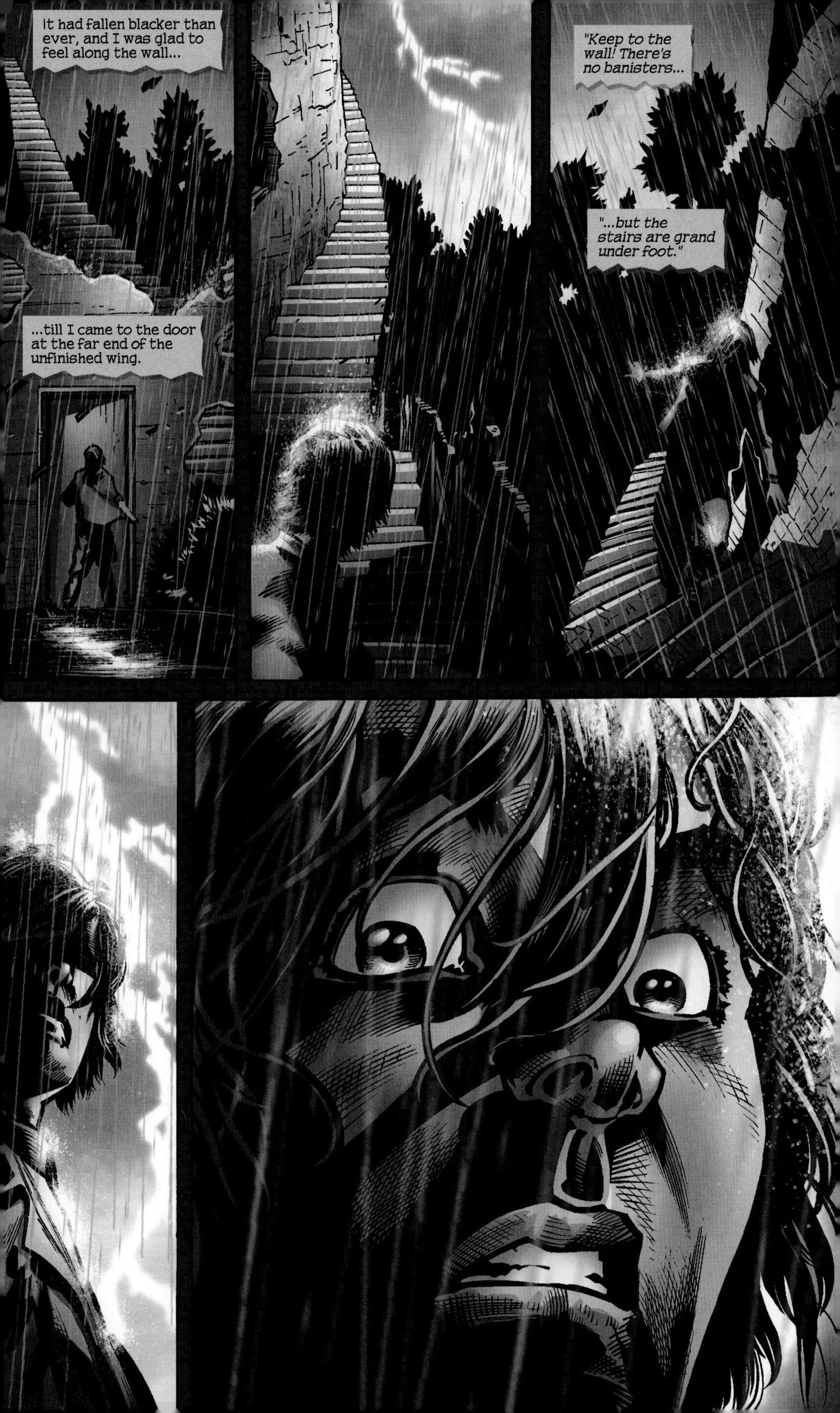
It had fallen blacker than ever, and I was glad to feel along the wall...
...till I came to the door at the far end of the unfinished wing.
"Keep to the wall! There's no banisters...
"...but the stairs are grand under foot."

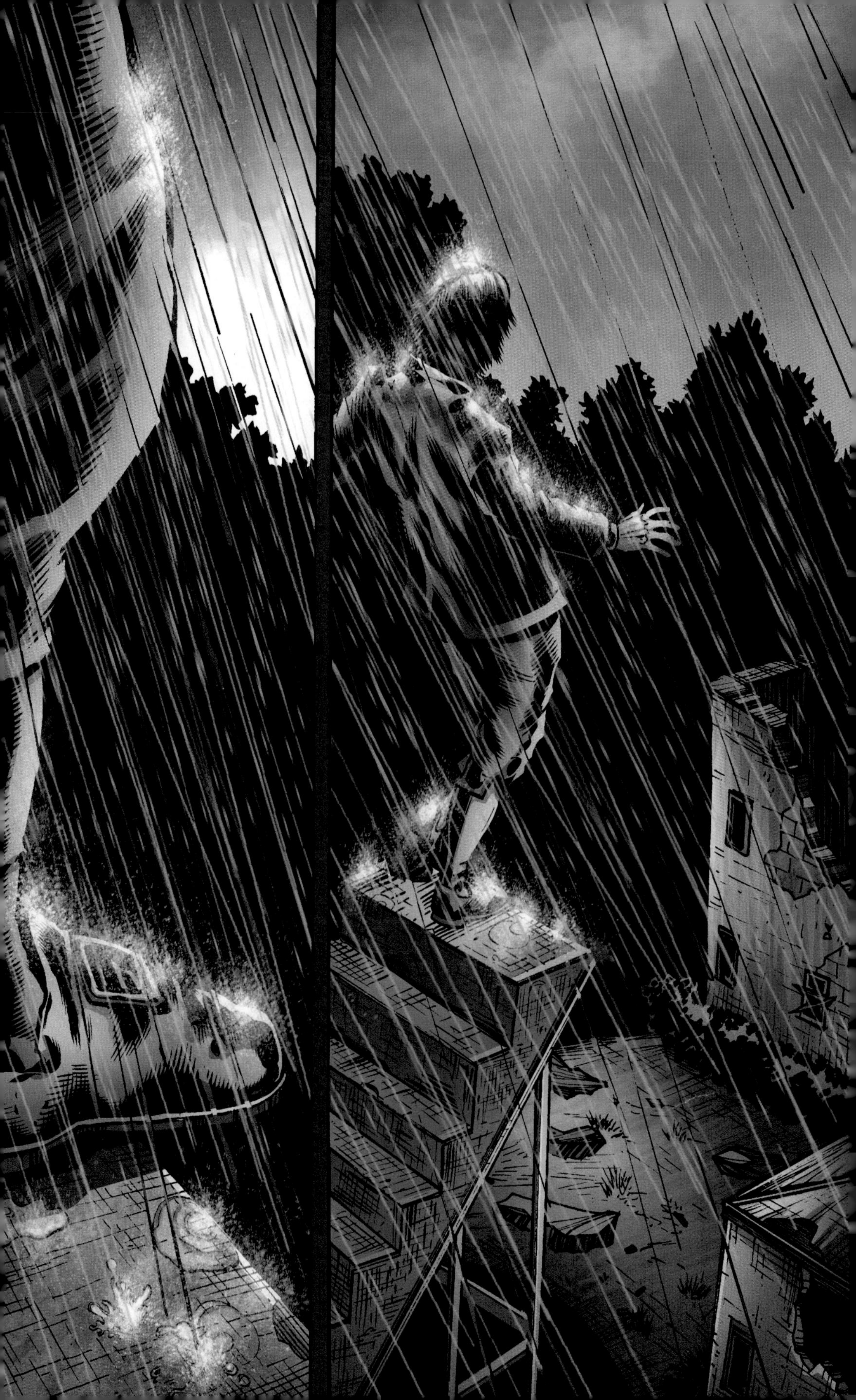

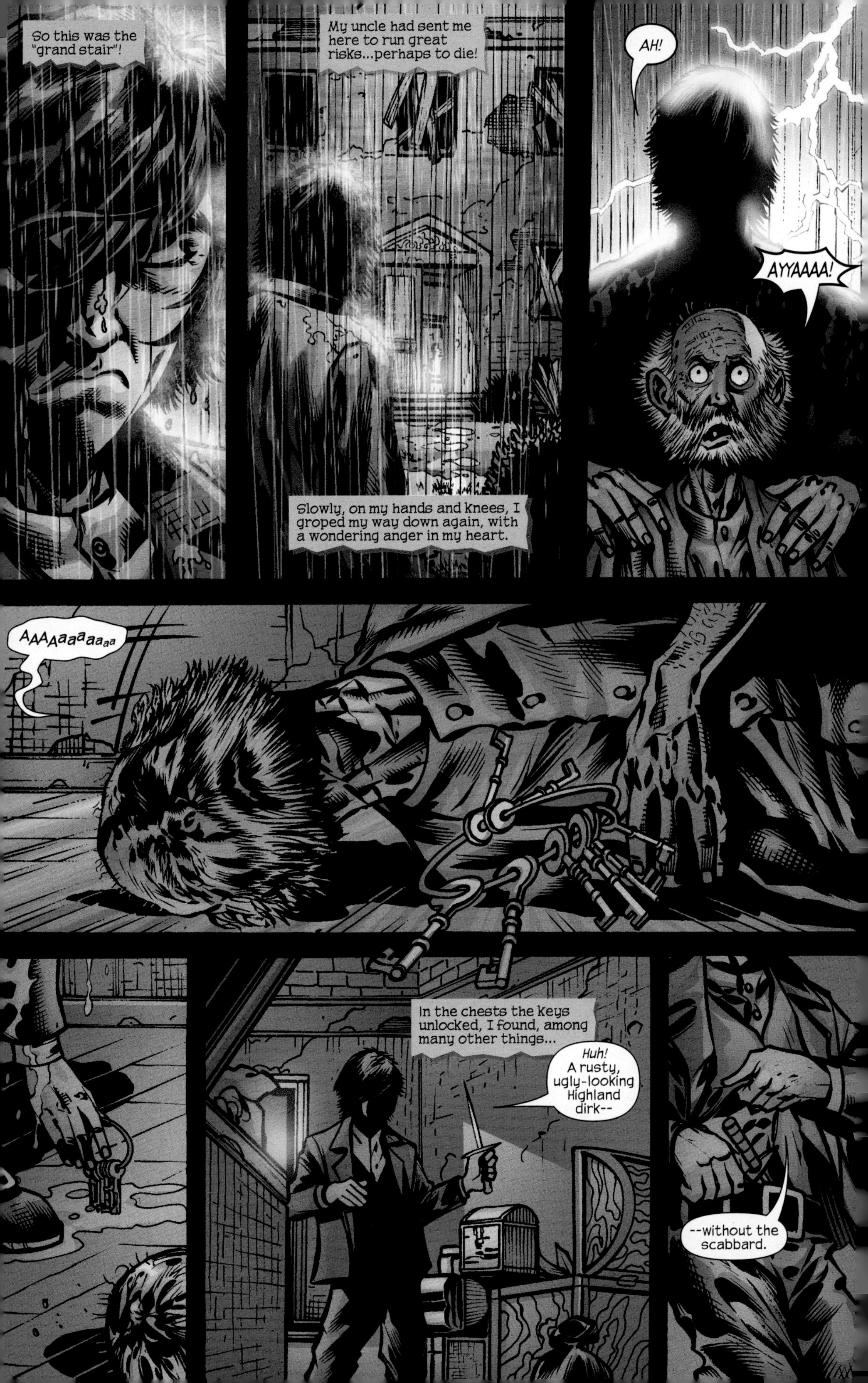
So this was the "grand stair"!
My uncle had sent me here to run great risks...perhaps to die!
Slowly, on my hands and knees, I groped my way down again, with a wondering anger in my heart.
AH!
AYYAAAA!
AAAAaaaaaaa
In the chests the keys unlocked, I found, among many other things...
Huh! A rusty, ugly-looking Highland dirk--
--without the scabbard.

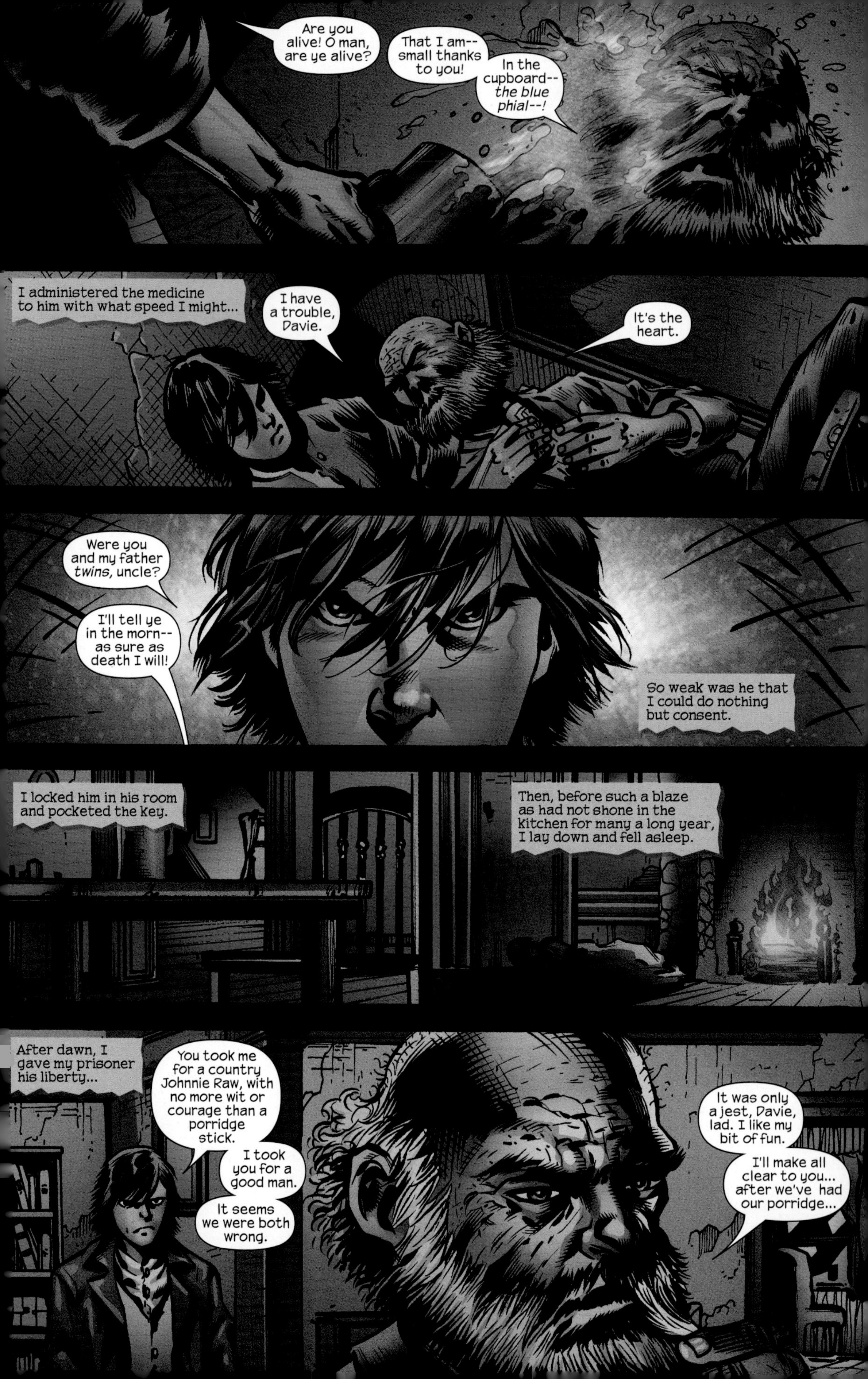

Are you alive! O man, are ye alive?
That I am--small thanks to you!
In the cupboard--*the blue phial*--!
I administered the medicine to him with what speed I might...
I have a trouble, Davie.
It's the heart.
Were you and my father *twins,* uncle?
I'll tell ye in the morn--as sure as death I will!
So weak was he that I could do nothing but consent.
I locked him in his room and pocketed the key.
Then, before such a blaze as had not shone in the kitchen for many a long year, I lay down and fell asleep.
After dawn, I gave my prisoner his liberty...
You took me for a country Johnnie Raw, with no more wit or courage than a porridge stick.
I took you for a good man.
It seems we were both wrong.
It was only a jest, Davie, lad. I like my bit of fun.
I'll make all clear to you... after we've had our porridge...

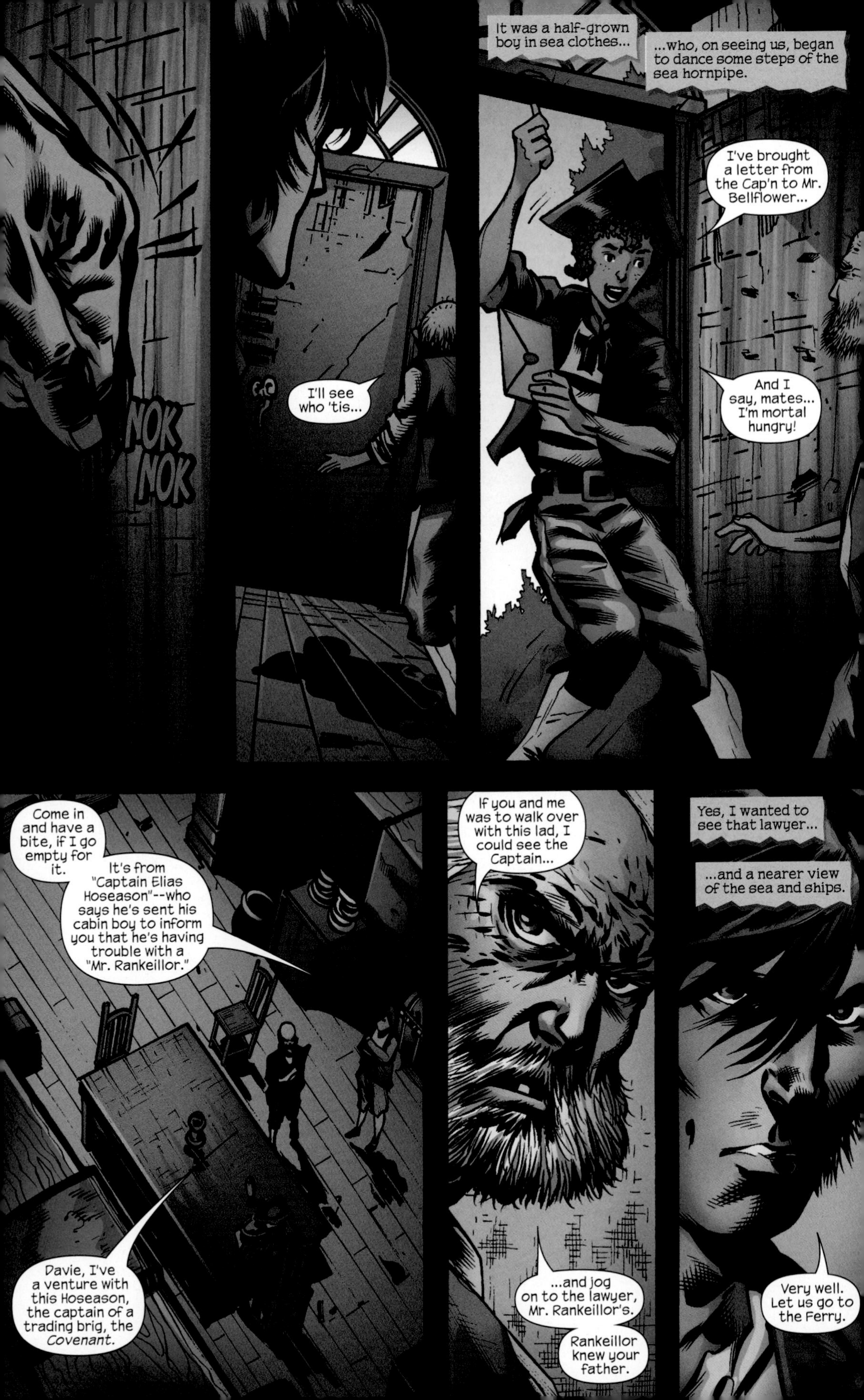
NOK
NOK
I'll see who 'tis...
It was a half-grown boy in sea clothes...
...who, on seeing us, began to dance some steps of the sea hornpipe.
I've brought a letter from the Cap'n to Mr. Bellflower...
And I say, mates... I'm mortal hungry!
Come in and have a bite, if I go empty for it.
It's from "Captain Elias Hoseason"--who says he's sent his cabin boy to inform you that he's having trouble with a "Mr. Rankeillor."
Davie, I've a venture with this Hoseason, the captain of a trading brig, the *Covenant*.
If you and me was to walk over with this lad, I could see the Captain...
...and jog on to the lawyer, Mr. Rankeillor's.
Rankeillor knew your father.
Yes, I wanted to see that lawyer...
...and a nearer view of the sea and ships.
Very well. Let us go to the Ferry.

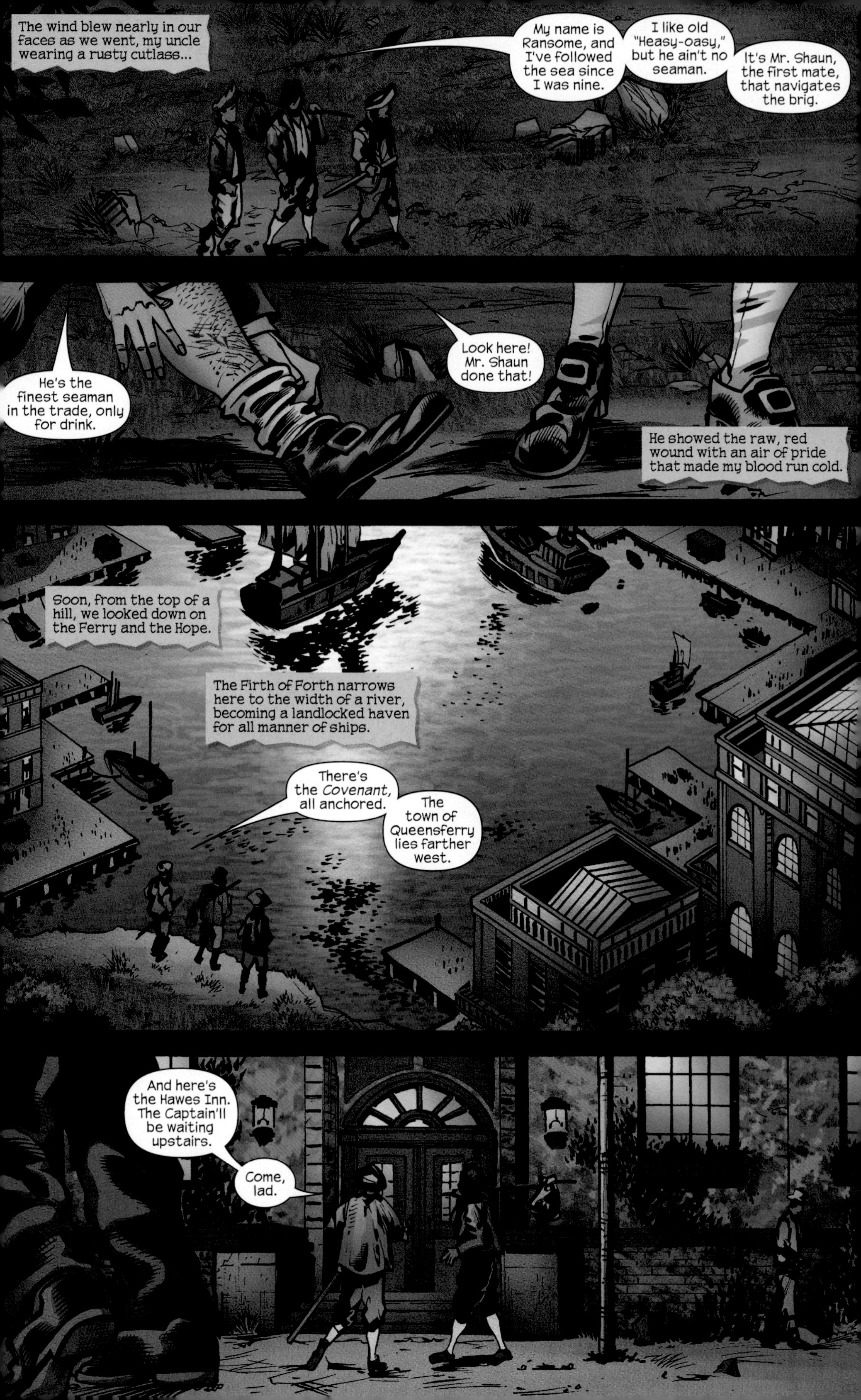
The wind blew nearly in our faces as we went, my uncle wearing a rusty cutlass...
My name is Ransome, and I've followed the sea since I was nine.
I like old "Heasy-oasy," but he ain't no seaman.
It's Mr. Shaun, the first mate, that navigates the brig.
He's the finest seaman in the trade, only for drink.
Look here! Mr. Shaun done that!
He showed the raw, red wound with an air of pride that made my blood run cold.
Soon, from the top of a hill, we looked down on the Ferry and the Hope.
The Firth of Forth narrows here to the width of a river, becoming a landlocked haven for all manner of ships.
There's the *Covenant*, all anchored.
The town of Queensferry lies farther west.
And here's the Hawes Inn. The Captain'll be waiting upstairs.
Come, lad.

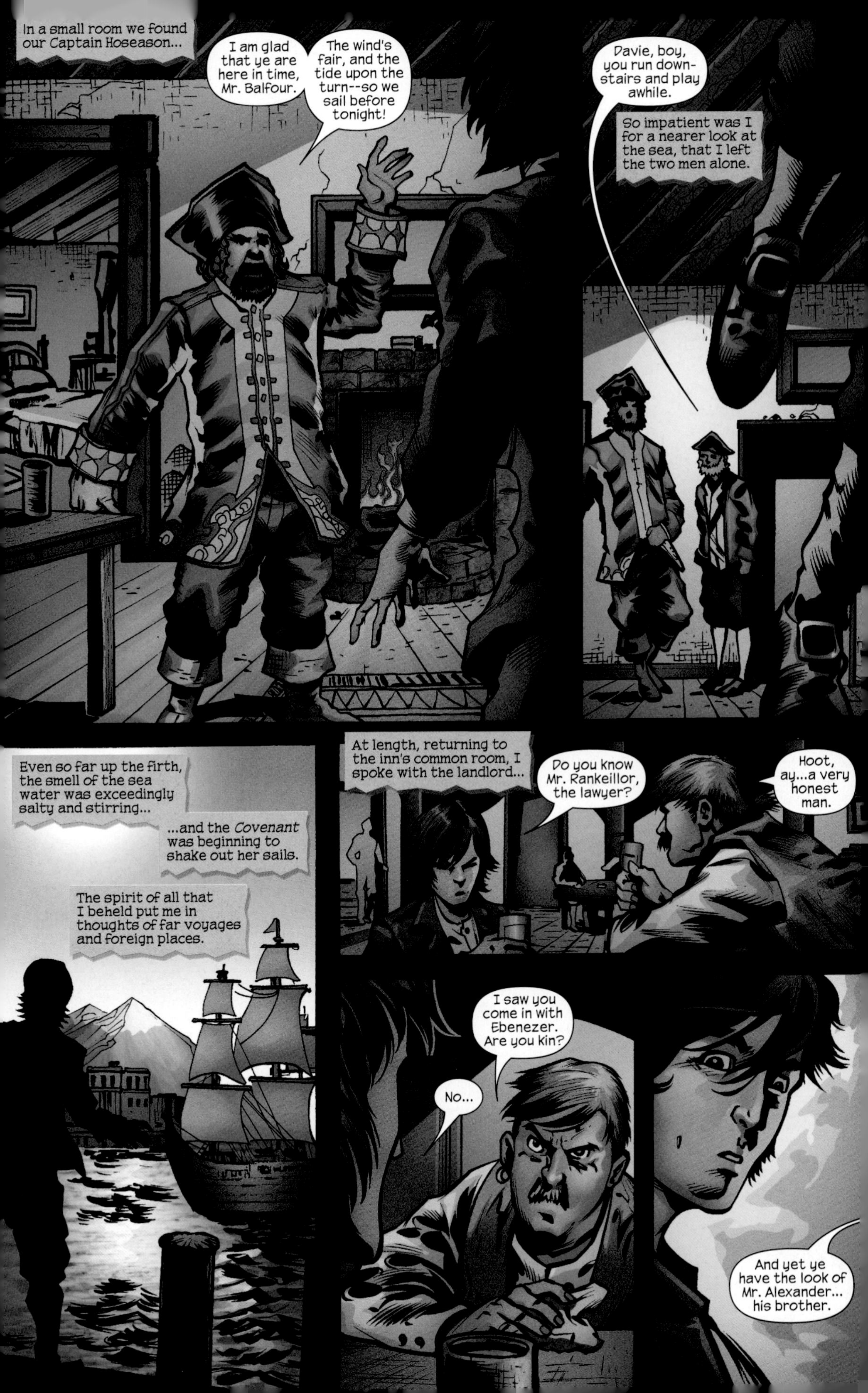

In a small room we found our Captain Hoseason...
I am glad that ye are here in time, Mr. Balfour.
The wind's fair, and the tide upon the turn--so we sail before tonight!
Davie, boy, you run down-stairs and play awhile.
So impatient was I for a nearer look at the sea, that I left the two men alone.
Even so far up the firth, the smell of the sea water was exceedingly salty and stirring...
...and the *Covenant* was beginning to shake out her sails.
The spirit of all that I beheld put me in thoughts of far voyages and foreign places.
At length, returning to the inn's common room, I spoke with the landlord...
Do you know Mr. Rankeillor, the lawyer?
Hoot, ay...a very honest man.
I saw you come in with Ebenezer. Are you kin?
No...
And yet ye have the look of Mr. Alexander... his brother.

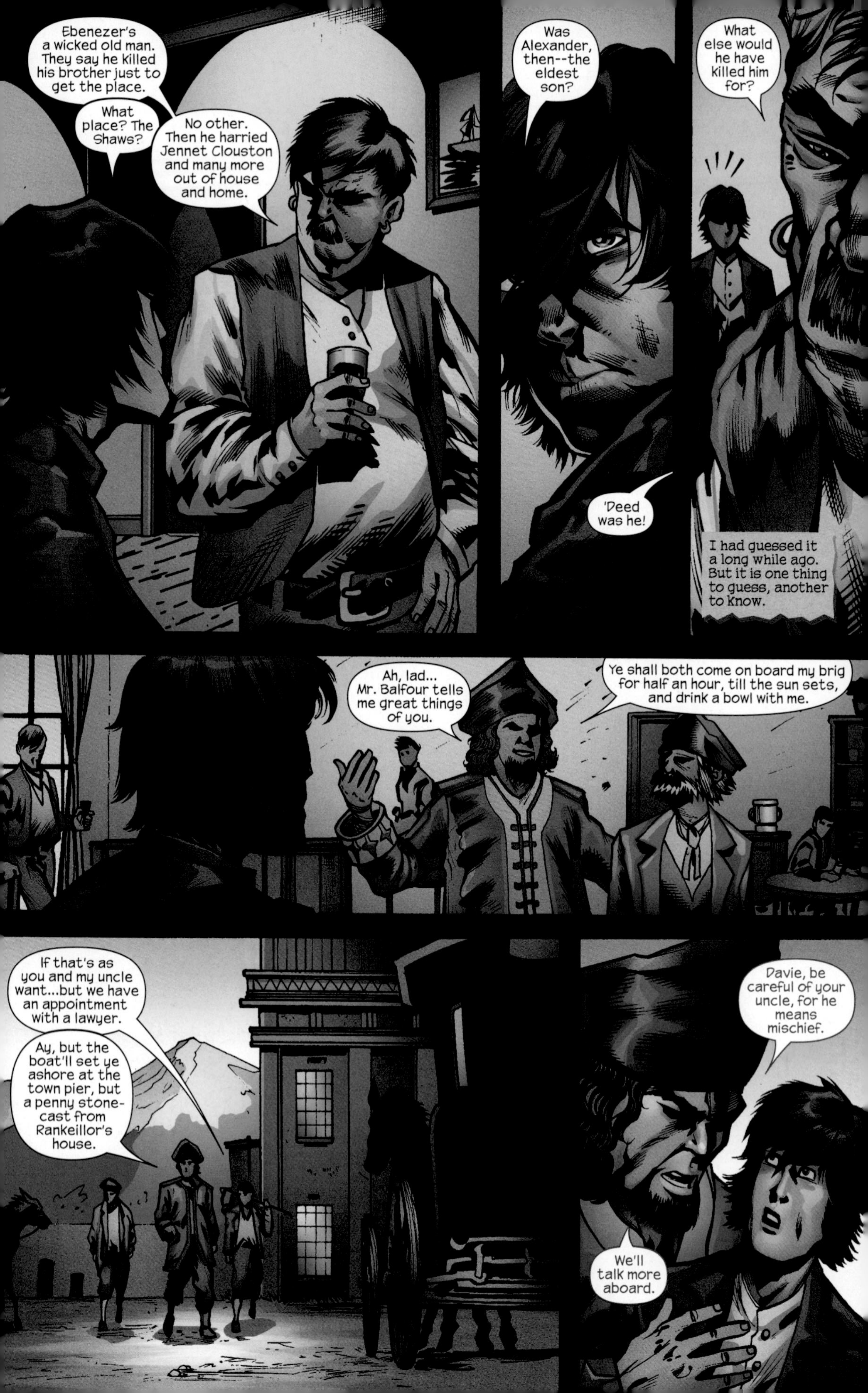
Ebenezer's a wicked old man. They say he killed his brother just to get the place.
What place? The Shaws?
No other. Then he harried Jennet Clouston and many more out of house and home.
Was Alexander, then--the eldest son?
'Deed was he!
What else would he have killed him for?
I had guessed it a long while ago. But it is one thing to guess, another to know.
Ah, lad... Mr. Balfour tells me great things of you.
Ye shall both come on board my brig for half an hour, till the sun sets, and drink a bowl with me.
If that's as you and my uncle want...but we have an appointment with a lawyer.
Ay, but the boat'll set ye ashore at the town pier, but a penny stone-cast from Rankeillor's house.
Davie, be careful of your uncle, for he means mischief.
We'll talk more aboard.

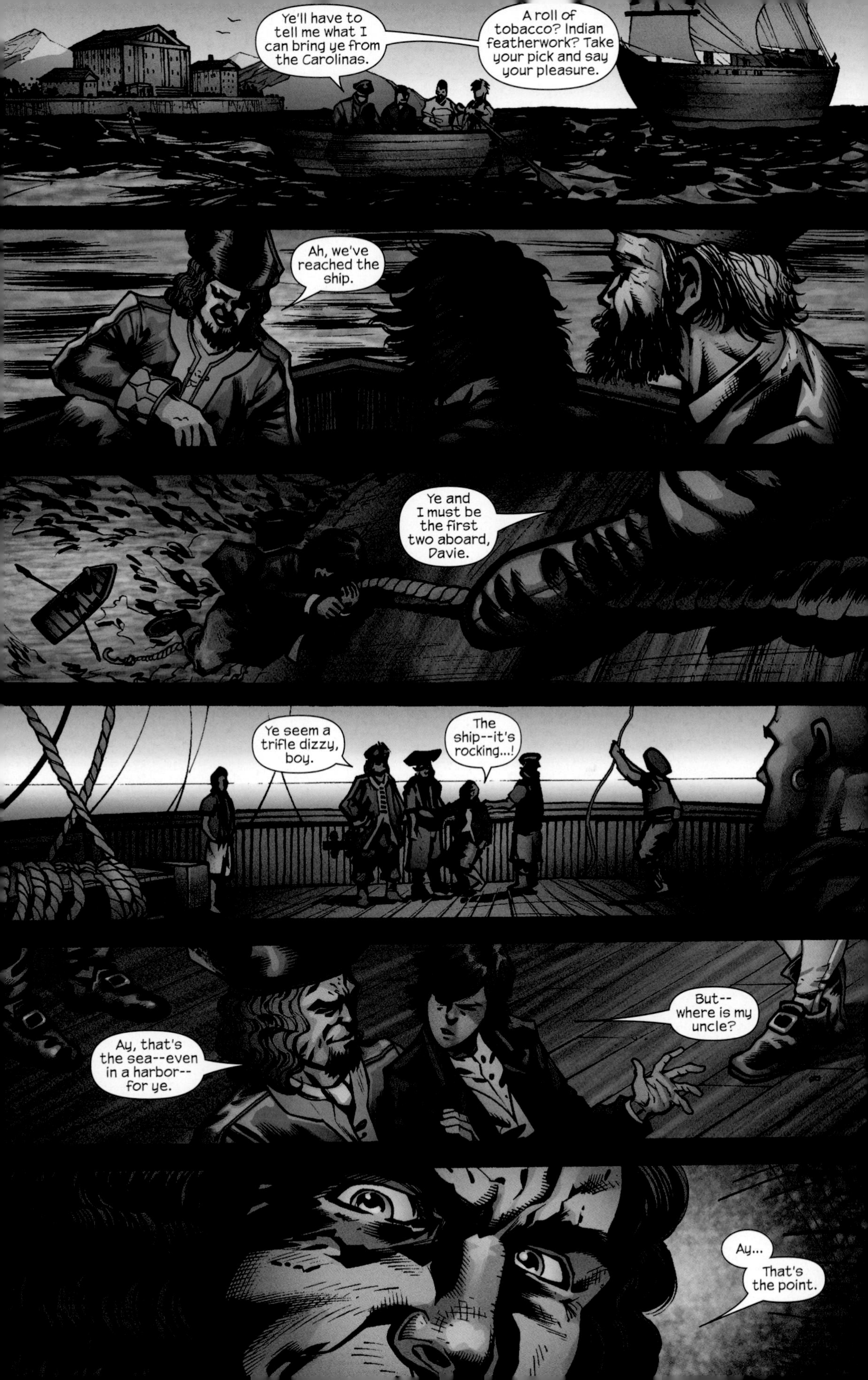
Ye'll have to tell me what I can bring ye from the Carolinas.
A roll of tobacco? Indian featherwork? Take your pick and say your pleasure.
Ah, we've reached the ship.
Ye and I must be the first two aboard, Davie.
Ye seem a trifle dizzy, boy.
The ship--it's rocking...!
But--where is my uncle?
Ay, that's the sea--even in a harbor--for ye.
Ay... That's the point.

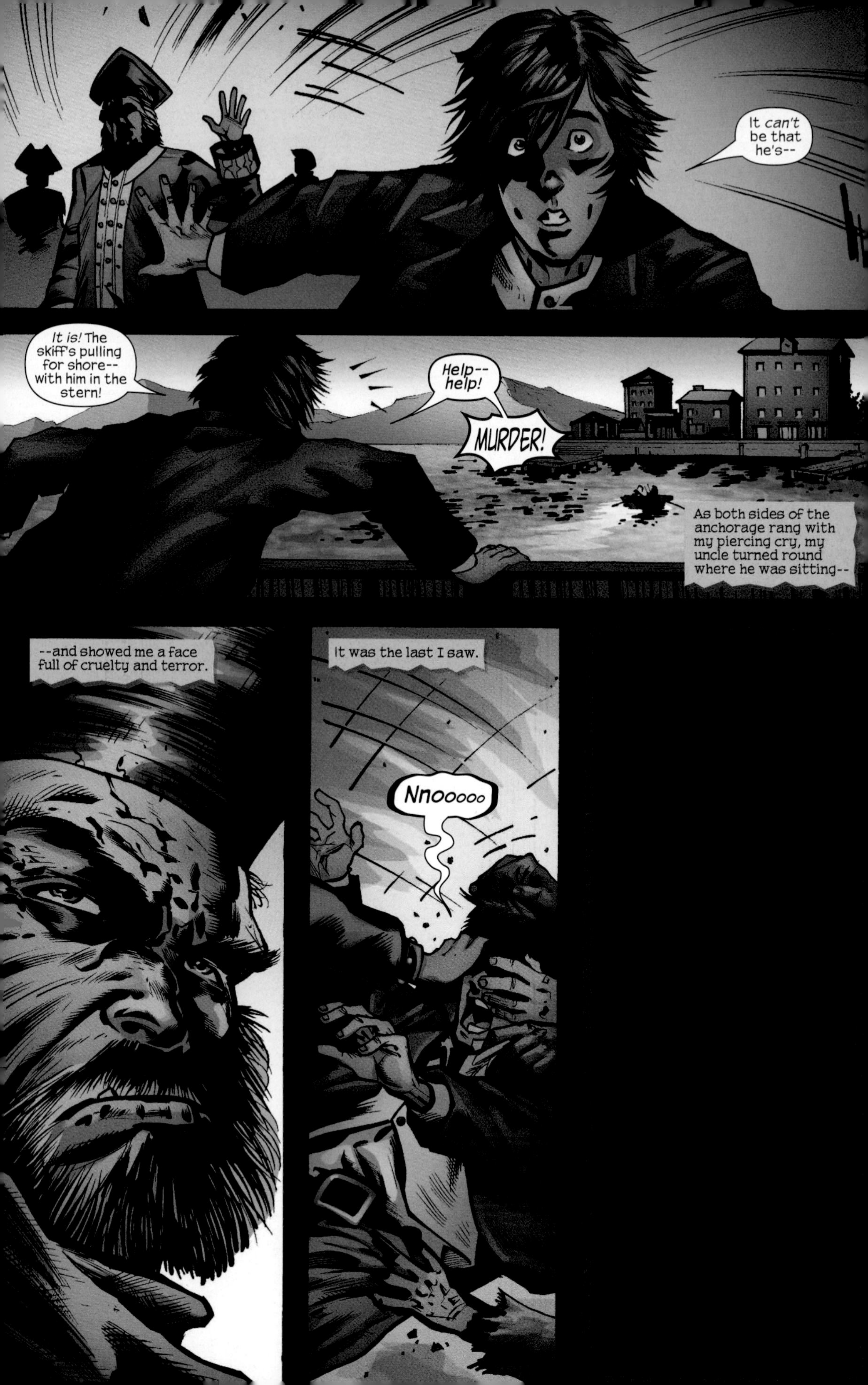
It can't be that he's--
It is! The skiff's pulling for shore--with him in the stern!
Help--help!
MURDER!
As both sides of the anchorage rang with my piercing cry, my uncle turned round where he was sitting--
--and showed me a face full of cruelty and terror.
It was the last I saw.
Nnooooo

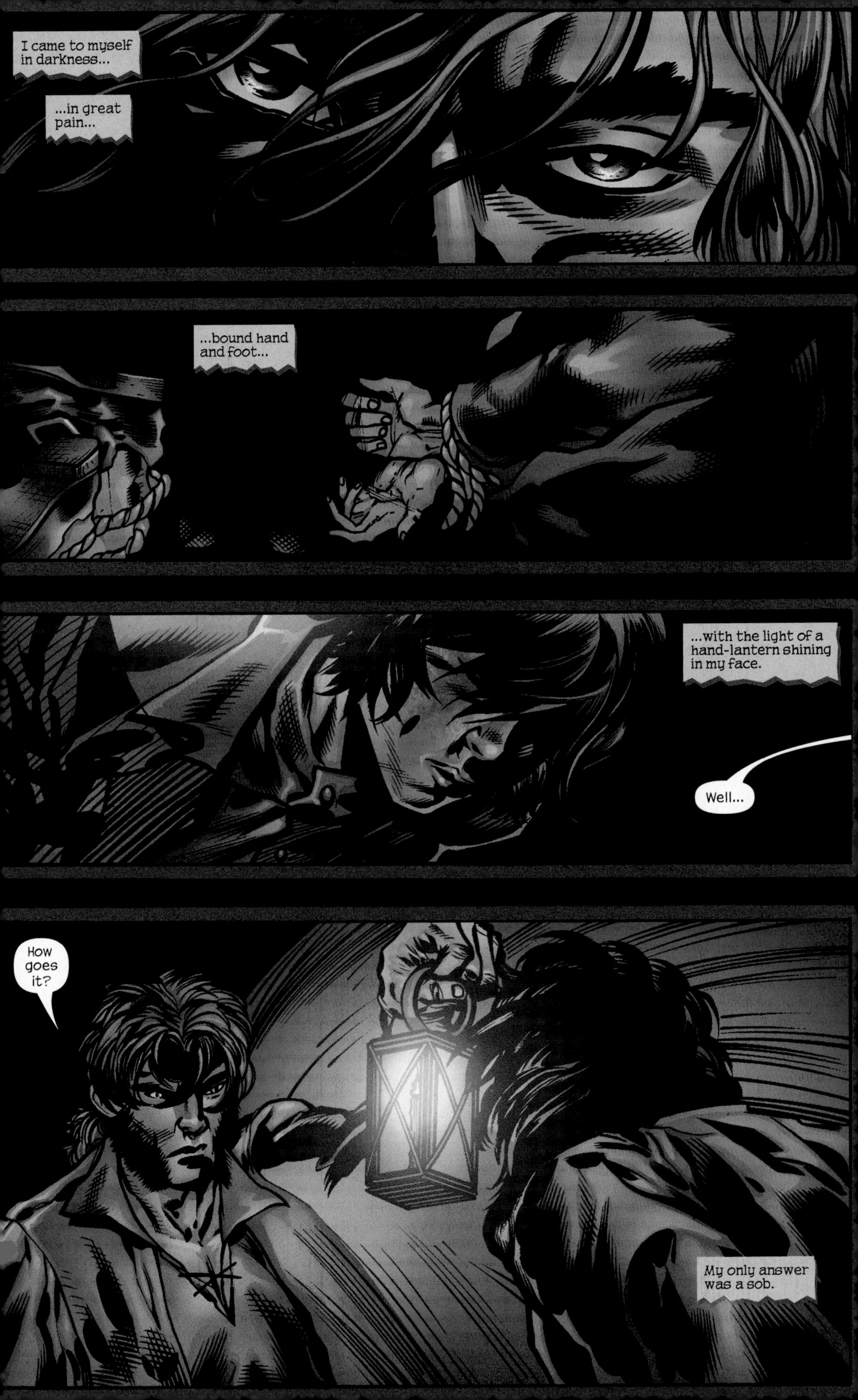
I came to myself in darkness...
...in great pain...
...bound hand and foot...
...with the light of a hand-lantern shining in my face.
Well...
How goes it?
My only answer was a sob.

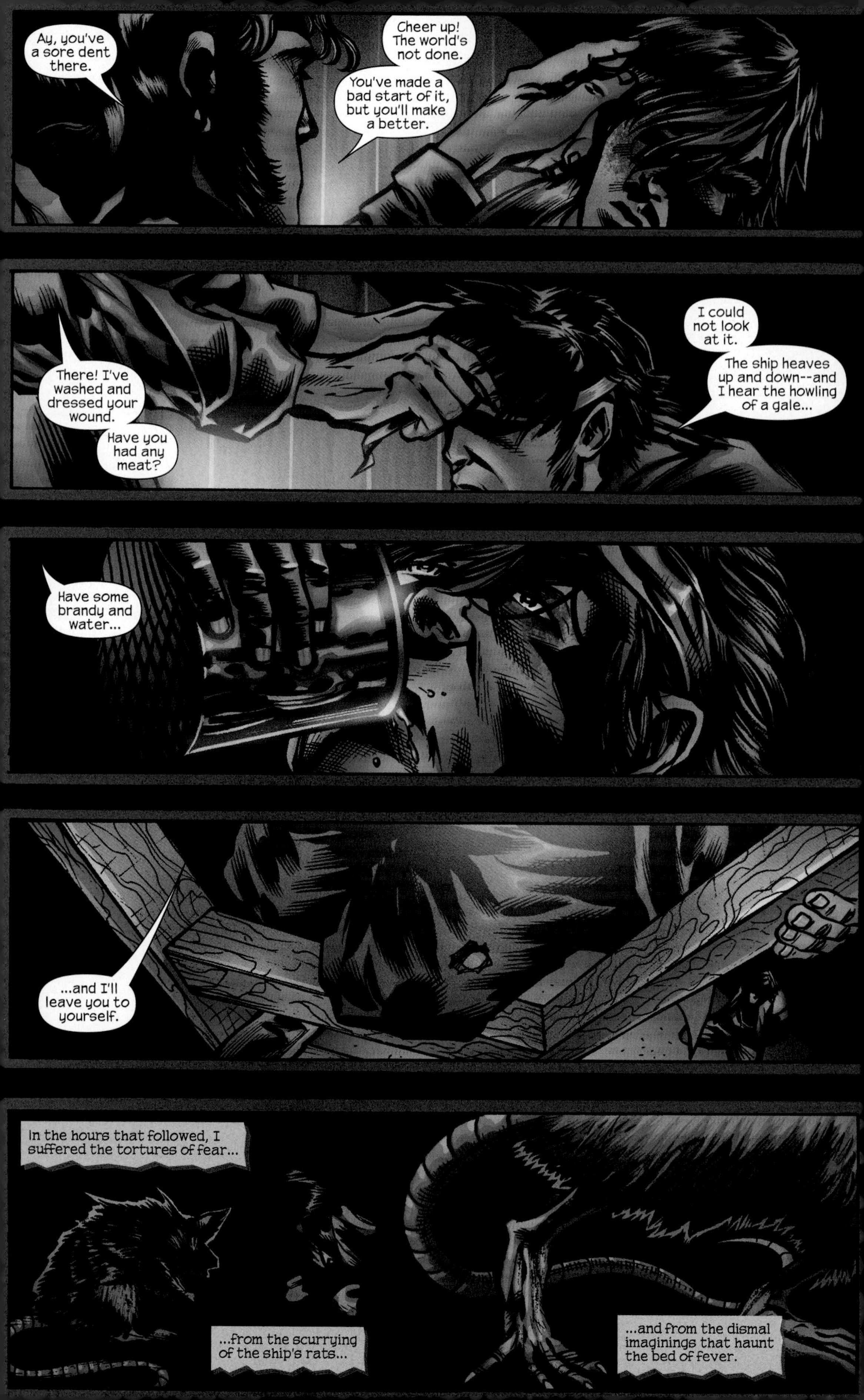

Ay, you've a sore dent there.
Cheer up! The world's not done.
You've made a bad start of it, but you'll make a better.
There! I've washed and dressed your wound.
Have you had any meat?
I could not look at it.
The ship heaves up and down--and I hear the howling of a gale...
Have some brandy and water...
...and I'll leave you to yourself.
In the hours that followed, I suffered the tortures of fear...
...from the scurrying of the ship's rats...
...and from the dismal imaginings that haunt the bed of fever.

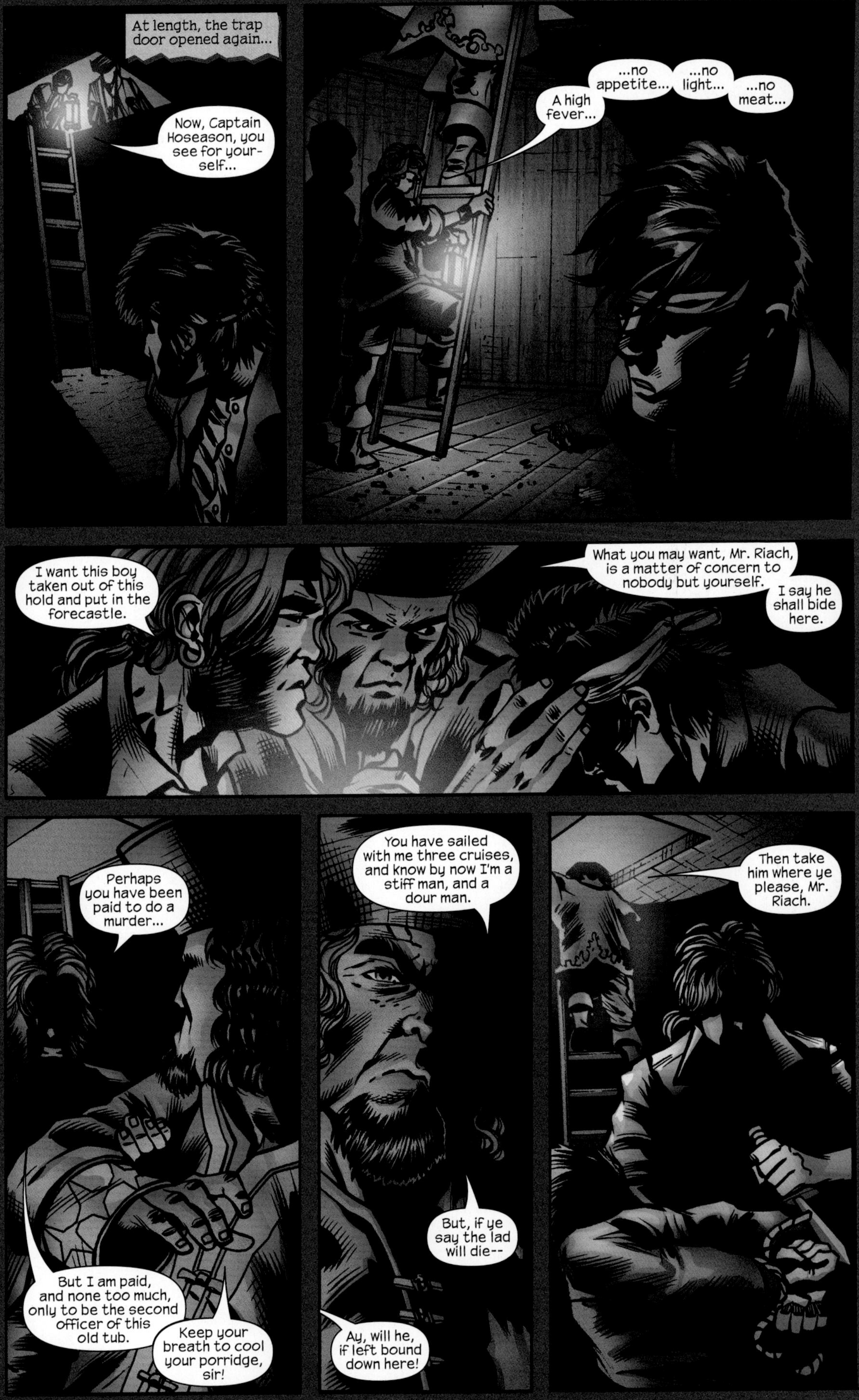
At length, the trap door opened again...
Now, Captain Hoseason, you see for your-self...
A high fever...
...no appetite...
...no light...
...no meat...
I want this boy taken out of this hold and put in the forecastle.
What you may want, Mr. Riach, is a matter of concern to nobody but yourself.
I say he shall bide here.
Perhaps you have been paid to do a murder...
But I am paid, and none too much, only to be the second officer of this old tub.
Keep your breath to cool your porridge, sir!
You have sailed with me three cruises, and know by now I'm a stiff man, and a dour man.
But, if ye say the lad will die--
Ay, will he, if left bound down here!
Then take him where ye please, Mr. Riach.

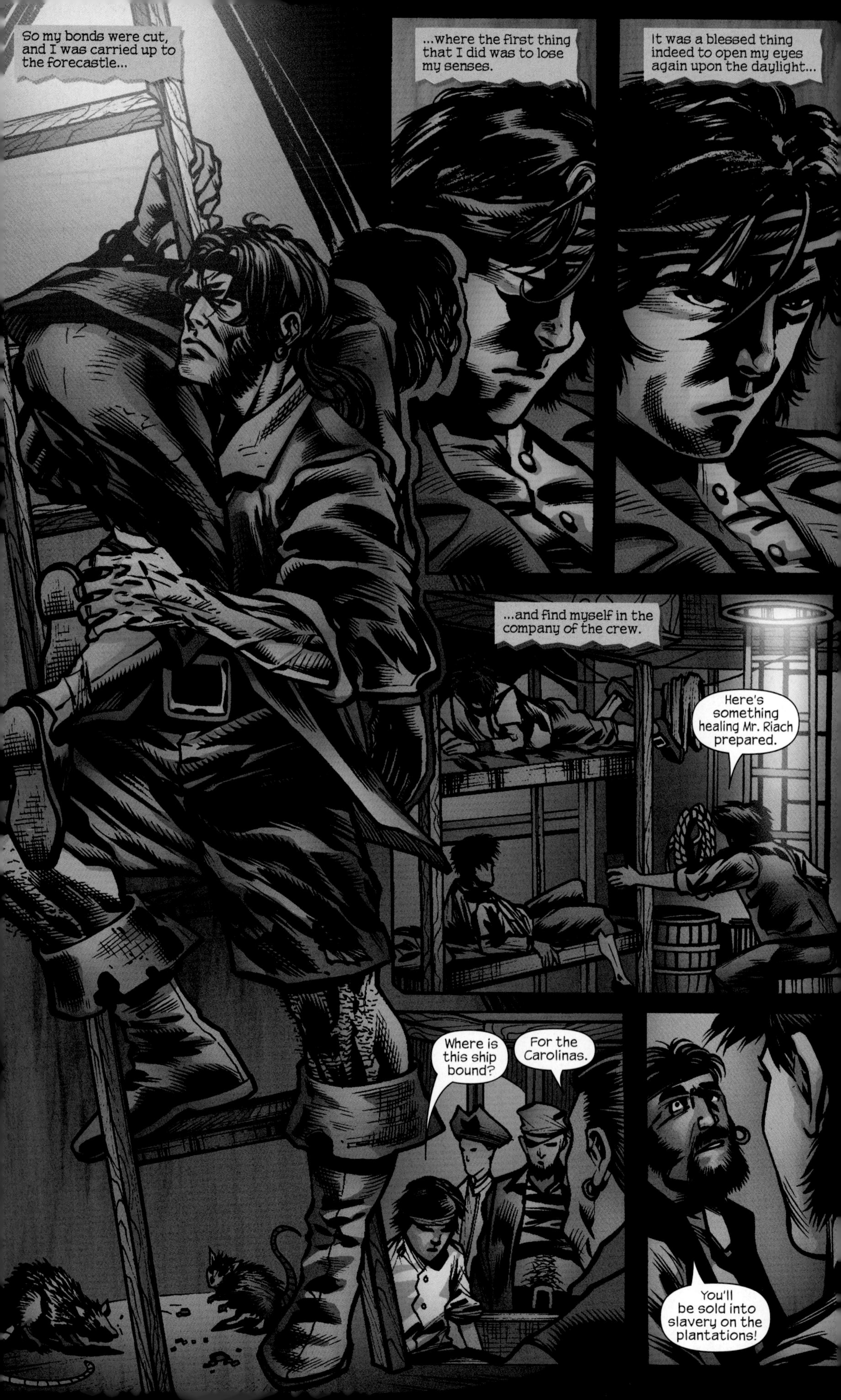
So my bonds were cut, and I was carried up to the forecastle...
...where the first thing that I did was to lose my senses.
It was a blessed thing indeed to open my eyes again upon the daylight...
...and find myself in the company of the crew.
Here's something healing Mr. Riach prepared.
Where is this ship bound?
For the Carolinas.
You'll be sold into slavery on the plantations!

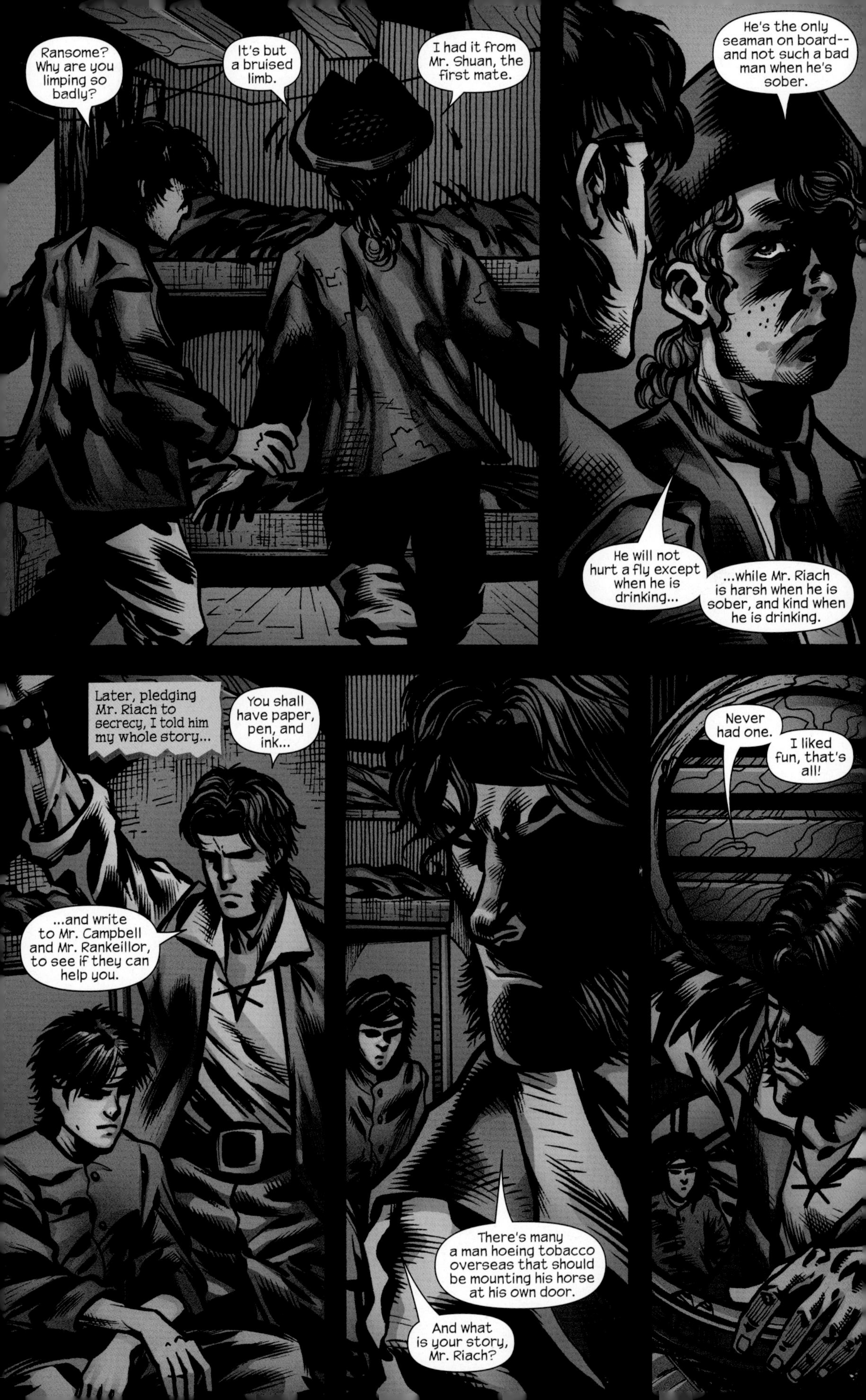
Ransome? Why are you limping so badly?
It's but a bruised limb.
I had it from Mr. Shuan, the first mate.
He's the only seaman on board-- and not such a bad man when he's sober.
He will not hurt a fly except when he is drinking...
...while Mr. Riach is harsh when he is sober, and kind when he is drinking.
Later, pledging Mr. Riach to secrecy, I told him my whole story...
You shall have paper, pen, and ink...
...and write to Mr. Campbell and Mr. Rankeillor, to see if they can help you.
And what is your story, Mr. Riach?
There's many a man hoeing tobacco overseas that should be mounting his horse at his own door.
Never had one.
I liked fun, that's all!

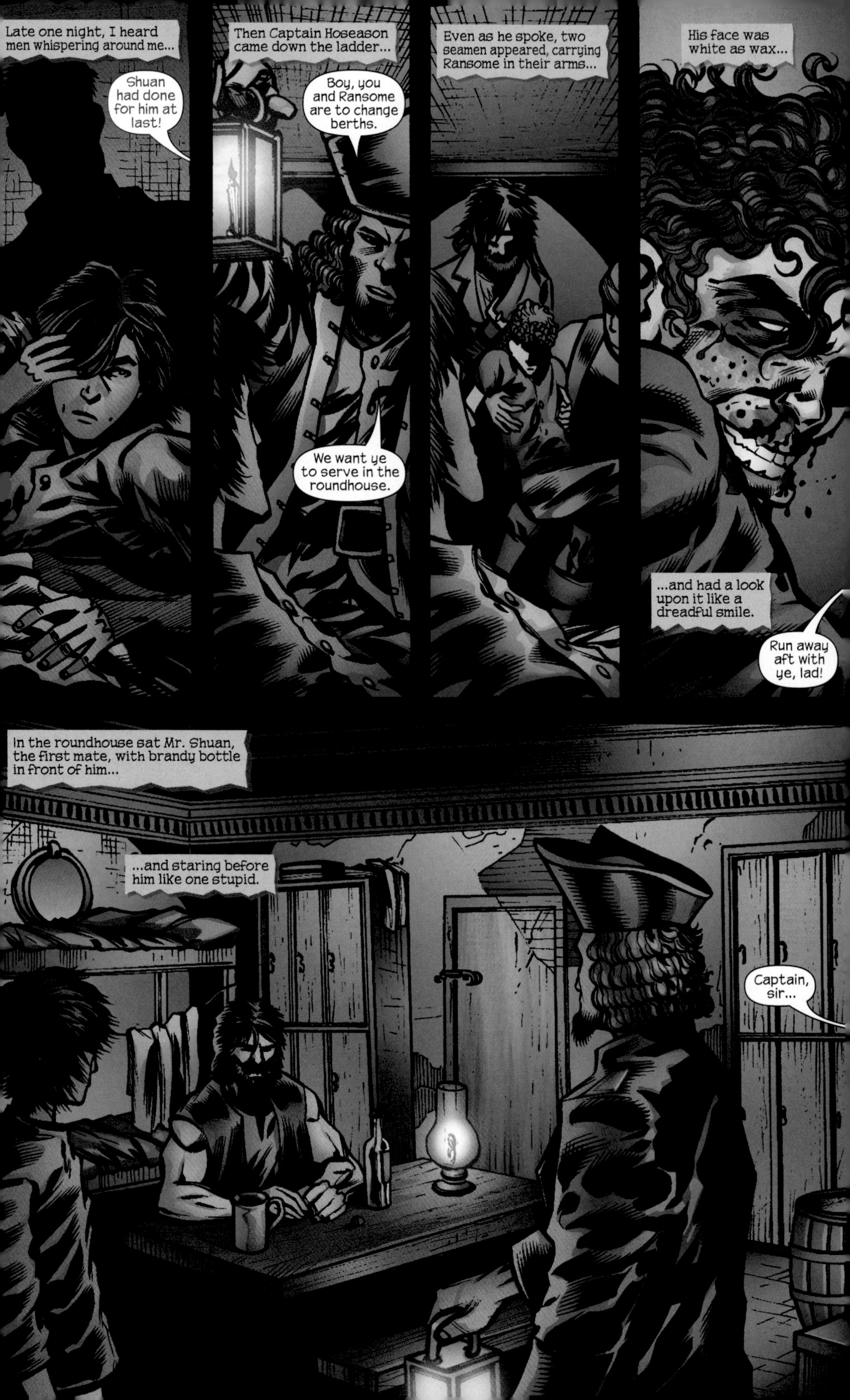
Late one night, I heard men whispering around me...
Shuan had done for him at last!
Then Captain Hoseason came down the ladder...
Boy, you and Ransome are to change berths.
We want ye to serve in the roundhouse.
Even as he spoke, two seamen appeared, carrying Ransome in their arms...
His face was white as wax...
...and had a look upon it like a dreadful smile.
Run away aft with ye, lad!
In the roundhouse sat Mr. Shuan, the first mate, with brandy bottle in front of him...
...and staring before him like one stupid.
Captain, sir...

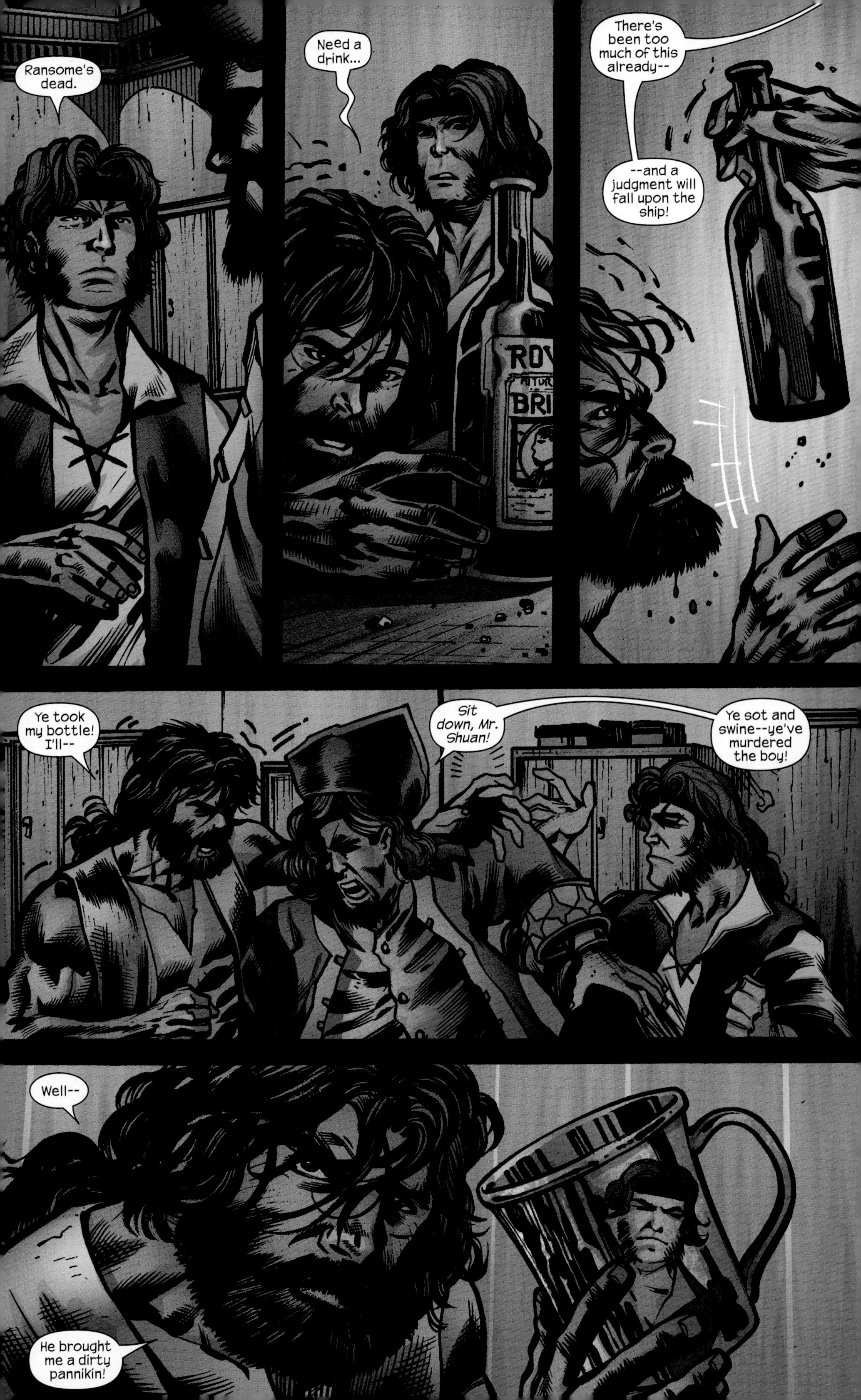
Ransome's dead.
Need a drink...
There's been too much of this already--
--and a judgment will fall upon the ship!
Ye took my bottle! I'll--
Sit down, Mr. Shuan!
Ye sot and swine--ye've murdered the boy!
Well--
He brought me a dirty pannikin!

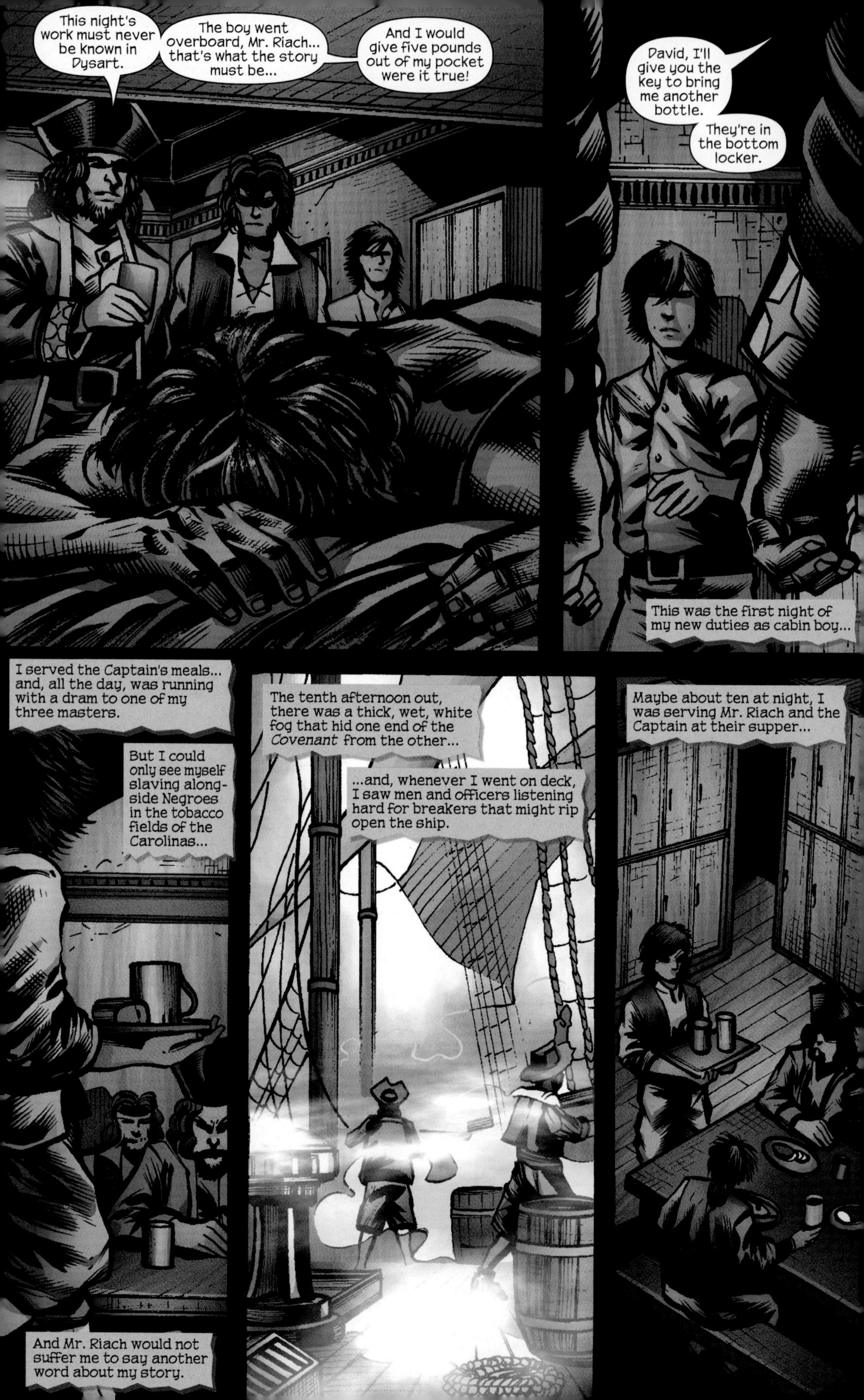
This night's work must never be known in Dysart.
The boy went overboard, Mr. Riach... that's what the story must be...
And I would give five pounds out of my pocket were it true!
David, I'll give you the key to bring me another bottle.
They're in the bottom locker.
This was the first night of my new duties as cabin boy...
I served the Captain's meals... and, all the day, was running with a dram to one of my three masters.
But I could only see myself slaving along-side Negroes in the tobacco fields of the Carolinas...
And Mr. Riach would not suffer me to say another word about my story.
The tenth afternoon out, there was a thick, wet, white fog that hid one end of the *Covenant* from the other...
...and, whenever I went on deck, I saw men and officers listening hard for breakers that might rip open the ship.
Maybe about ten at night, I was serving Mr. Riach and the Captain at their supper...

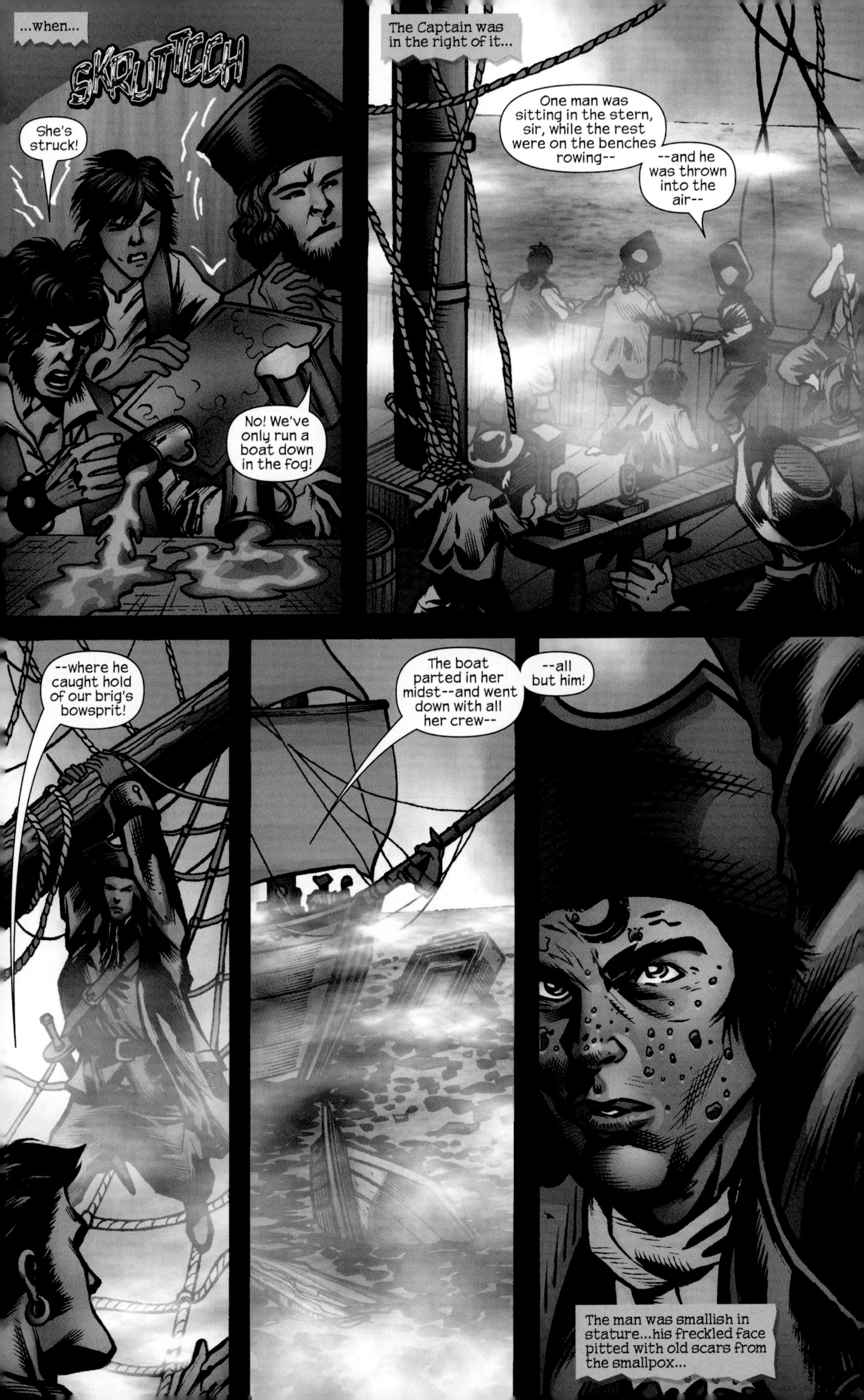
...when...
SKRUTTCCH
She's struck!
No! We've only run a boat down in the fog!
The Captain was in the right of it...
One man was sitting in the stern, sir, while the rest were on the benches rowing--
--and he was thrown into the air--
--where he caught hold of our brig's bowsprit!
The boat parted in her midst--and went down with all her crew--
--all but him!
The man was smallish in stature...his freckled face pitted with old scars from the smallpox...

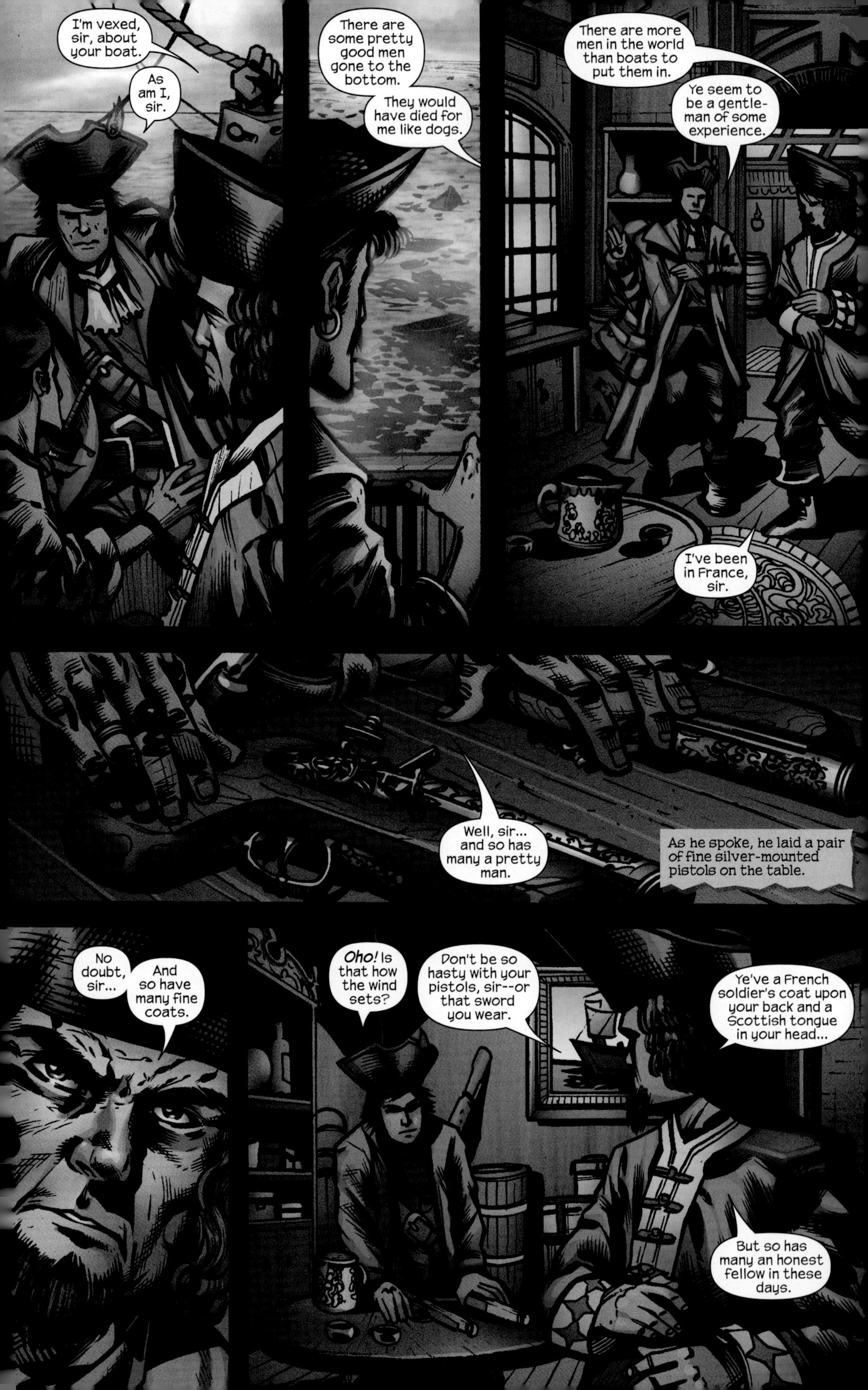
I'm vexed, sir, about your boat.
As am I, sir.
There are some pretty good men gone to the bottom.
They would have died for me like dogs.
There are more men in the world than boats to put them in.
Ye seem to be a gentle-man of some experience.
I've been in France, sir.
Well, sir... and so has many a pretty man.
As he spoke, he laid a pair of fine silver-mounted pistols on the table.
No doubt, sir...
And so have many fine coats.
Oho! Is that how the wind sets?
Don't be so hasty with your pistols, sir--or that sword you wear.
Ye've a French soldier's coat upon your back and a Scottish tongue in your head...
But so has many an honest fellow in these days.

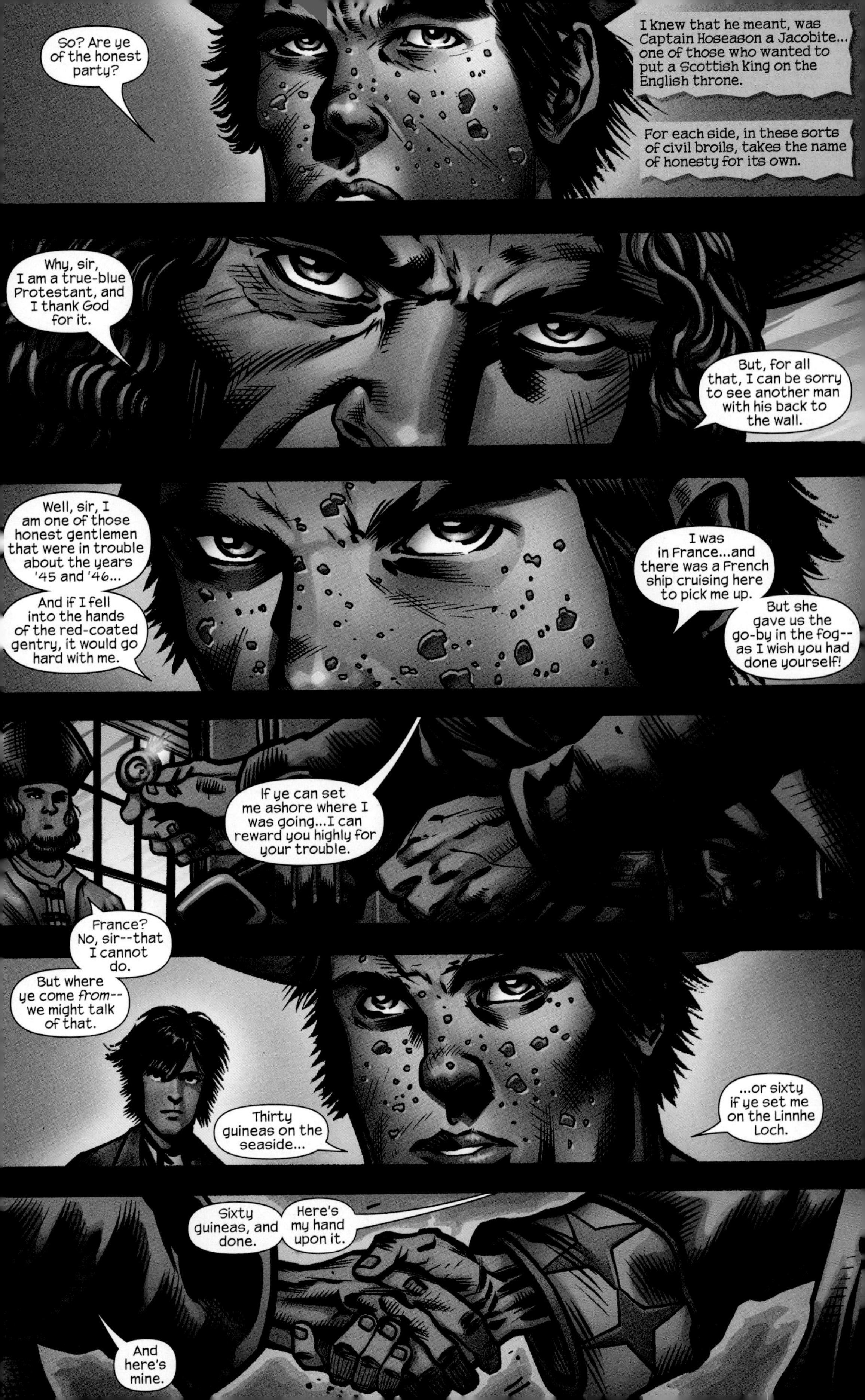

So? Are ye of the honest party?
I knew that he meant, was Captain Hoseason a Jacobite... one of those who wanted to put a Scottish King on the English throne.
For each side, in these sorts of civil broils, takes the name of honesty for its own.
Why, sir, I am a true-blue Protestant, and I thank God for it.
But, for all that, I can be sorry to see another man with his back to the wall.
Well, sir, I am one of those honest gentlemen that were in trouble about the years '45 and '46...
And if I fell into the hands of the red-coated gentry, it would go hard with me.
I was in France...and there was a French ship cruising here to pick me up.
But she gave us the go-by in the fog--as I wish you had done yourself!
If ye can set me ashore where I was going...I can reward you highly for your trouble.
France? No, sir--that I cannot do.
But where ye come *from*--we might talk of that.
Thirty guineas on the seaside...
...or sixty if ye set me on the Linnhe Loch.
Sixty guineas, and done.
Here's my hand upon it.
And here's mine.

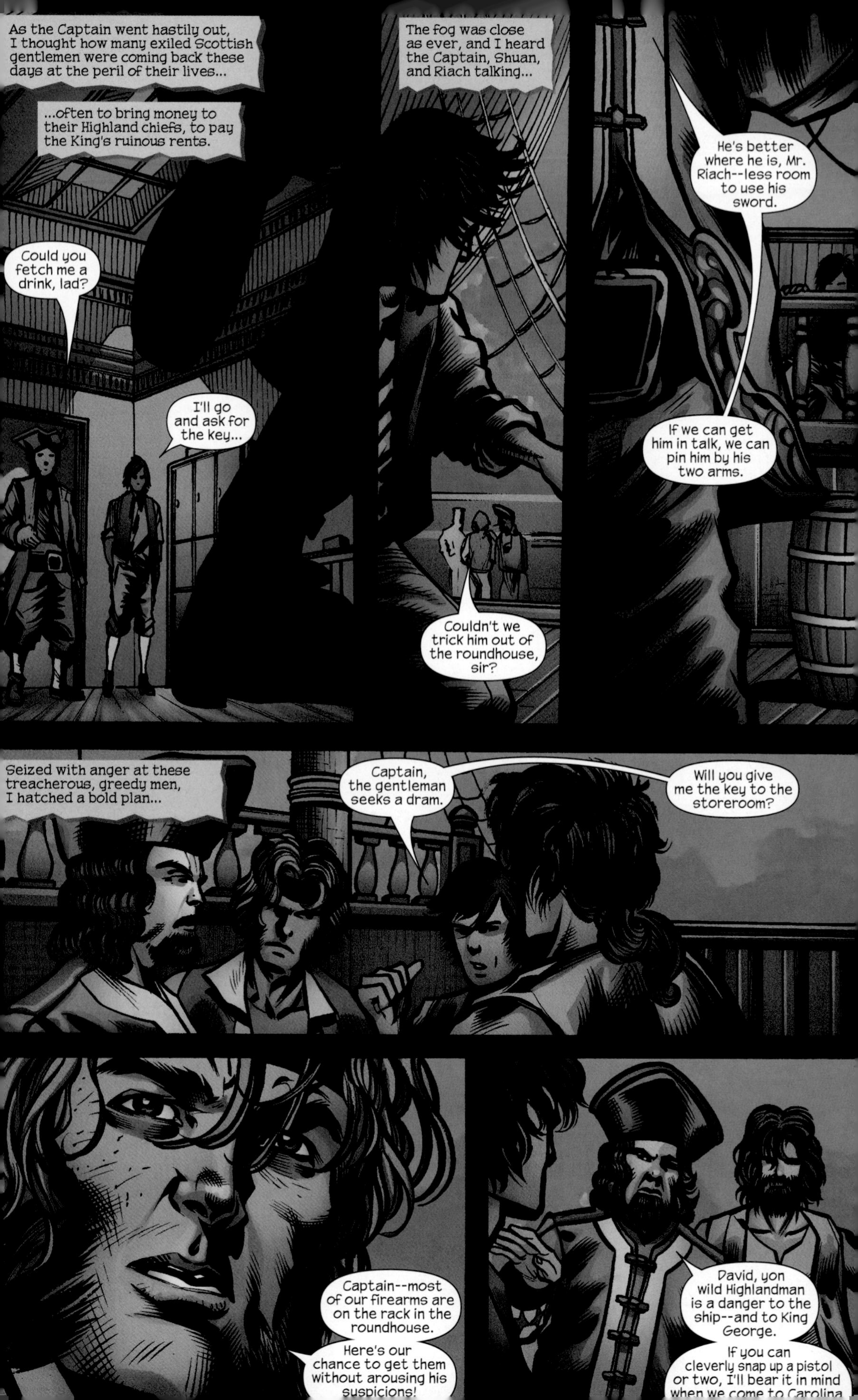
As the Captain went hastily out, I thought how many exiled Scottish gentlemen were coming back these days at the peril of their lives...
...often to bring money to their Highland chiefs, to pay the King's ruinous rents.
Could you fetch me a drink, lad?
I'll go and ask for the key...
The fog was close as ever, and I heard the Captain, Shuan, and Riach talking...
Couldn't we trick him out of the roundhouse, sir?
He's better where he is, Mr. Riach--less room to use his sword.
If we can get him in talk, we can pin him by his two arms.
Seized with anger at these treacherous, greedy men, I hatched a bold plan...
Captain, the gentleman seeks a dram.
Will you give me the key to the storeroom?
Captain--most of our firearms are on the rack in the roundhouse.
Here's our chance to get them without arousing his suspicions!
David, yon wild Highlandman is a danger to the ship--and to King George.
If you can cleverly snap up a pistol or two, I'll bear it in mind when we come to Carolina.

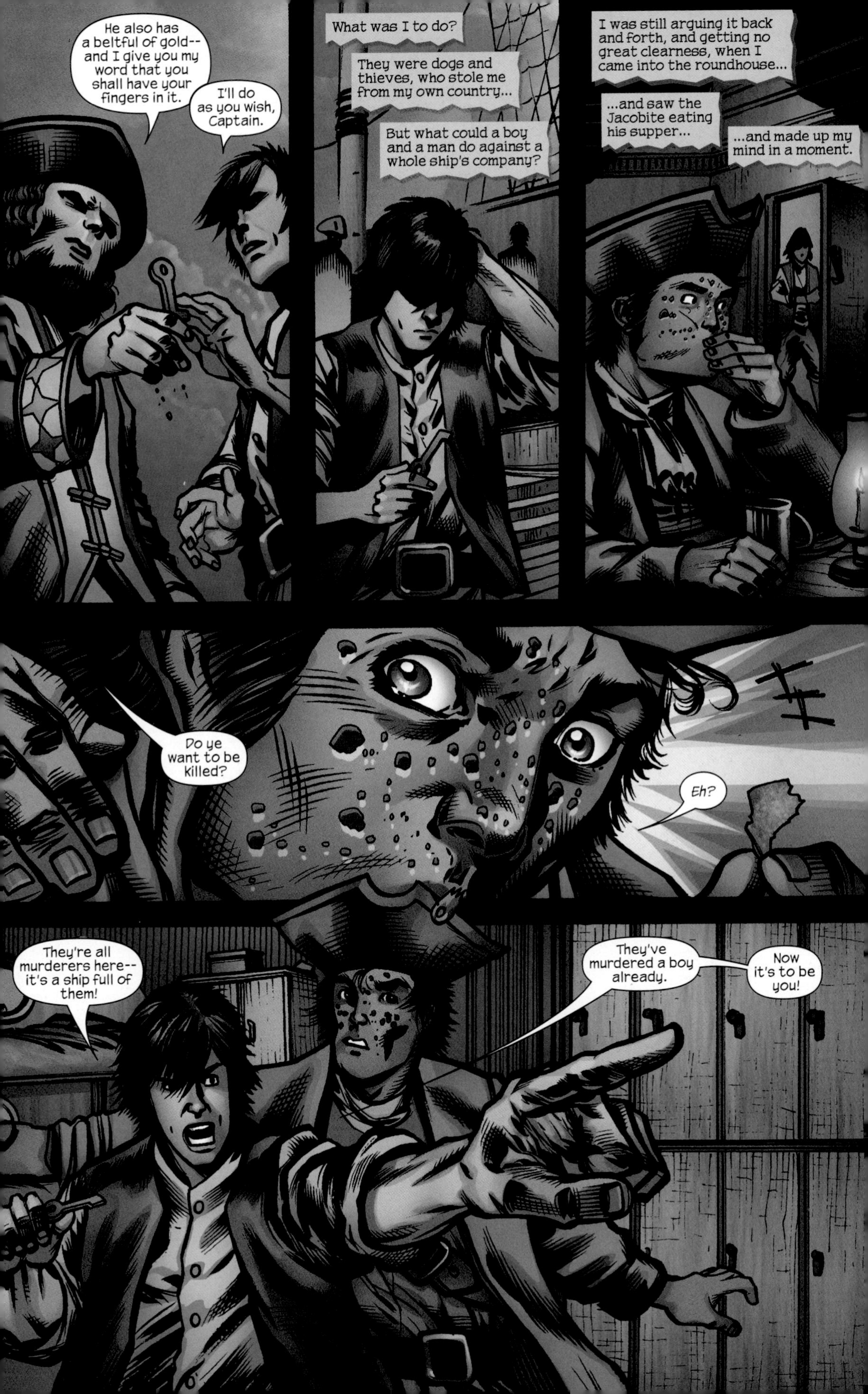
He also has a beltful of gold--and I give you my word that you shall have your fingers in it.
I'll do as you wish, Captain.
What was I to do?
They were dogs and thieves, who stole me from my own country...
But what could a boy and a man do against a whole ship's company?
I was still arguing it back and forth, and getting no great clearness, when I came into the roundhouse...
...and saw the Jacobite eating his supper...
...and made up my mind in a moment.
Do ye want to be killed?
Eh?
They're all murderers here--it's a ship full of them!
They've murdered a boy already.
Now it's to be you!

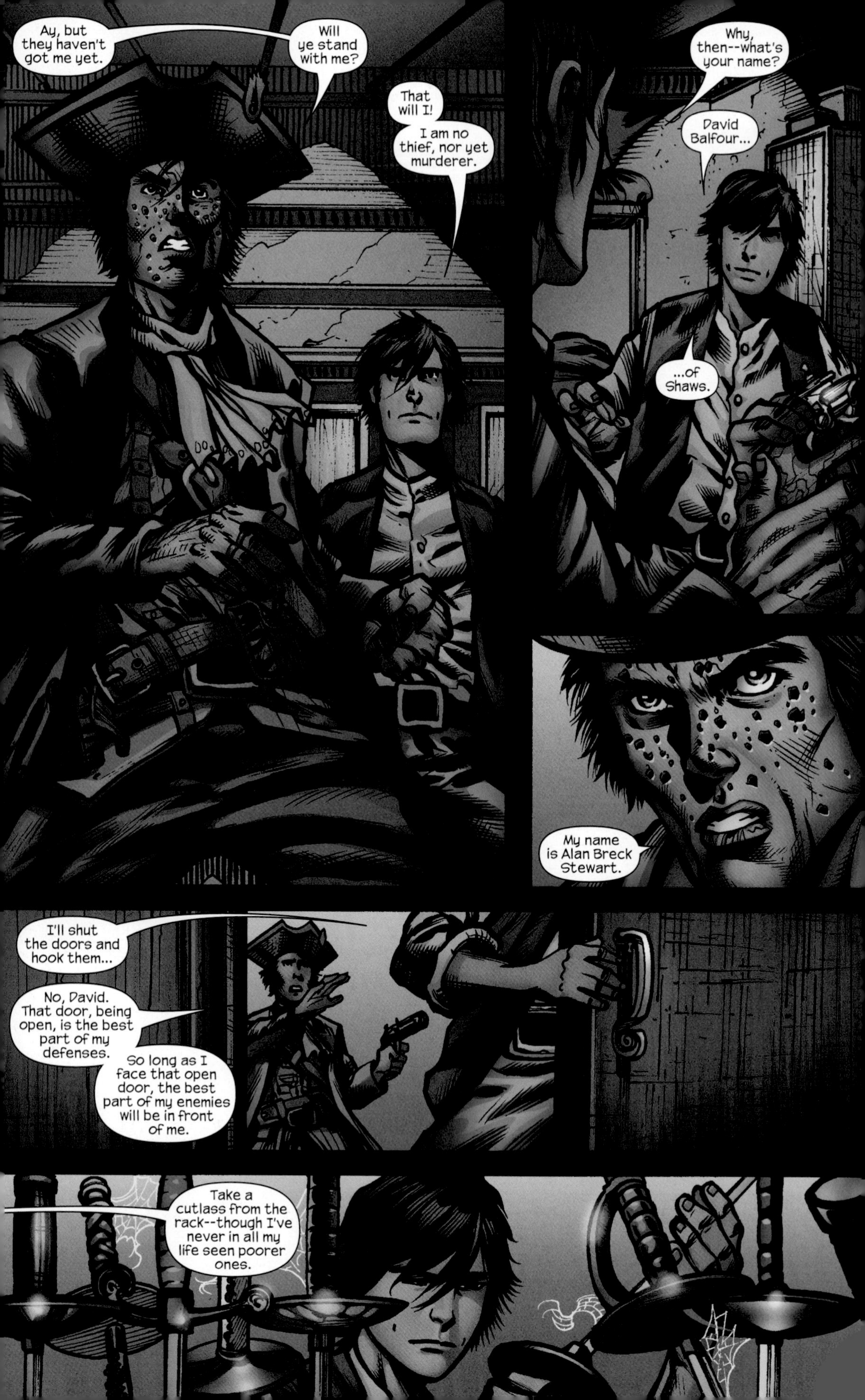
Ay, but they haven't got me yet.
Will ye stand with me?
That will I!
I am no thief, nor yet murderer.
Why, then--what's your name?
David Balfour...
...of Shaws.
My name is Alan Breck Stewart.
I'll shut the doors and hook them...
No, David. That door, being open, is the best part of my defenses.
So long as I face that open door, the best part of my enemies will be in front of me.
Take a cutlass from the rack--though I've never in all my life seen poorer ones.

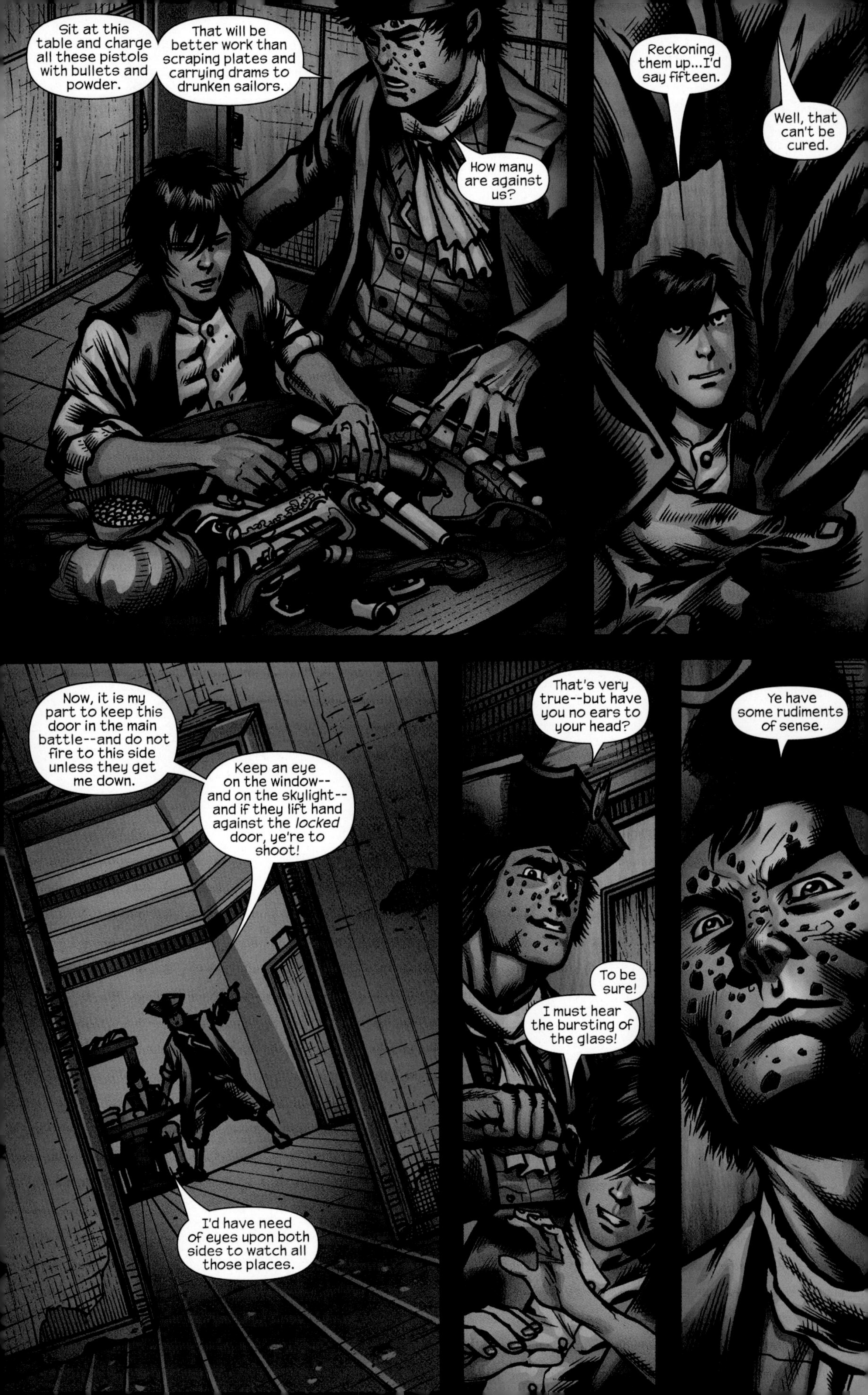
Sit at this table and charge all these pistols with bullets and powder.
That will be better work than scraping plates and carrying drams to drunken sailors.
How many are against us?
Reckoning them up...I'd say fifteen.
Well, that can't be cured.
Now, it is my part to keep this door in the main battle--and do not fire to this side unless they get me down.
Keep an eye on the window--and on the skylight--and if they lift hand against the *locked* door, ye're to shoot!
I'd have need of eyes upon both sides to watch all those places.
That's very true--but have you no ears to your head?
To be sure!
I must hear the bursting of the glass!
Ye have some rudiments of sense.

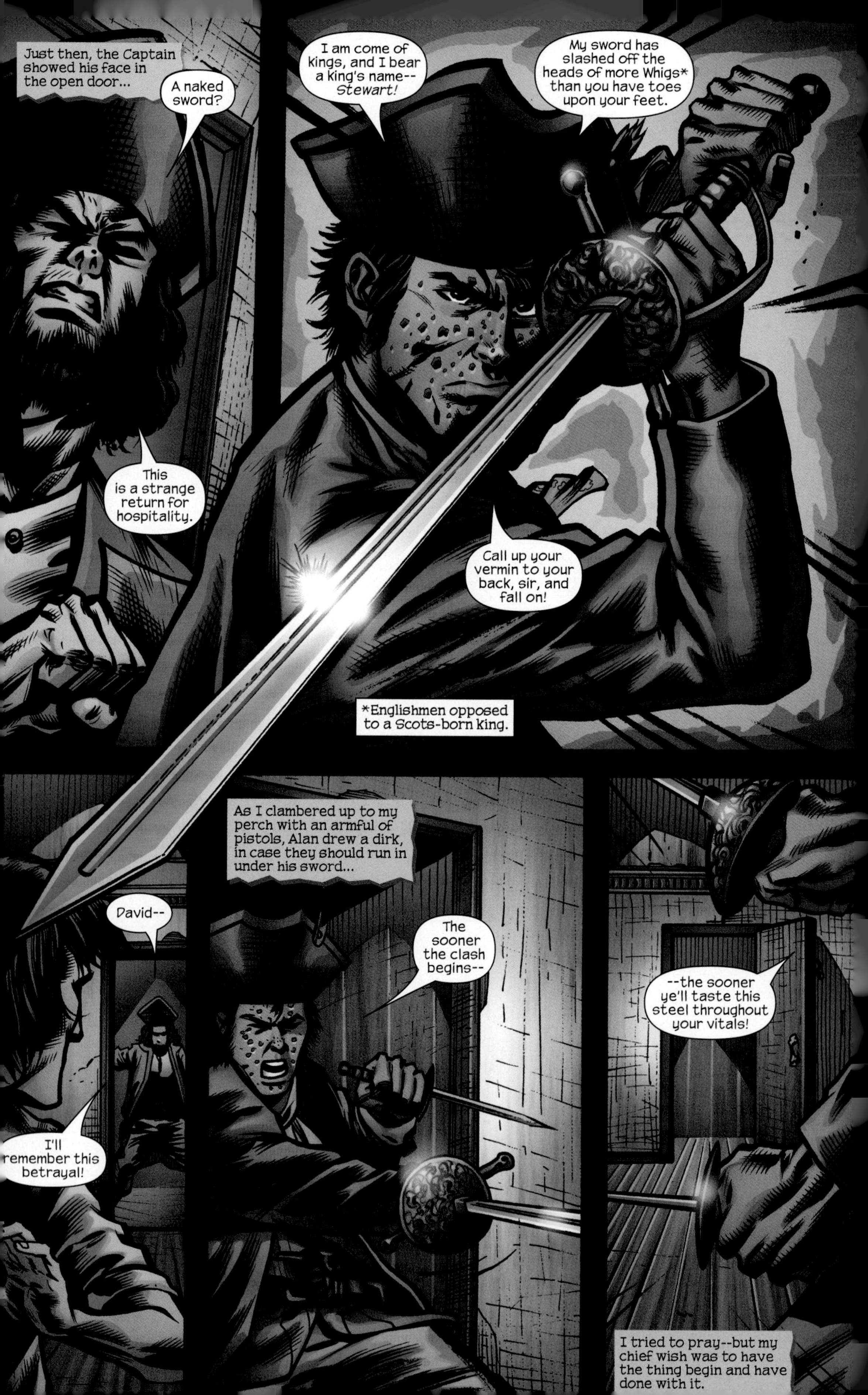
Just then, the Captain showed his face in the open door...
A naked sword?
I am come of kings, and I bear a king's name-- Stewart!
My sword has slashed off the heads of more Whigs* than you have toes upon your feet.
This is a strange return for hospitality.
Call up your vermin to your back, sir, and fall on!
*Englishmen opposed to a Scots-born king.
David--
I'll remember this betrayal!
As I clambered up to my perch with an armful of pistols, Alan drew a dirk, in case they should run in under his sword...
The sooner the clash begins--
--the sooner ye'll taste this steel throughout your vitals!
I tried to pray--but my chief wish was to have the thing begin and have done with it.

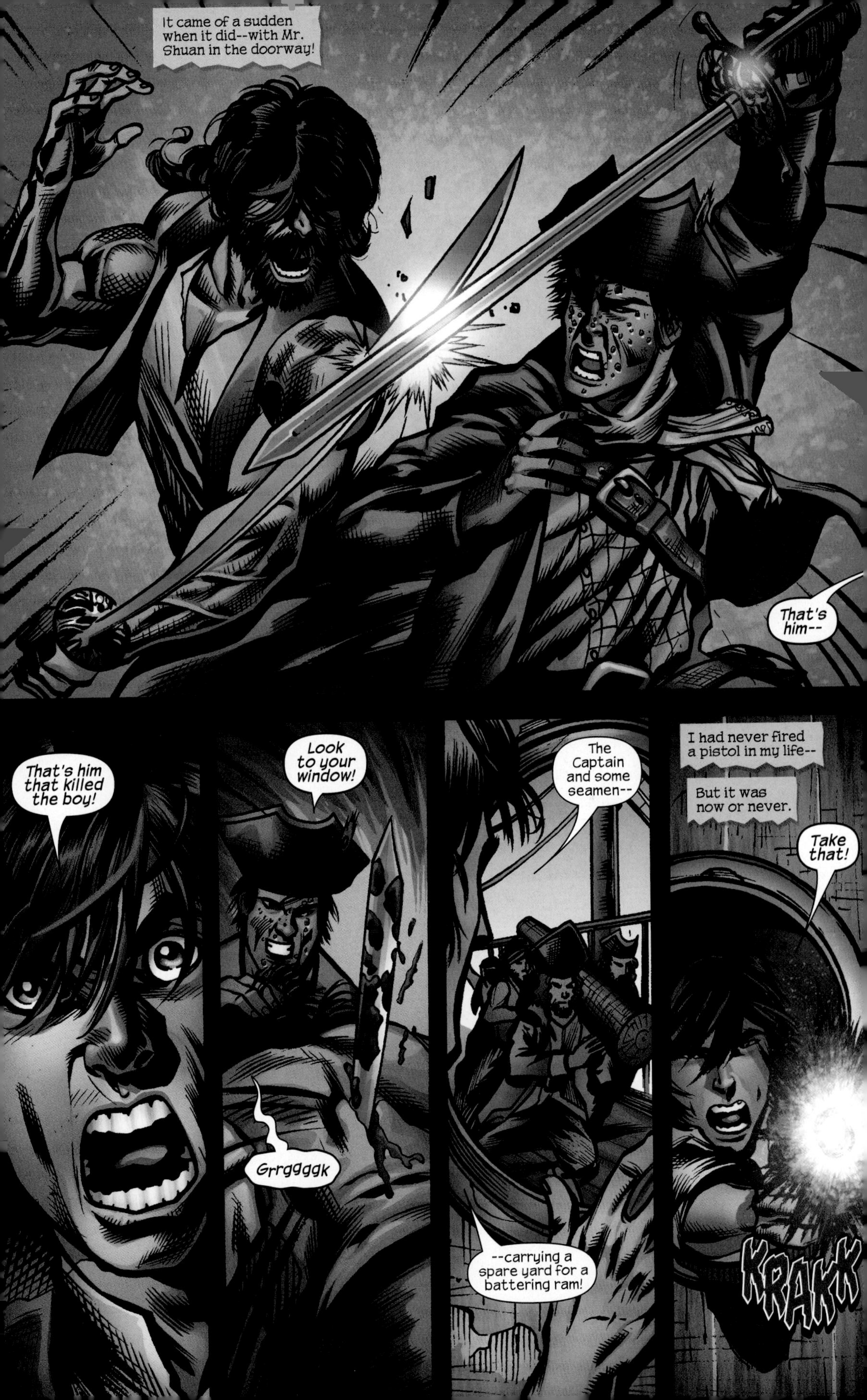
It came of a sudden when it did--with Mr. Shuan in the doorway!
That's him--
That's him that killed the boy!
Look to your window!
Grrggggk
The Captain and some seamen--
--carrying a spare yard for a battering ram!
I had never fired a pistol in my life--
But it was now or never.
Take that!
KRAKK

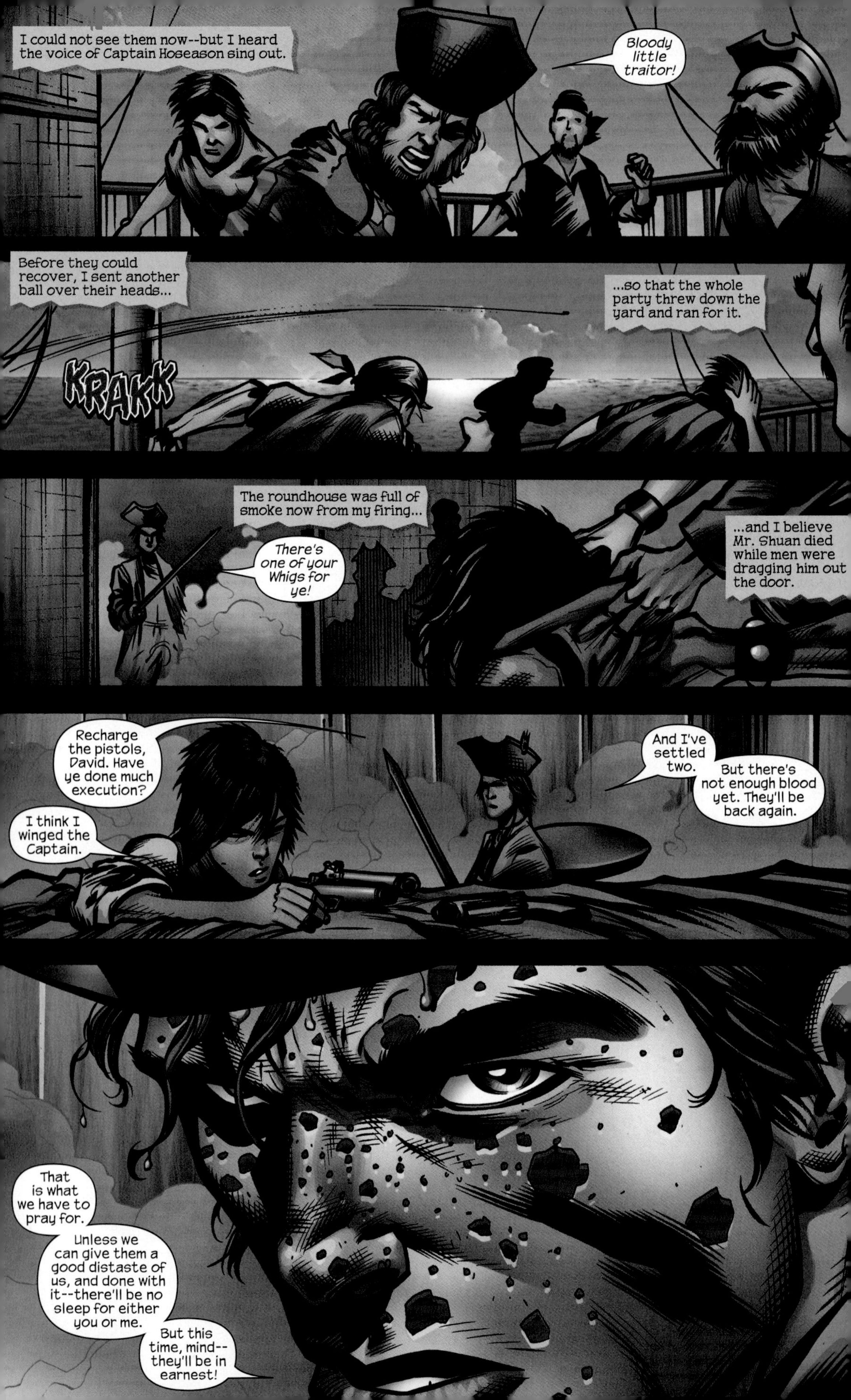
I could not see them now--but I heard the voice of Captain Hoseason sing out.
Bloody little traitor!
Before they could recover, I sent another ball over their heads...
KRAKK
...so that the whole party threw down the yard and ran for it.
The roundhouse was full of smoke now from my firing...
There's one of your Whigs for ye!
...and I believe Mr. Shuan died while men were dragging him out the door.
Recharge the pistols, David. Have ye done much execution?
I think I winged the Captain.
And I've settled two.
But there's not enough blood yet. They'll be back again.
That is what we have to pray for.
Unless we can give them a good distaste of us, and done with it--there'll be no sleep for either you or me.
But this time, mind--they'll be in earnest!

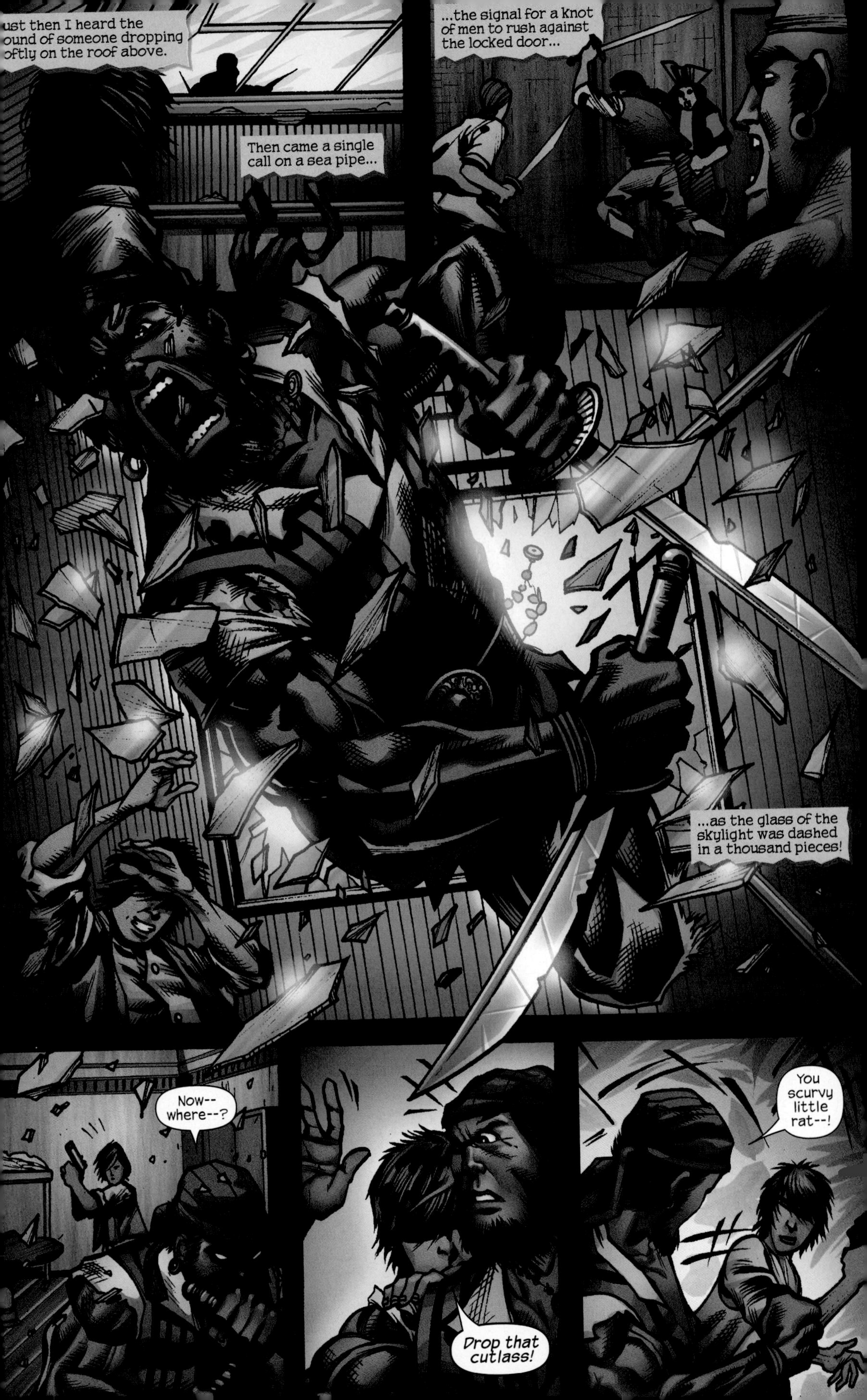
ust then I heard the
ound of someone dropping
oftly on the roof above.
Then came a single
call on a sea pipe...
...the signal for a knot
of men to rush against
the locked door...
...as the glass of the
skylight was dashed
in a thousand pieces!
Now--
where--?
Drop that
cutlass!
You
scurvy
little
rat--!

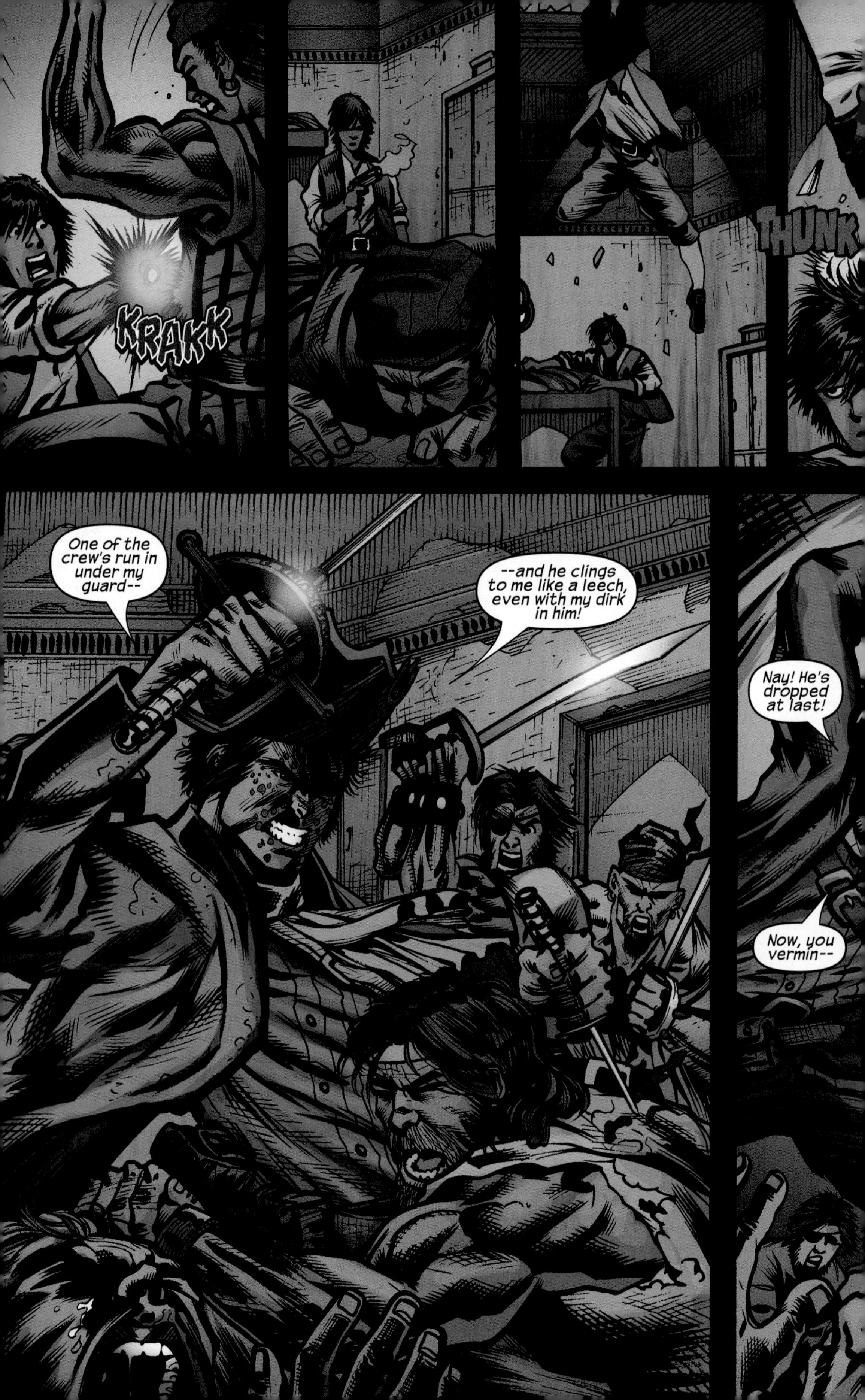
KRAKK
THUNK
One of the crew's run in under my guard--
--and he clings to me like a leech, even with my dirk in him!
Nay! He's dropped at last!
Now, you vermin--

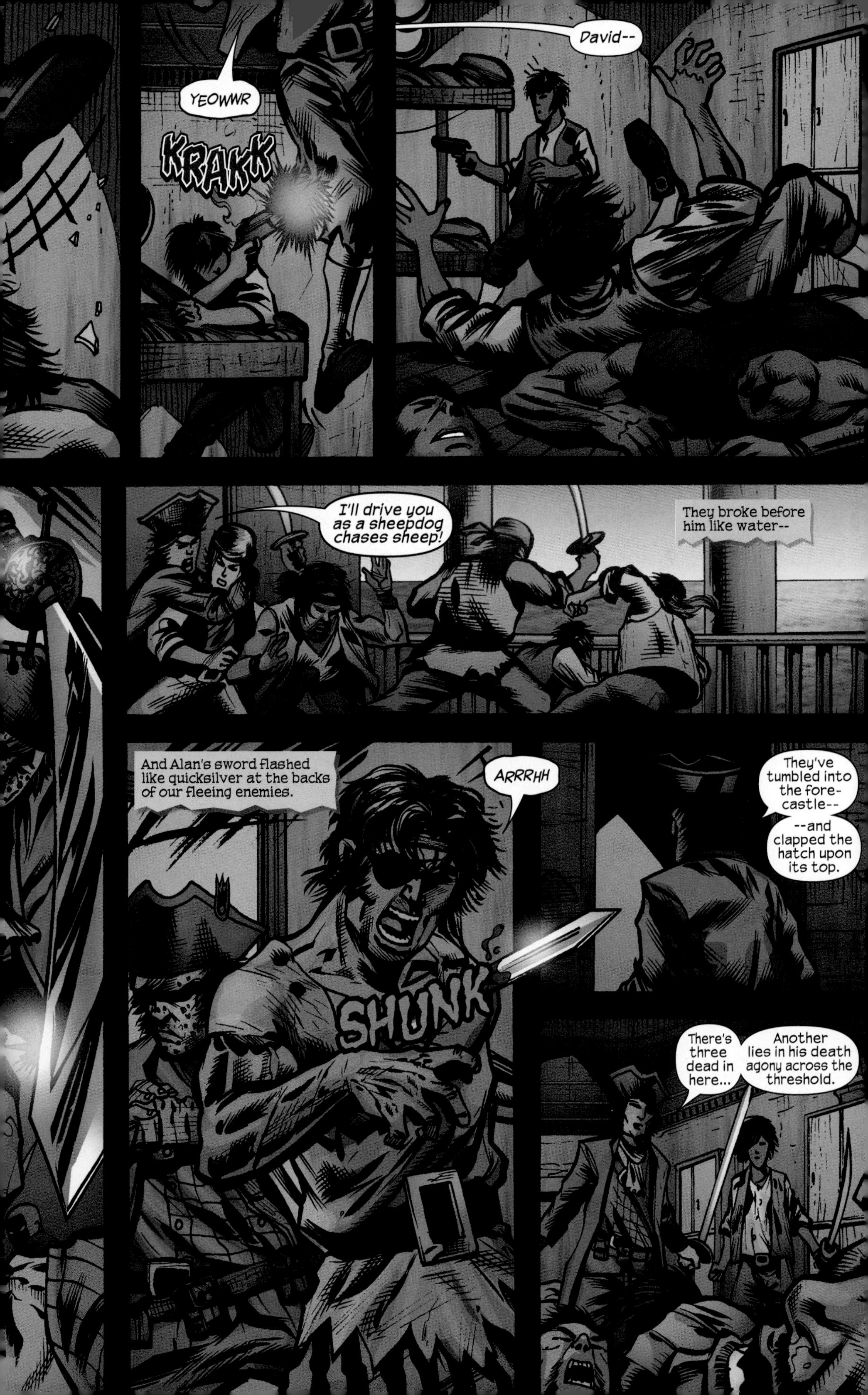
YEOWWR
KRAKK
David--
I'll drive you as a sheepdog chases sheep!
They broke before him like water--
And Alan's sword flashed like quicksilver at the backs of our fleeing enemies.
ARRRHH
SHUNK
They've tumbled into the fore-castle--
--and clapped the hatch upon its top.
There's three dead in here...
Another lies in his death agony across the threshold.

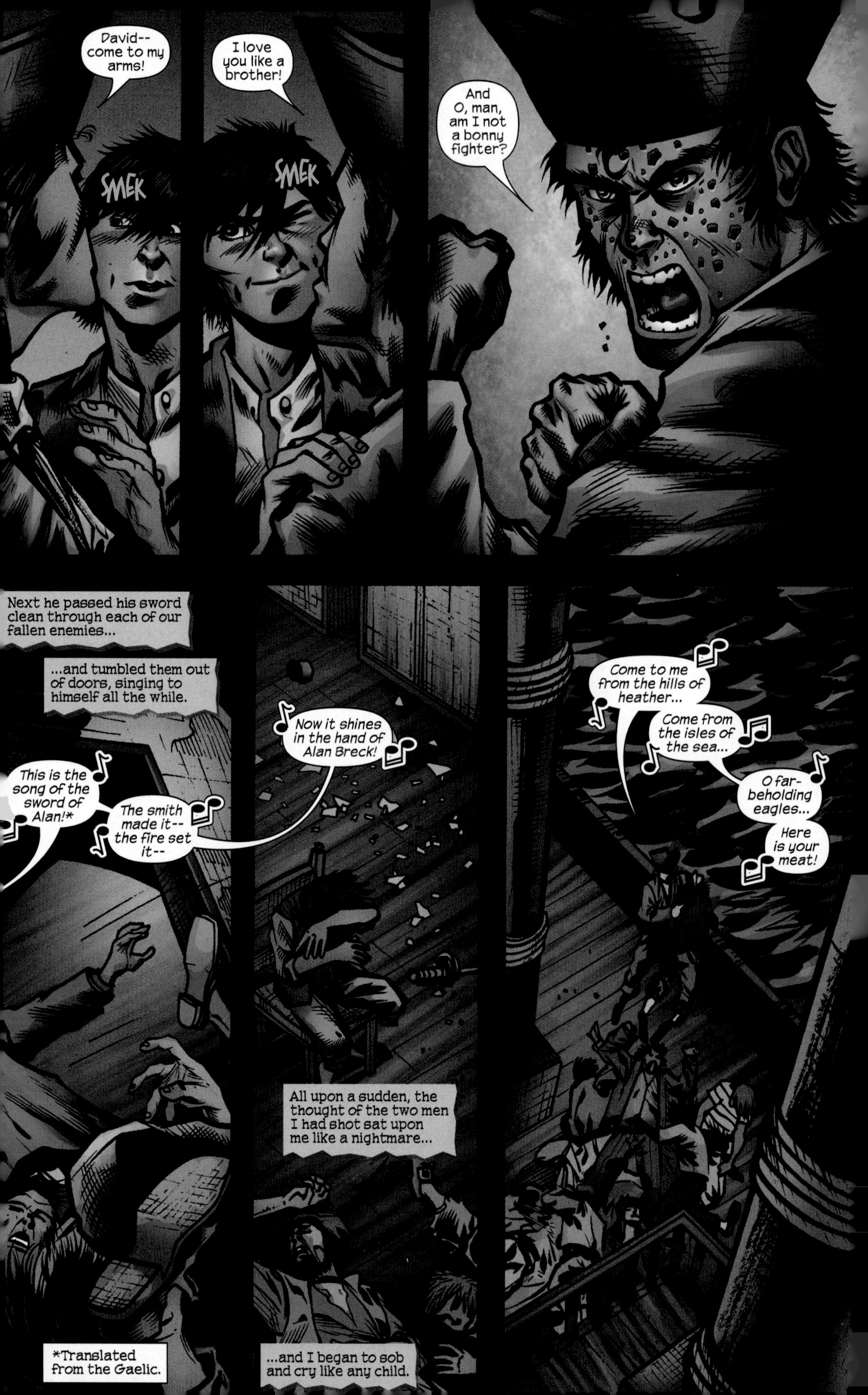
David-- come to my arms!
SMEK
I love you like a brother!
SMEK
And O, man, am I not a bonny fighter?
Next he passed his sword clean through each of our fallen enemies...
...and tumbled them out of doors, singing to himself all the while.
This is the song of the sword of Alan!*
The smith made it-- the fire set it--
Now it shines in the hand of Alan Breck!
Come to me from the hills of heather...
Come from the isles of the sea...
O far-beholding eagles...
Here is your meat!
All upon a sudden, the thought of the two men I had shot sat upon me like a nightmare...
*Translated from the Gaelic.
...and I began to sob and cry like any child.

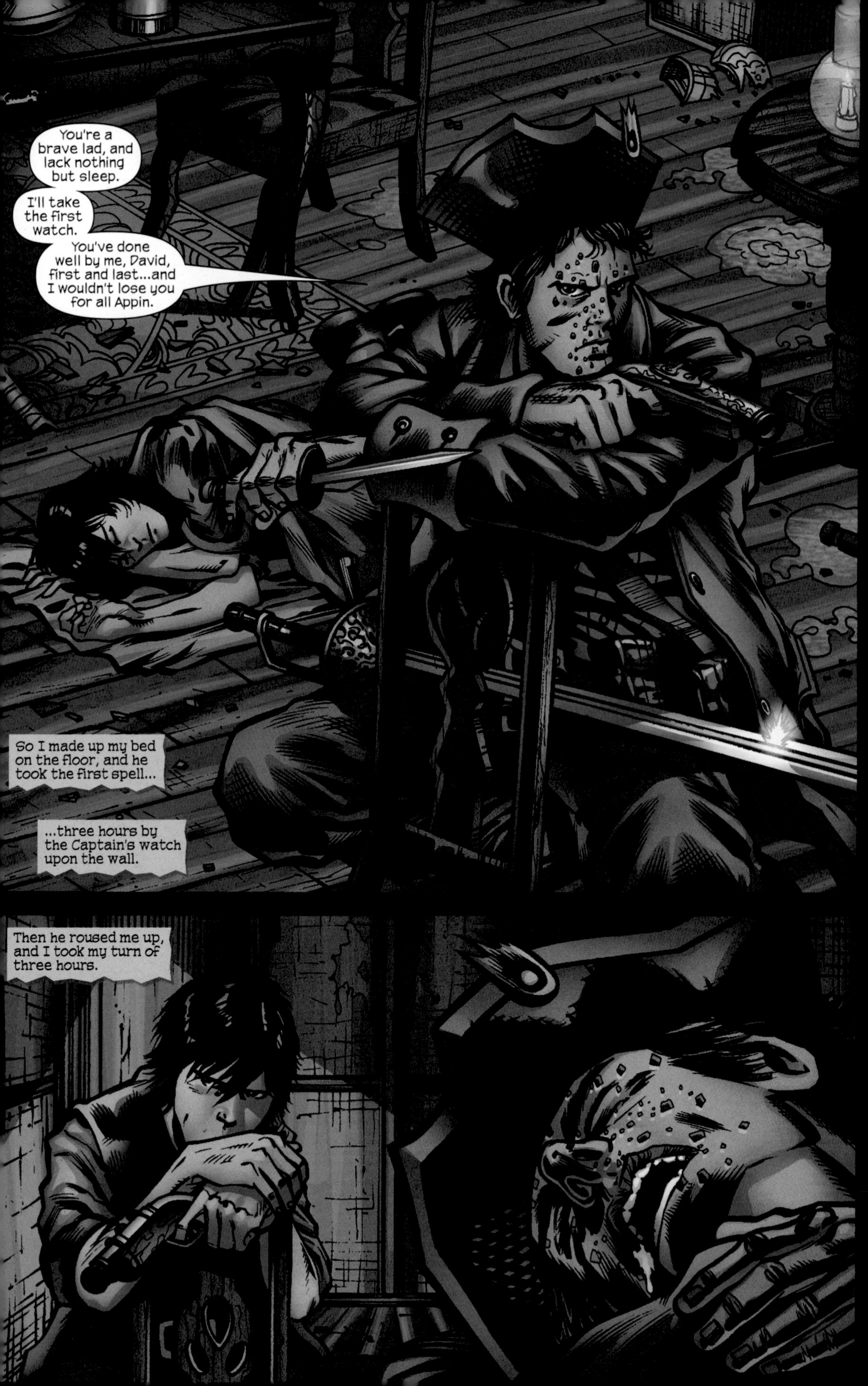
You're a brave lad, and lack nothing but sleep.
I'll take the first watch.
You've done well by me, David, first and last...and I wouldn't lose you for all Appin.
So I made up my bed on the floor, and he took the first spell...
...three hours by the Captain's watch upon the wall.
Then he roused me up, and I took my turn of three hours.

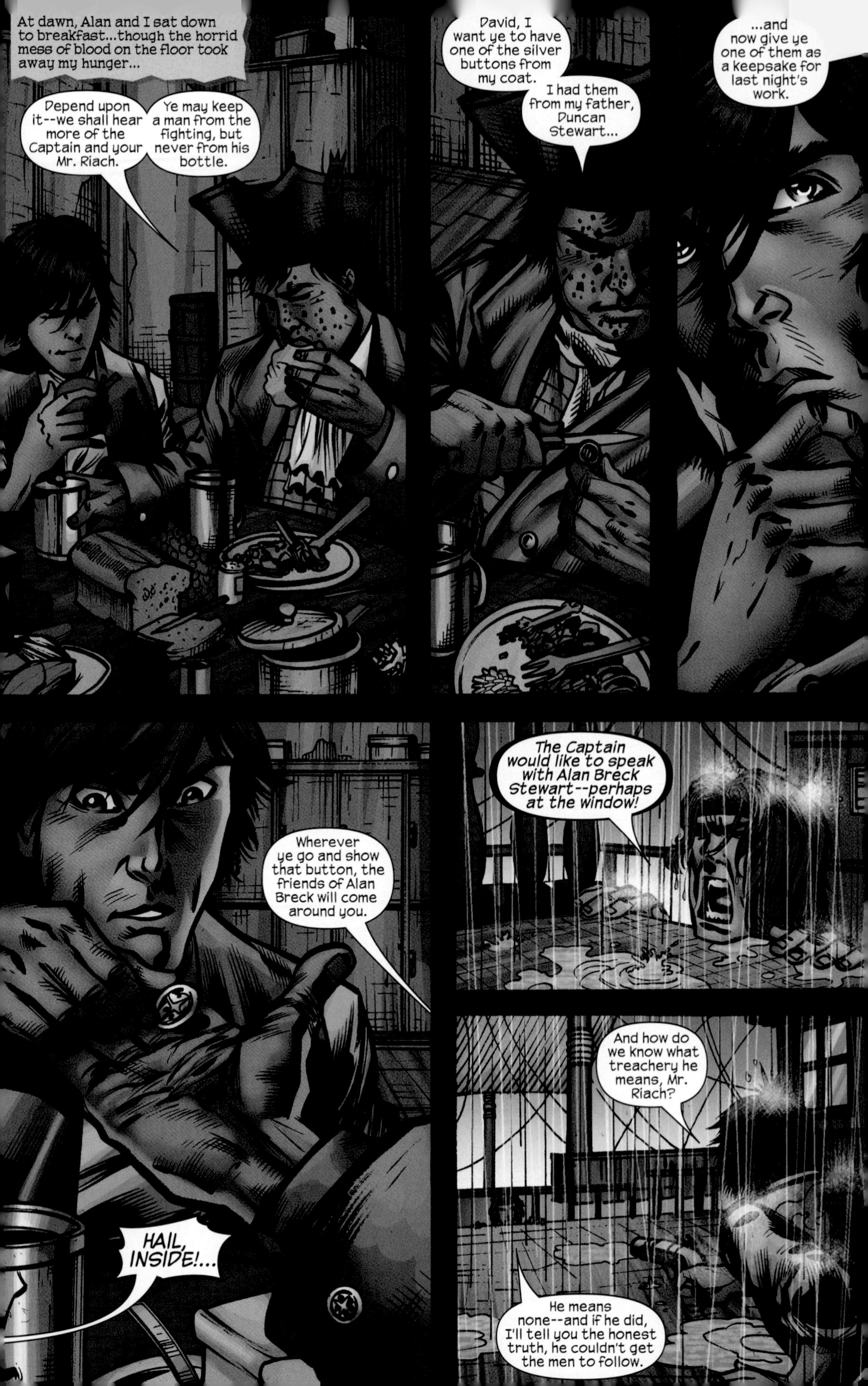
At dawn, Alan and I sat down to breakfast...though the horrid mess of blood on the floor took away my hunger...
Depend upon it--we shall hear more of the Captain and your Mr. Riach.
Ye may keep a man from the fighting, but never from his bottle.
David, I want ye to have one of the silver buttons from my coat.
I had them from my father, Duncan Stewart...
...and now give ye one of them as a keepsake for last night's work.
Wherever ye go and show that button, the friends of Alan Breck will come around you.
HAIL, INSIDE!...
The Captain would like to speak with Alan Breck Stewart--perhaps at the window!
And how do we know what treachery he means, Mr. Riach?
He means none--and if he did, I'll tell you the honest truth, he couldn't get the men to follow.

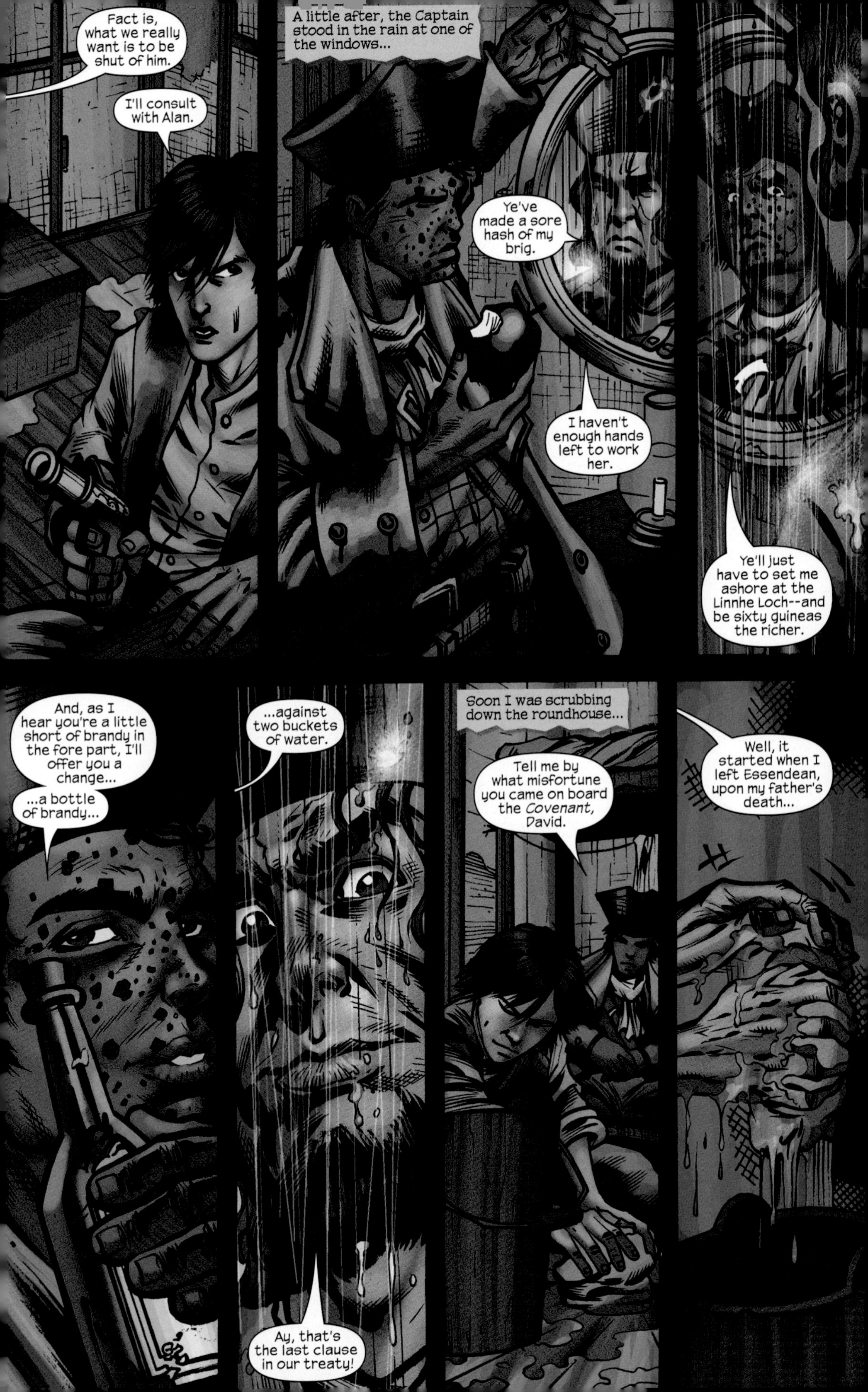
Fact is, what we really want is to be shut of him.
I'll consult with Alan.
A little after, the Captain stood in the rain at one of the windows...
Ye've made a sore hash of my brig.
I haven't enough hands left to work her.
Ye'll just have to set me ashore at the Linnhe Loch--and be sixty guineas the richer.
And, as I hear you're a little short of brandy in the fore part, I'll offer you a change...
...a bottle of brandy...
...against two buckets of water.
Ay, that's the last clause in our treaty!
Soon I was scrubbing down the roundhouse...
Tell me by what misfortune you came on board the *Covenant*, David.
Well, it started when I left Essendean, upon my father's death...

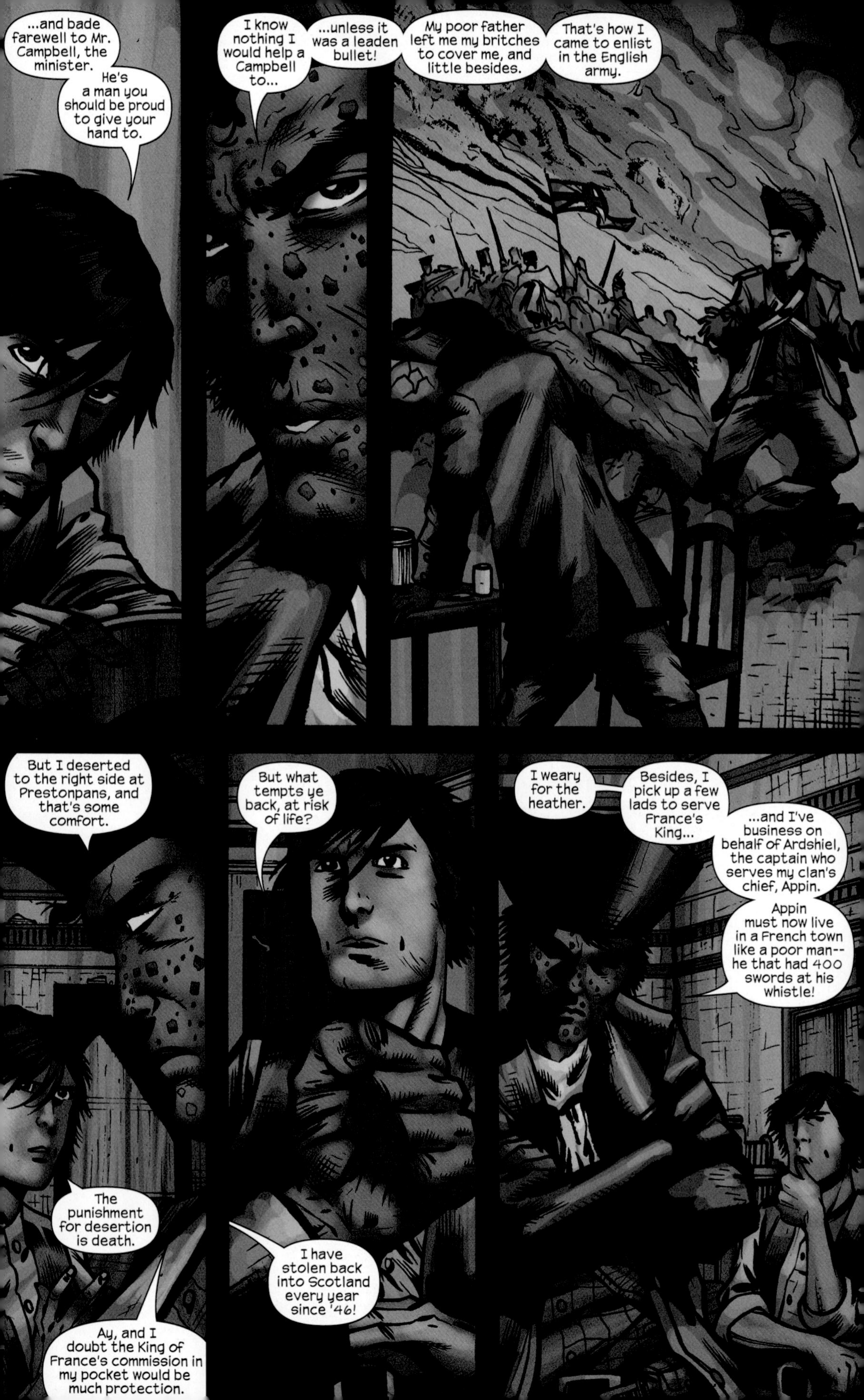
...and bade farewell to Mr. Campbell, the minister.
He's a man you should be proud to give your hand to.
I know nothing I would help a Campbell to...
...unless it was a leaden bullet!
My poor father left me my britches to cover me, and little besides.
That's how I came to enlist in the English army.
But I deserted to the right side at Prestonpans, and that's some comfort.
The punishment for desertion is death.
Ay, and I doubt the King of France's commission in my pocket would be much protection.
But what tempts ye back, at risk of life?
I have stolen back into Scotland every year since '46!
I weary for the heather.
Besides, I pick up a few lads to serve France's King...
...and I've business on behalf of Ardshiel, the captain who serves my clan's chief, Appin.
Appin must now live in a French town like a poor man--he that had 400 swords at his whistle!

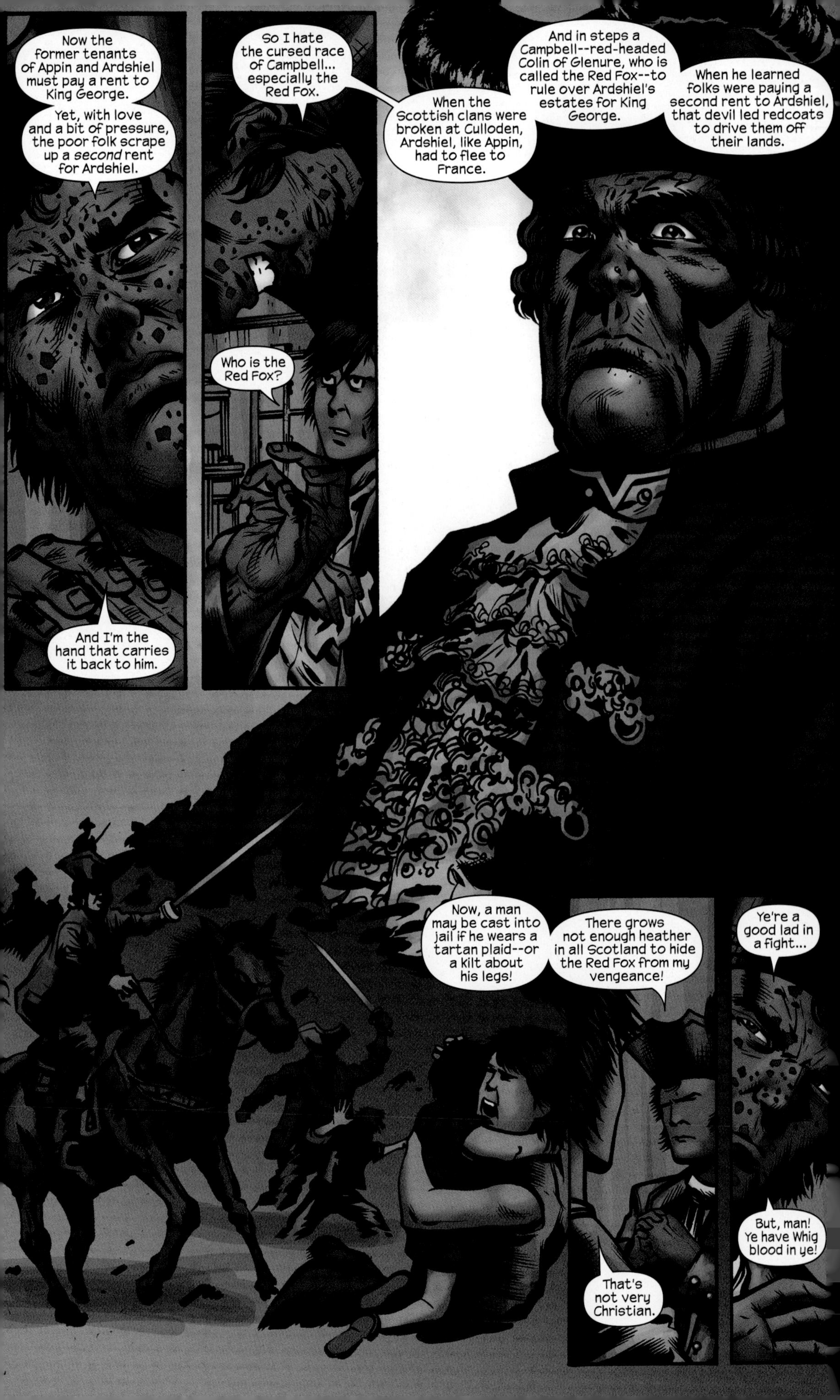

Now the former tenants of Appin and Ardshiel must pay a rent to King George.
Yet, with love and a bit of pressure, the poor folk scrape up a *second* rent for Ardshiel.
And I'm the hand that carries it back to him.
So I hate the cursed race of Campbell... especially the Red Fox.
Who is the Red Fox?
When the Scottish clans were broken at Culloden, Ardshiel, like Appin, had to flee to France.
And in steps a Campbell--red-headed Colin of Glenure, who is called the Red Fox--to rule over Ardshiel's estates for King George.
When he learned folks were paying a second rent to Ardshiel, that devil led redcoats to drive them off their lands.
Now, a man may be cast into jail if he wears a tartan plaid--or a kilt about his legs!
There grows not enough heather in all Scotland to hide the Red Fox from my vengeance!
That's not very Christian.
Ye're a good lad in a fight...
But, man! Ye have Whig blood in ye!

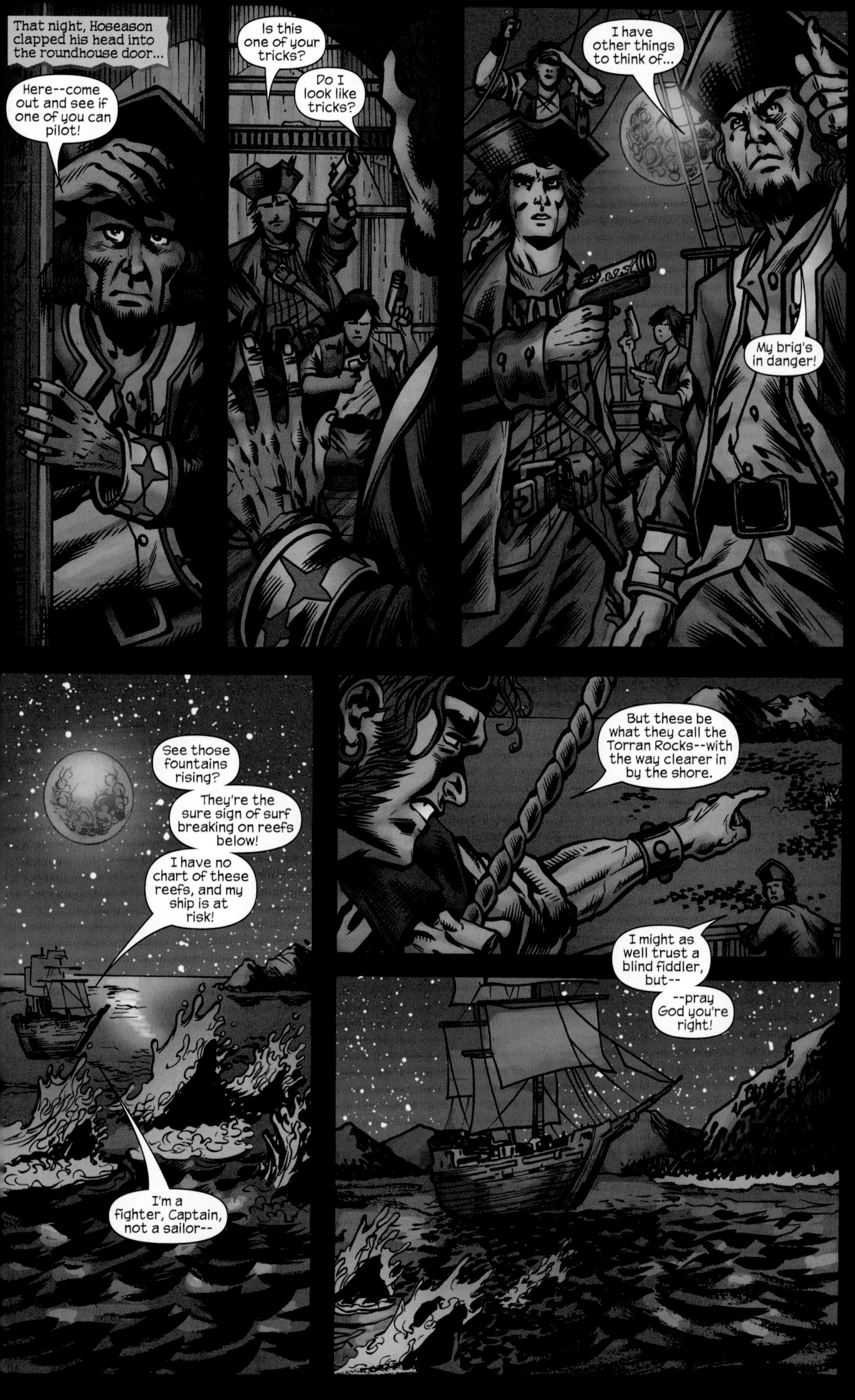
That night, Hoseason clapped his head into the roundhouse door...
Here--come out and see if one of you can pilot!
Is this one of your tricks?
Do I look like tricks?
I have other things to think of...
My brig's in danger!
See those fountains rising?
They're the sure sign of surf breaking on reefs below!
I have no chart of these reefs, and my ship is at risk!
I'm a fighter, Captain, not a sailor--
But these be what they call the Torran Rocks--with the way clearer in by the shore.
I might as well trust a blind fiddler, but--
--pray God you're right!

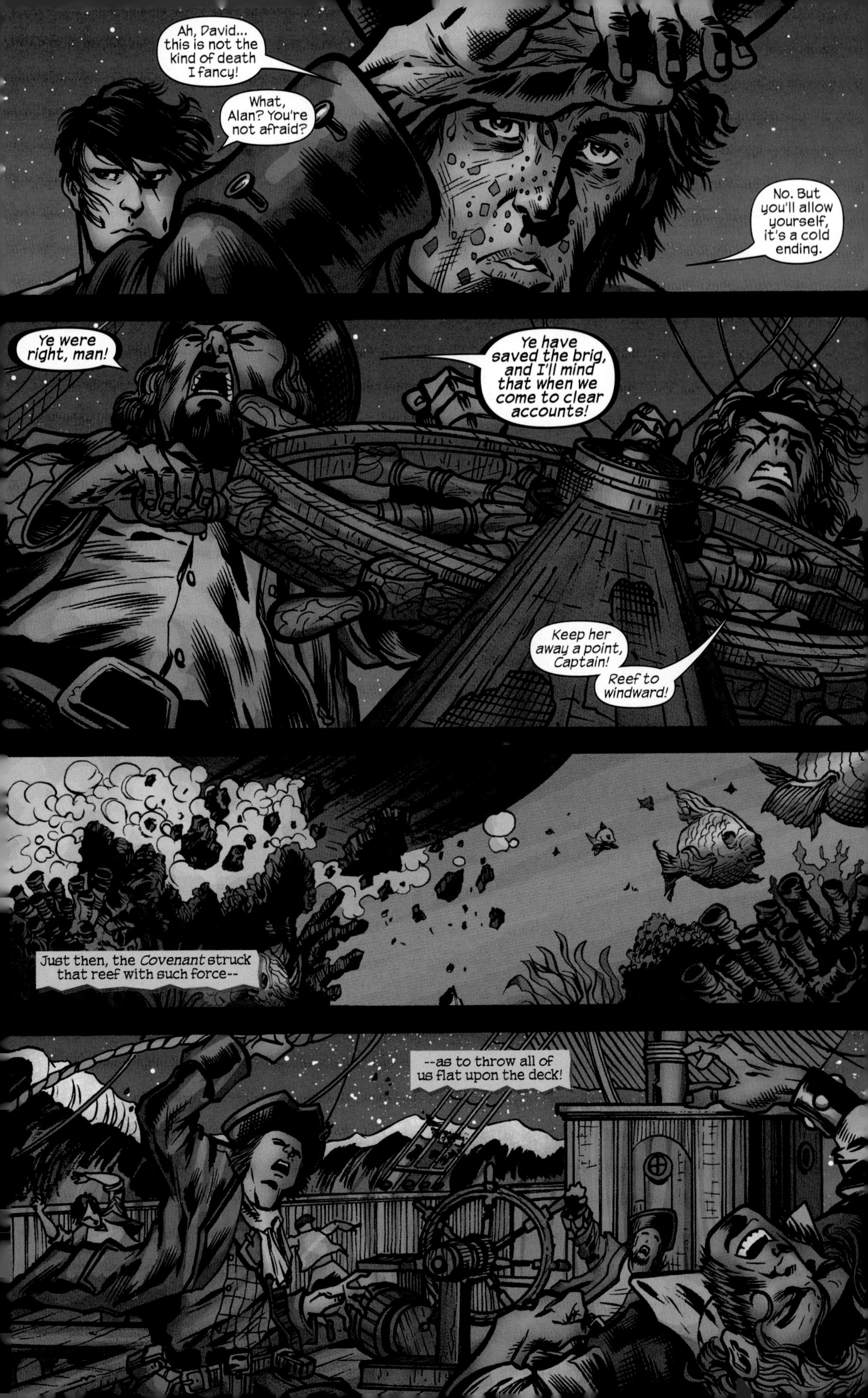
Ah, David... this is not the kind of death I fancy!
What, Alan? You're not afraid?
No. But you'll allow yourself, it's a cold ending.
Ye were right, man!
Ye have saved the brig, and I'll mind that when we come to clear accounts!
Keep her away a point, Captain!
Reef to windward!
Just then, the *Covenant* struck that reef with such force--
--as to throw all of us flat upon the deck!

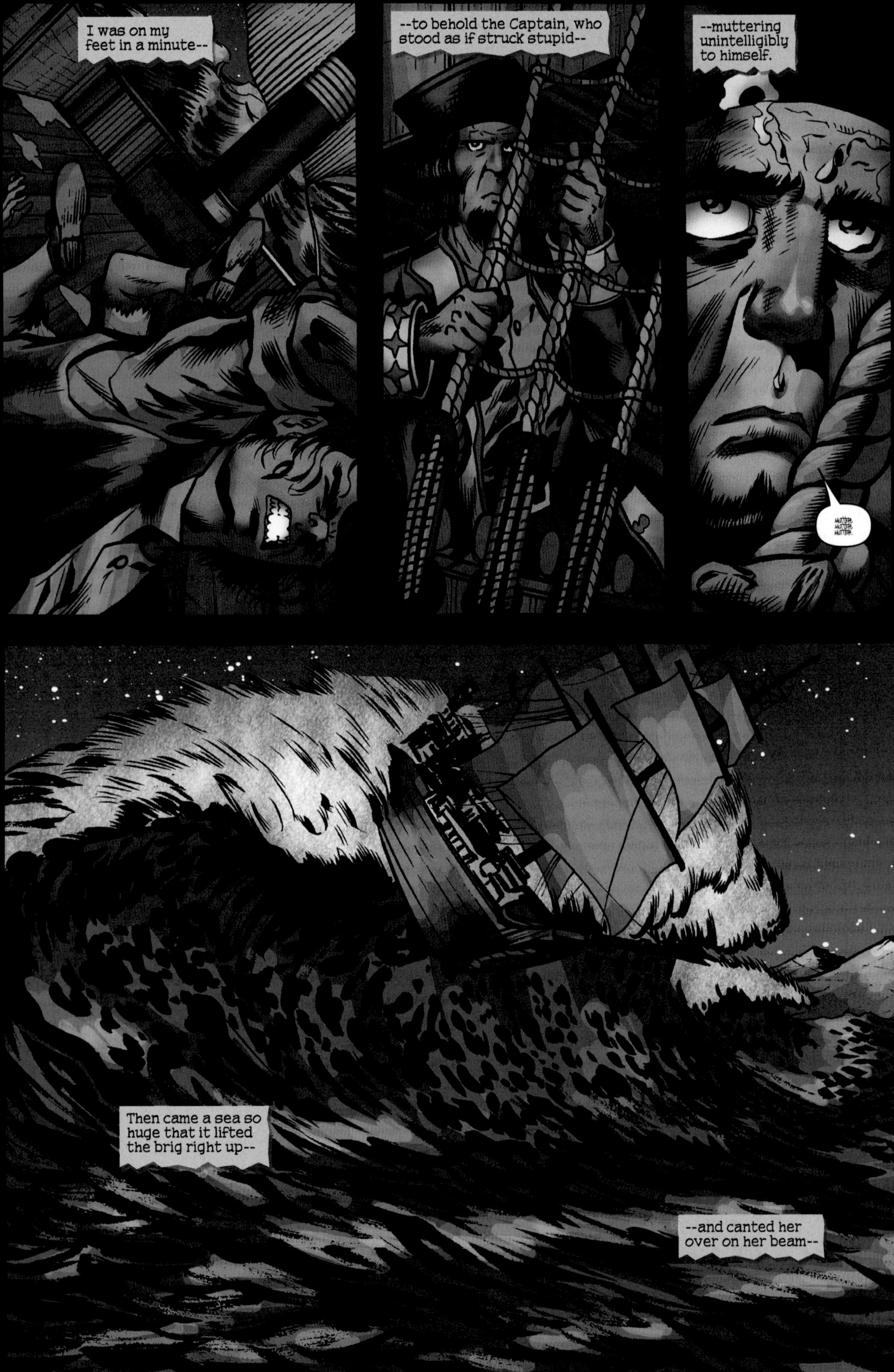
I was on my feet in a minute--
--to behold the Captain, who stood as if struck stupid--
--muttering unintelligibly to himself.
MUTTER, MUTTER, MUTTER...
Then came a sea so huge that it lifted the brig right up--
--and canted her over on her beam--

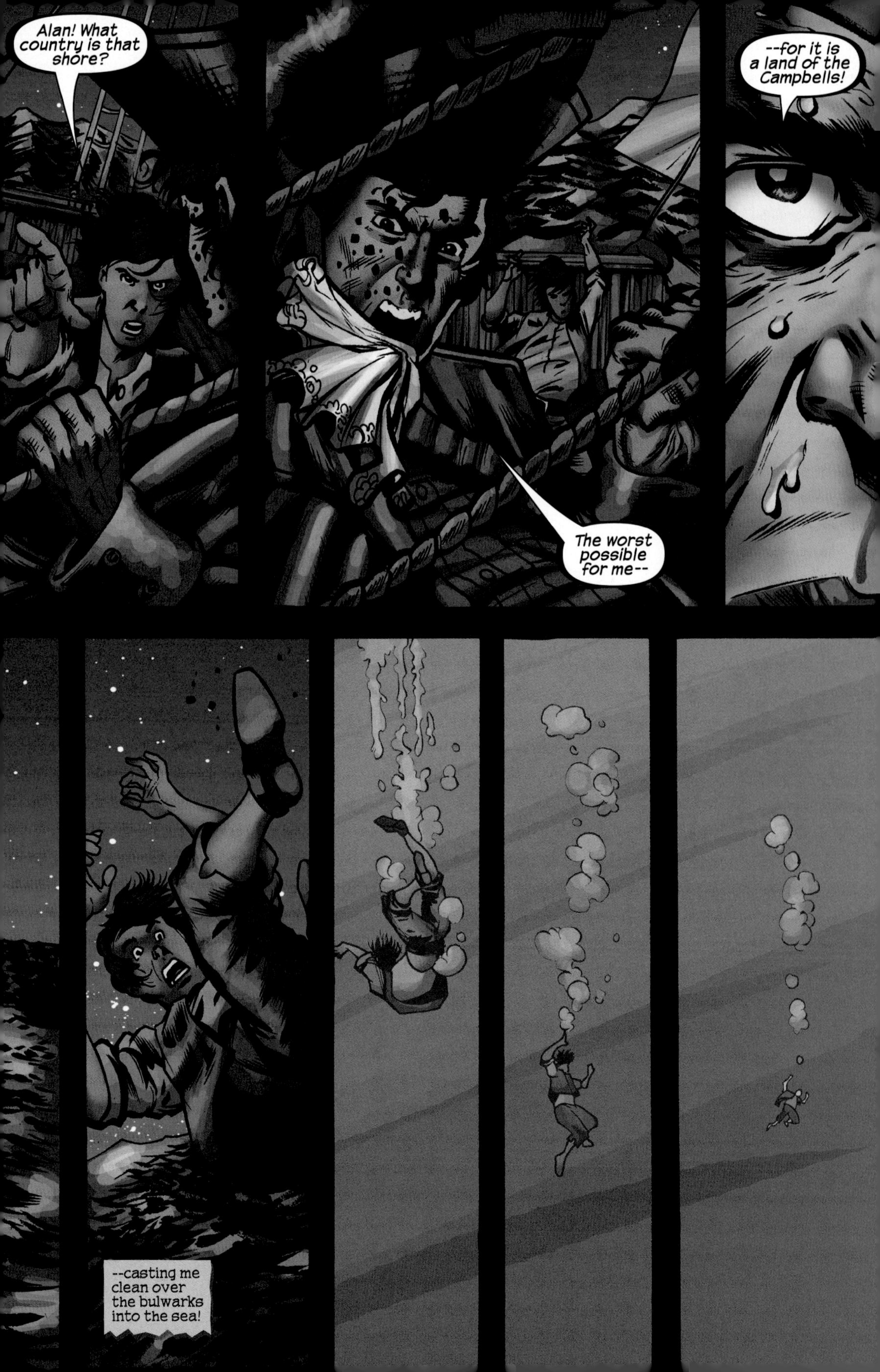
Alan! What country is that shore?
The worst possible for me--
--for it is a land of the Campbells!
--casting me clean over the bulwarks into the sea!

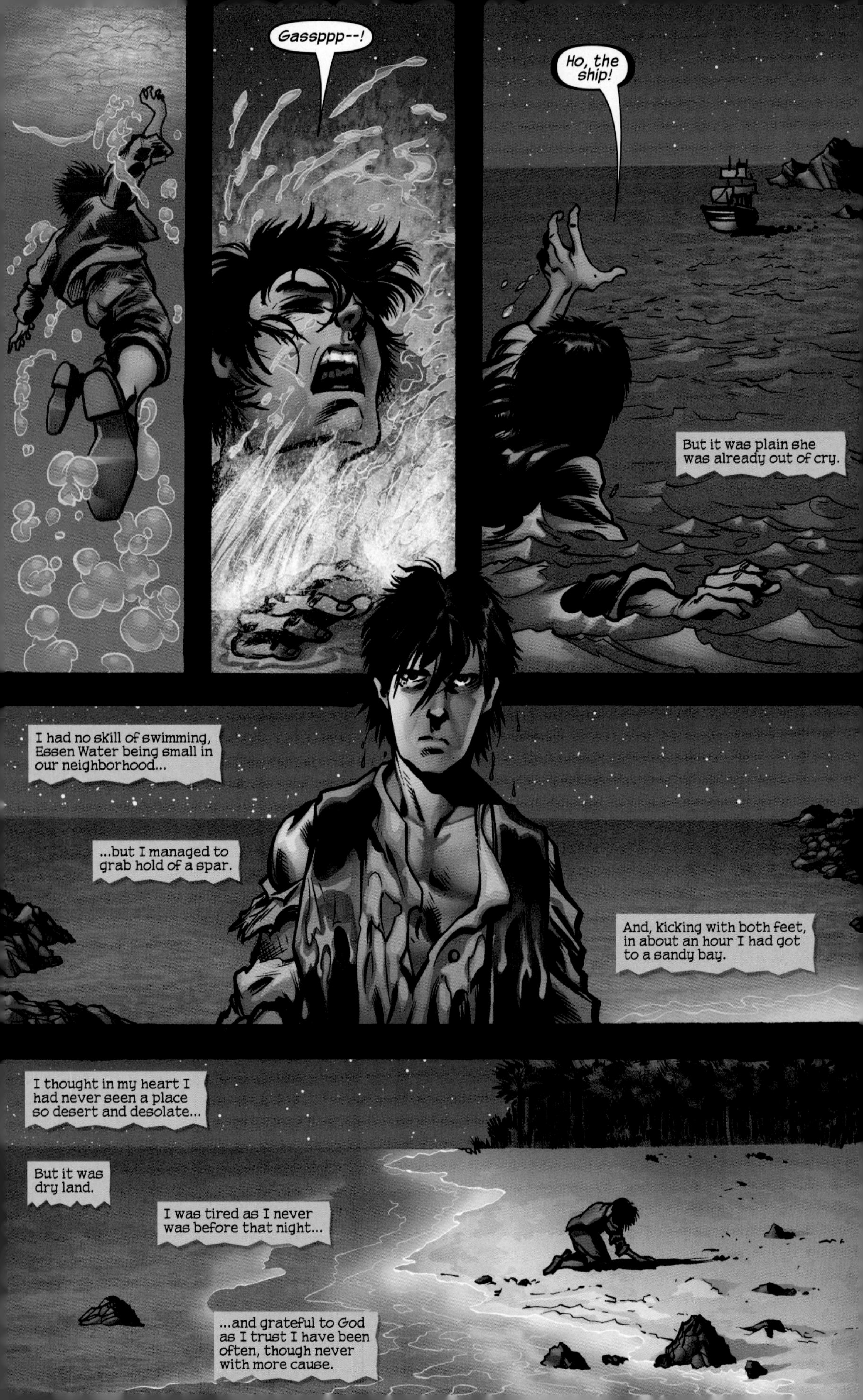

Gassppp--!
Ho, the ship!
But it was plain she was already out of cry.
I had no skill of swimming, Essen Water being small in our neighborhood...
...but I managed to grab hold of a spar.
And, kicking with both feet, in about an hour I had got to a sandy bay.
I thought in my heart I had never seen a place so desert and desolate...
But it was dry land.
I was tired as I never was before that night...
...and grateful to God as I trust I have been often, though never with more cause.

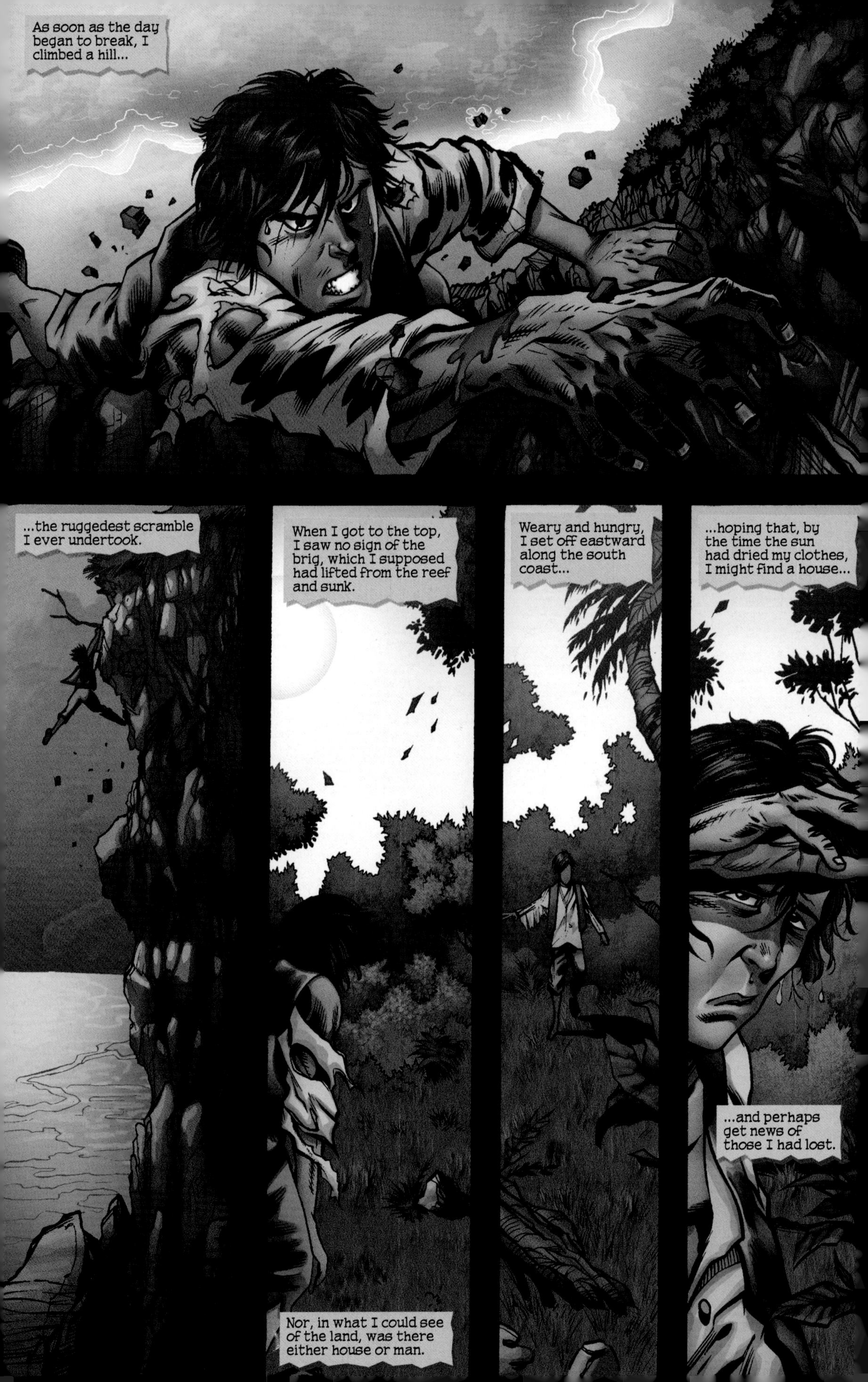
As soon as the day began to break, I climbed a hill...
...the ruggedest scramble I ever undertook.
When I got to the top, I saw no sign of the brig, which I supposed had lifted from the reef and sunk.
Nor, in what I could see of the land, was there either house or man.
Weary and hungry, I set off eastward along the south coast...
...hoping that, by the time the sun had dried my clothes, I might find a house...
...and perhaps get news of those I had lost.

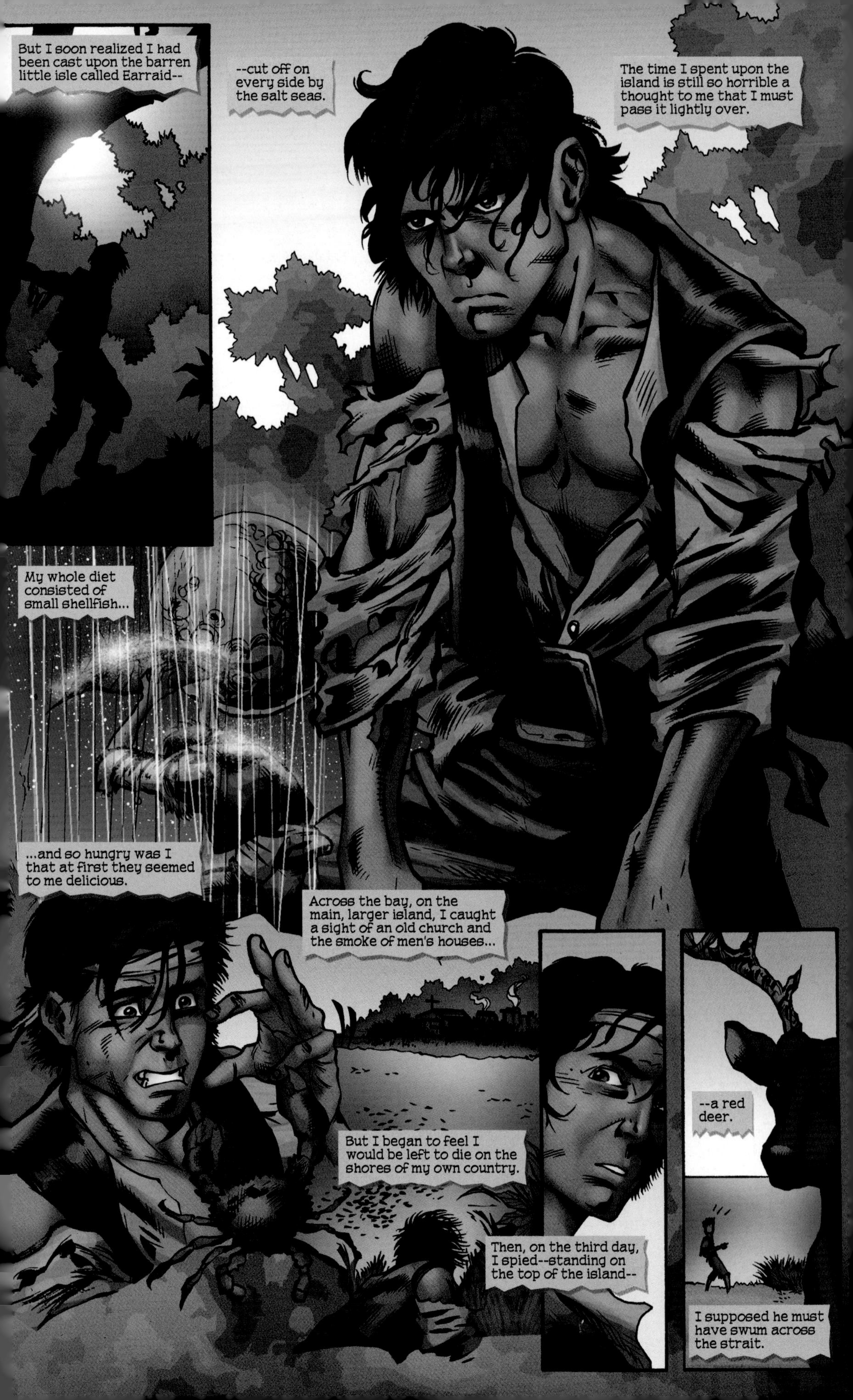
But I soon realized I had been cast upon the barren little isle called Earraid--
--cut off on every side by the salt seas.
The time I spent upon the island is still so horrible a thought to me that I must pass it lightly over.
My whole diet consisted of small shellfish...
...and so hungry was I that at first they seemed to me delicious.
Across the bay, on the main, larger island, I caught a sight of an old church and the smoke of men's houses...
But I began to feel I would be left to die on the shores of my own country.
Then, on the third day, I spied--standing on the top of the island--
--a red deer.
I supposed he must have swum across the strait.

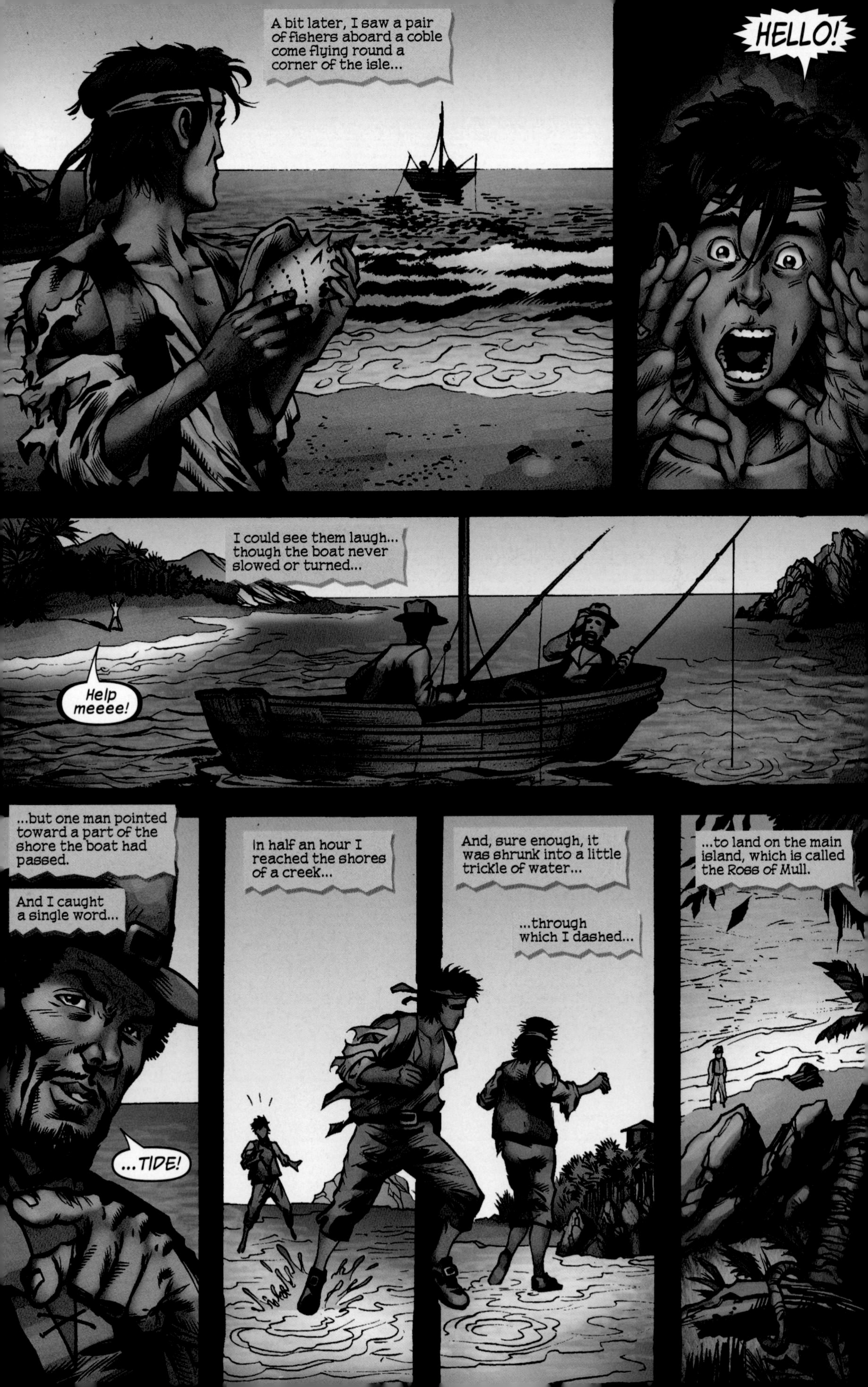
A bit later, I saw a pair of fishers aboard a coble come flying round a corner of the isle...
HELLO!
I could see them laugh... though the boat never slowed or turned...
Help meeee!
...but one man pointed toward a part of the shore the boat had passed.
And I caught a single word...
...TIDE!
In half an hour I reached the shores of a creek...
And, sure enough, it was shrunk into a little trickle of water...
...through which I dashed...
...to land on the main island, which is called the Ross of Mull.

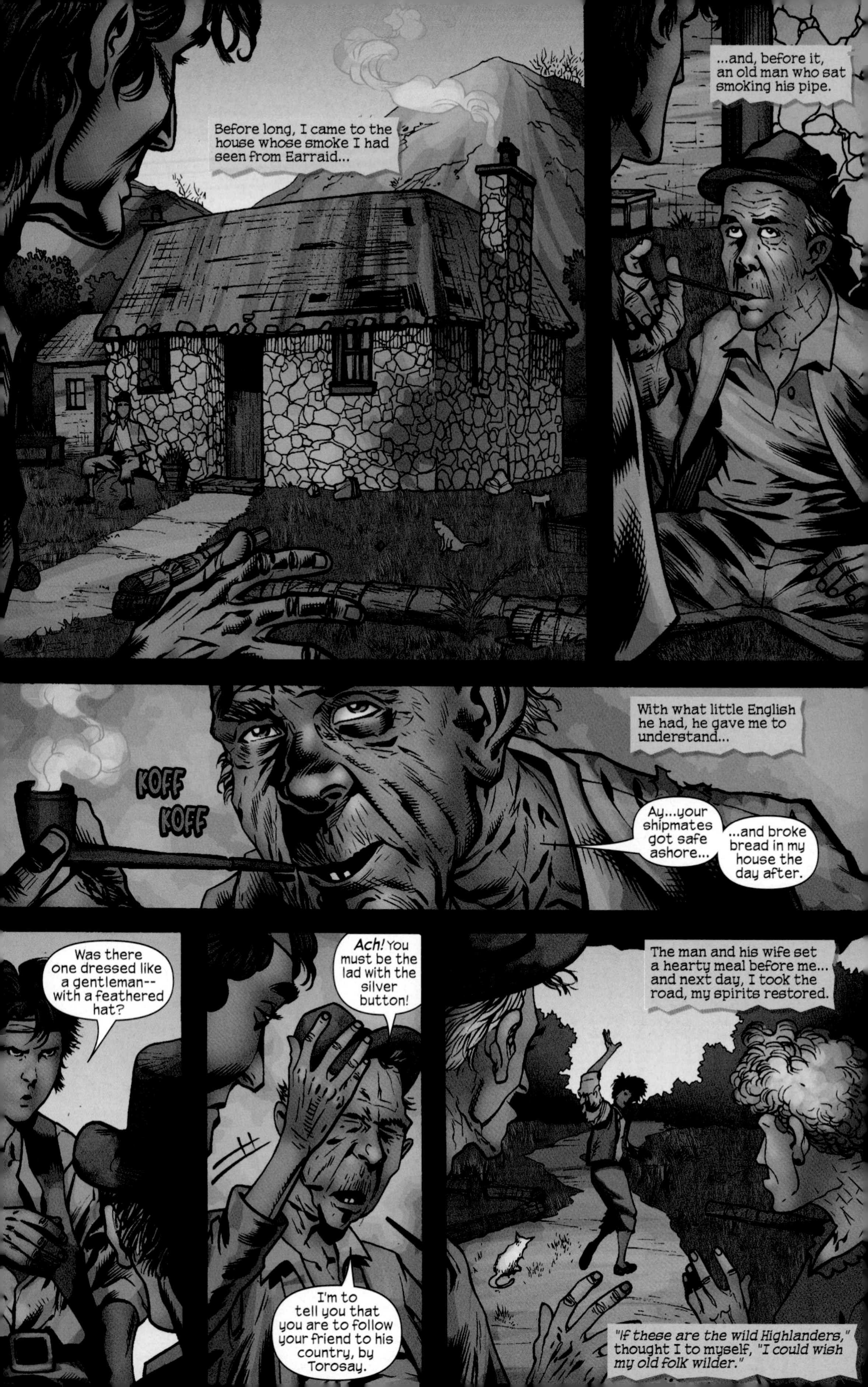
Before long, I came to the house whose smoke I had seen from Earraid...
...and, before it, an old man who sat smoking his pipe.
With what little English he had, he gave me to understand...
KOFF KOFF
Ay...your shipmates got safe ashore...
...and broke bread in my house the day after.
Was there one dressed like a gentleman--with a feathered hat?
Ach! You must be the lad with the silver button!
I'm to tell you that you are to follow your friend to his country, by Torosay.
The man and his wife set a hearty meal before me... and next day, I took the road, my spirits restored.
"If these are the wild Highlanders," thought I to myself, "I could wish my old folk wilder."

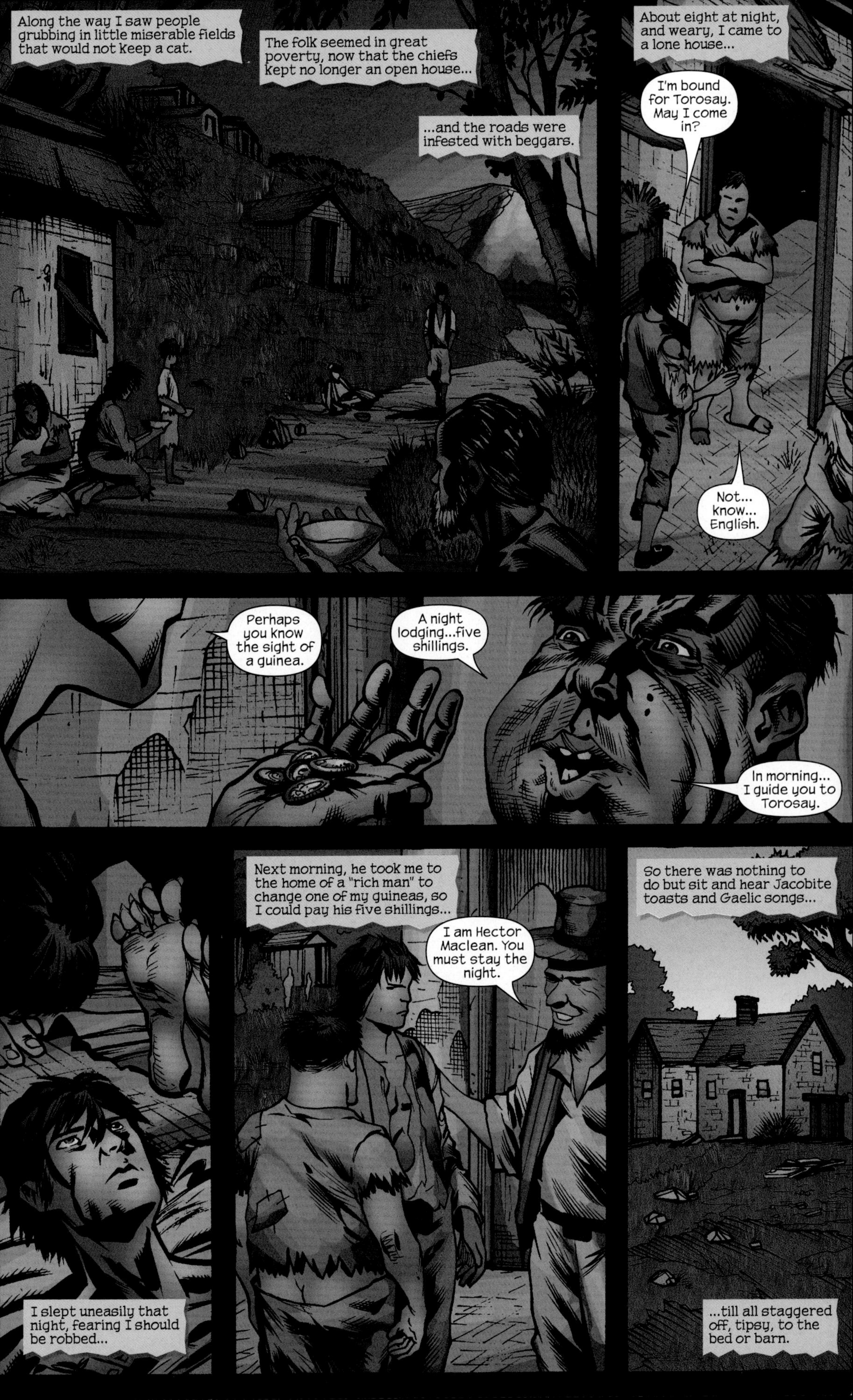
Along the way I saw people grubbing in little miserable fields that would not keep a cat.
The folk seemed in great poverty, now that the chiefs kept no longer an open house...
...and the roads were infested with beggars.
About eight at night, and weary, I came to a lone house...
I'm bound for Torosay. May I come in?
Not... know... English.
Perhaps you know the sight of a guinea.
A night lodging...five shillings.
In morning... I guide you to Torosay.
I slept uneasily that night, fearing I should be robbed...
Next morning, he took me to the home of a "rich man" to change one of my guineas, so I could pay his five shillings...
I am Hector Maclean. You must stay the night.
So there was nothing to do but sit and hear Jacobite toasts and Gaelic songs...
...till all staggered off, tipsy, to the bed or barn.

Next day, my rascal guide got to the bottle early...and it was three hours before I had him clear of the house.

We went down a heathery valley that lay before Mr. Maclean's home...

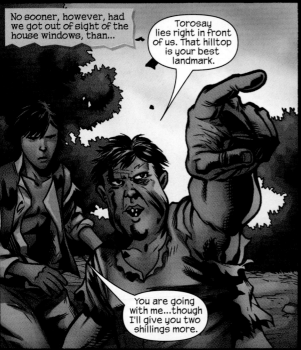

No sooner, however, had we got out of sight of the house windows, than...

Torosay lies right in front of us. That hilltop is your best landmark.

You are going with me...though I'll give you two shillings more.

Less than two miles later, he sat down and took off his brogues...

I must rest.

You'll go on, you lazy lout, if I have to strike you!

Five more shillings...

...or...

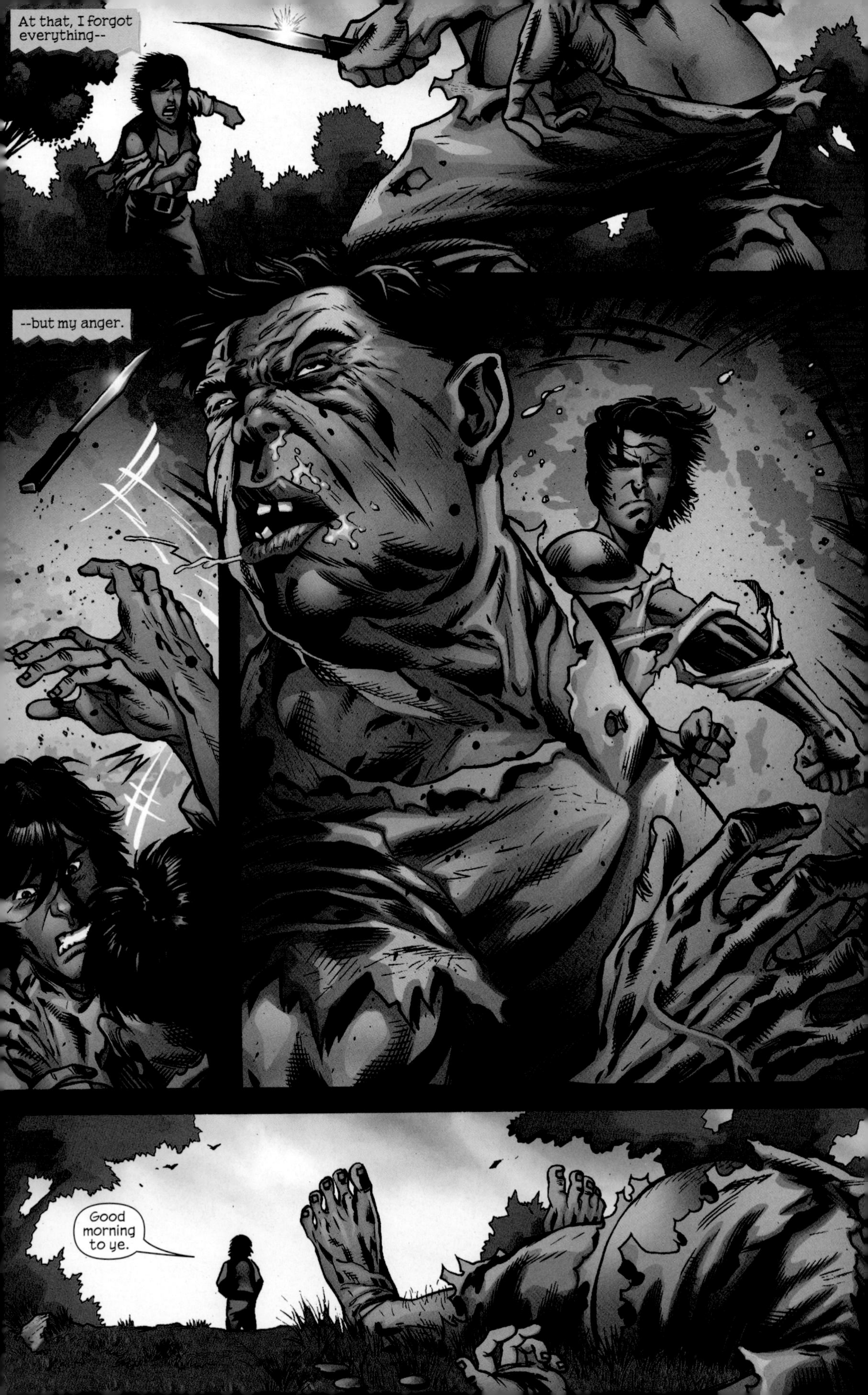
At that, I forgot everything--
--but my anger.
Good morning to ye.

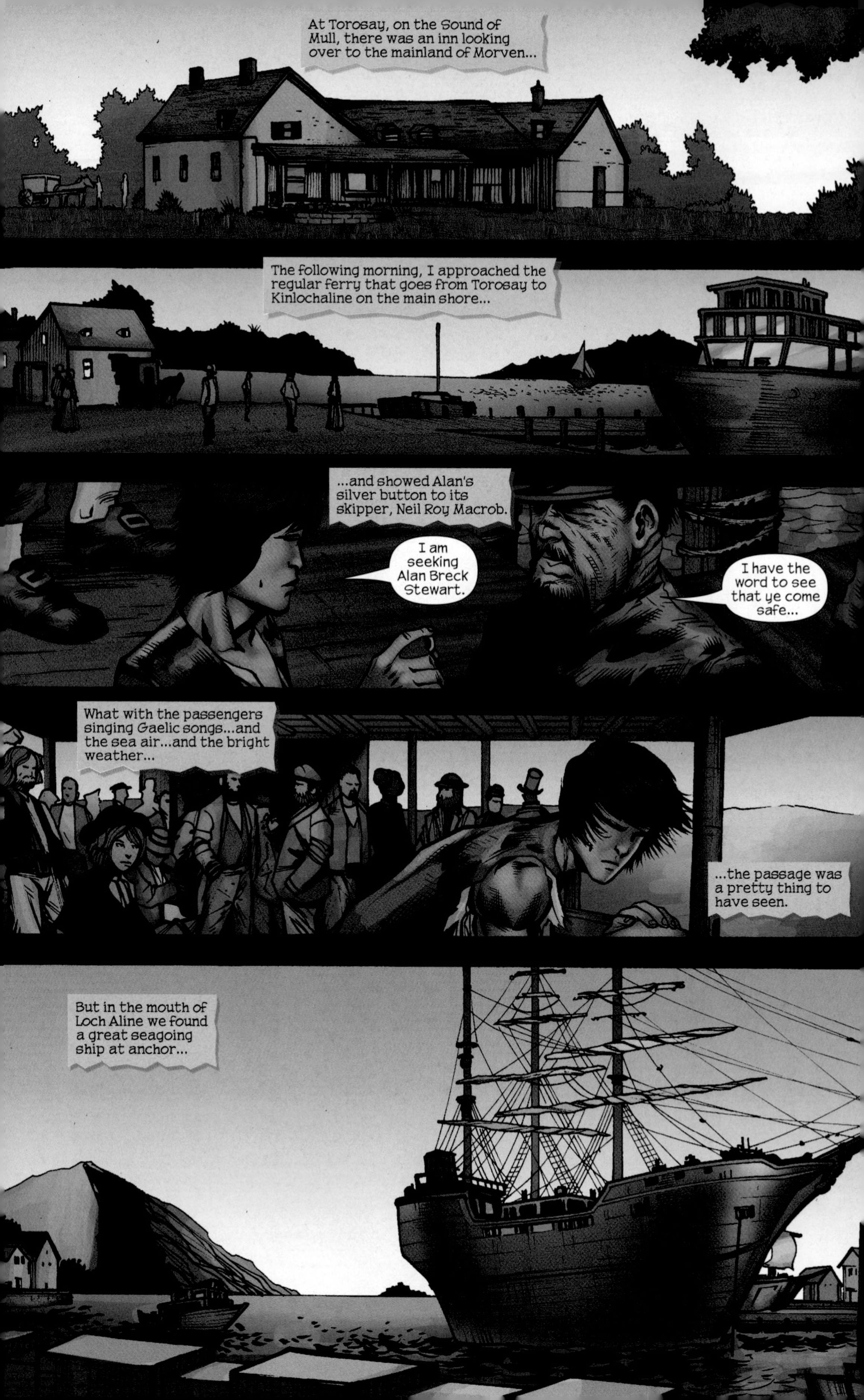
At Torosay, on the Sound of Mull, there was an inn looking over to the mainland of Morven...
The following morning, I approached the regular ferry that goes from Torosay to Kinlochaline on the main shore...
...and showed Alan's silver button to its skipper, Neil Roy Macrob.
I am seeking Alan Breck Stewart.
I have the word to see that ye come safe...
What with the passengers singing Gaelic songs...and the sea air...and the bright weather...
...the passage was a pretty thing to have seen.
But in the mouth of Loch Aline we found a great seagoing ship at anchor...

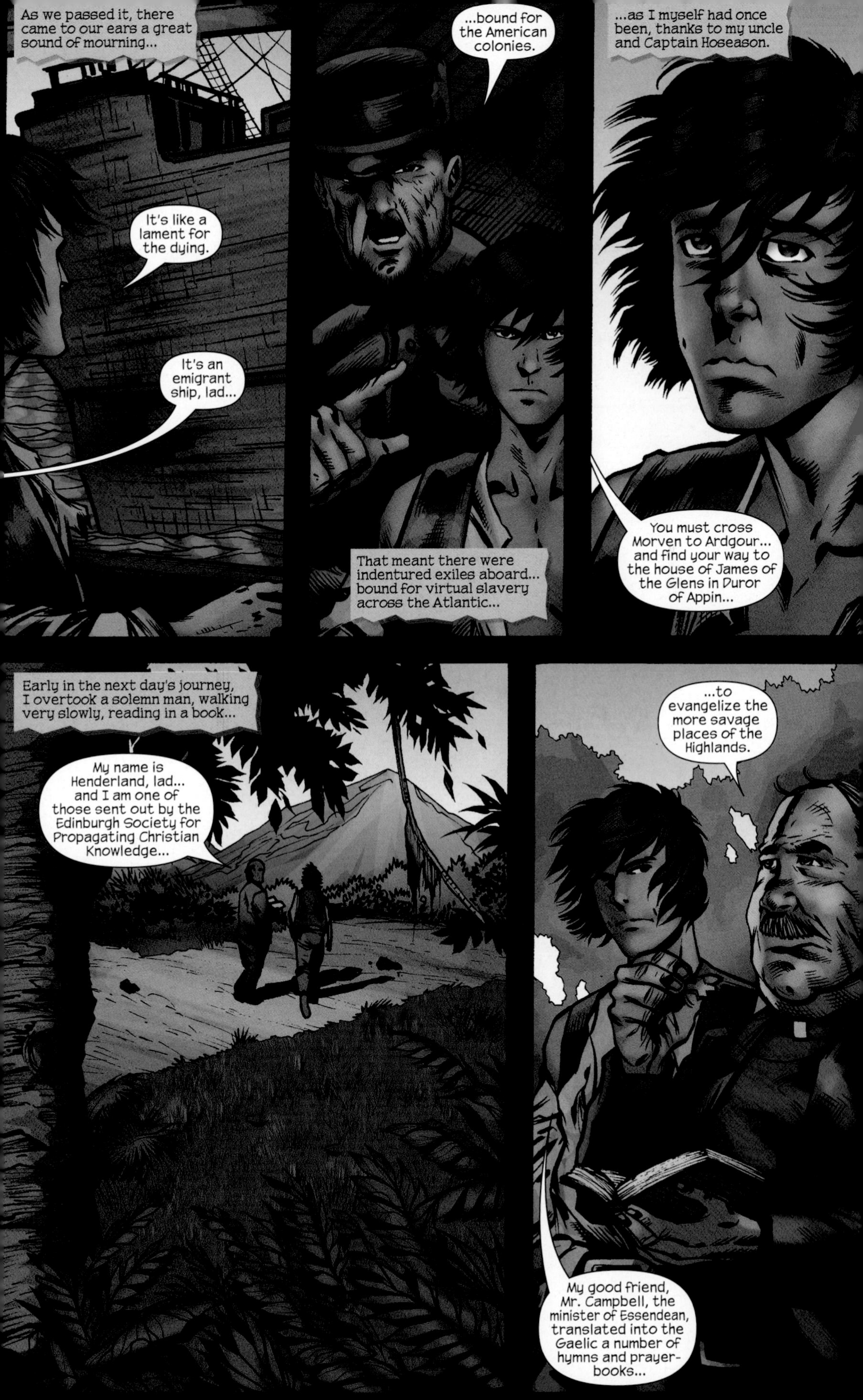
As we passed it, there came to our ears a great sound of mourning...
It's like a lament for the dying.
It's an emigrant ship, lad...
...bound for the American colonies.
That meant there were indentured exiles aboard... bound for virtual slavery across the Atlantic...
...as I myself had once been, thanks to my uncle and Captain Hoseason.
You must cross Morven to Ardgour... and find your way to the house of James of the Glens in Duror of Appin...
Early in the next day's journey, I overtook a solemn man, walking very slowly, reading in a book...
My name is Henderland, lad... and I am one of those sent out by the Edinburgh Society for Propagating Christian Knowledge...
...to evangelize the more savage places of the Highlands.
My good friend, Mr. Campbell, the minister of Essendean, translated into the Gaelic a number of hymns and prayer-books...

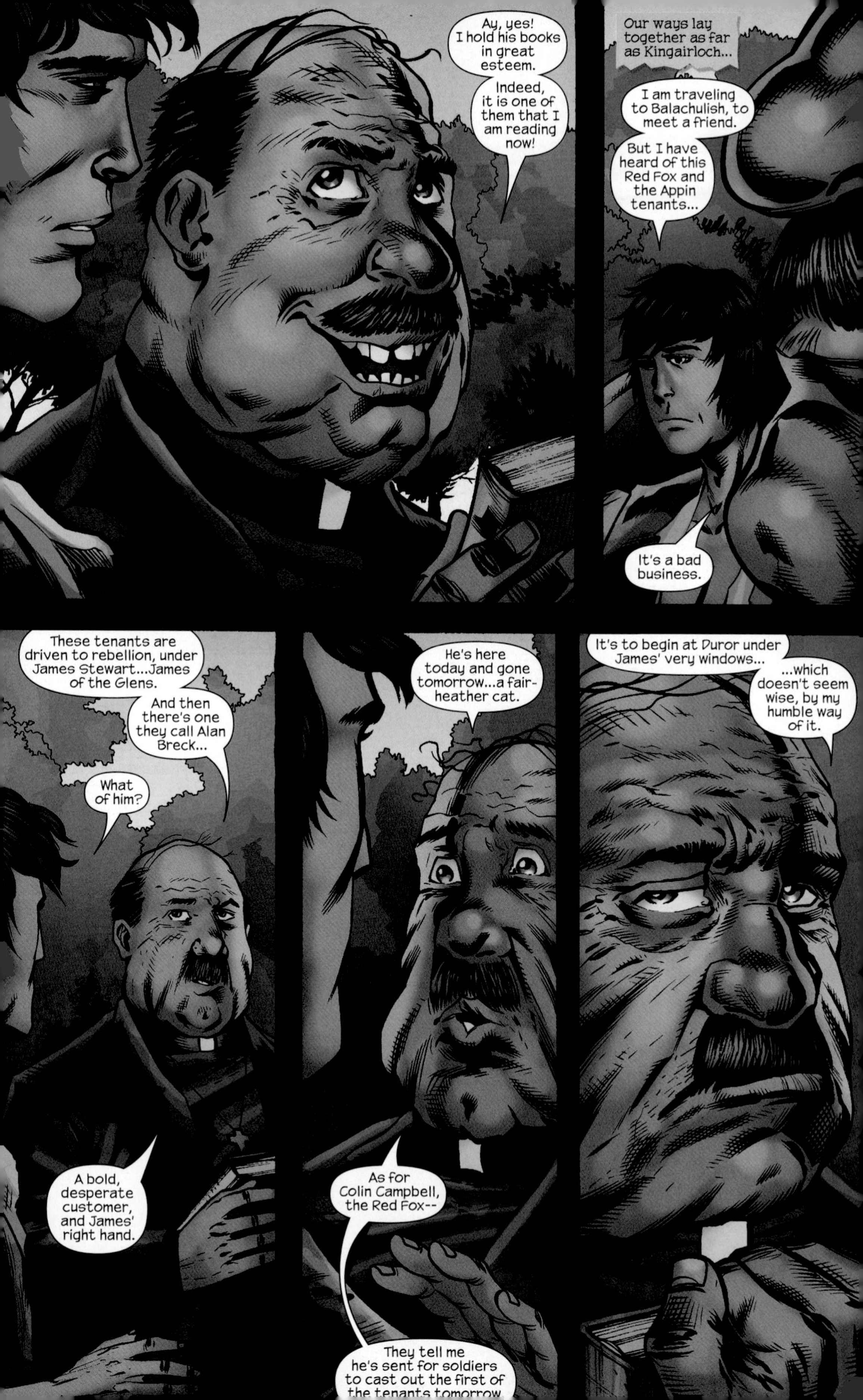
Ay, yes! I hold his books in great esteem.
Indeed, it is one of them that I am reading now!
Our ways lay together as far as Kingairloch...
I am traveling to Balachulish, to meet a friend.
But I have heard of this Red Fox and the Appin tenants...
It's a bad business.
These tenants are driven to rebellion, under James Stewart...James of the Glens.
And then there's one they call Alan Breck...
What of him?
A bold, desperate customer, and James' right hand.
He's here today and gone tomorrow...a fair-heather cat.
As for Colin Campbell, the Red Fox--
They tell me he's sent for soldiers to cast out the first of the tenants tomorrow
It's to begin at Duror under James' very windows...
...which doesn't seem wise, by my humble way of it.

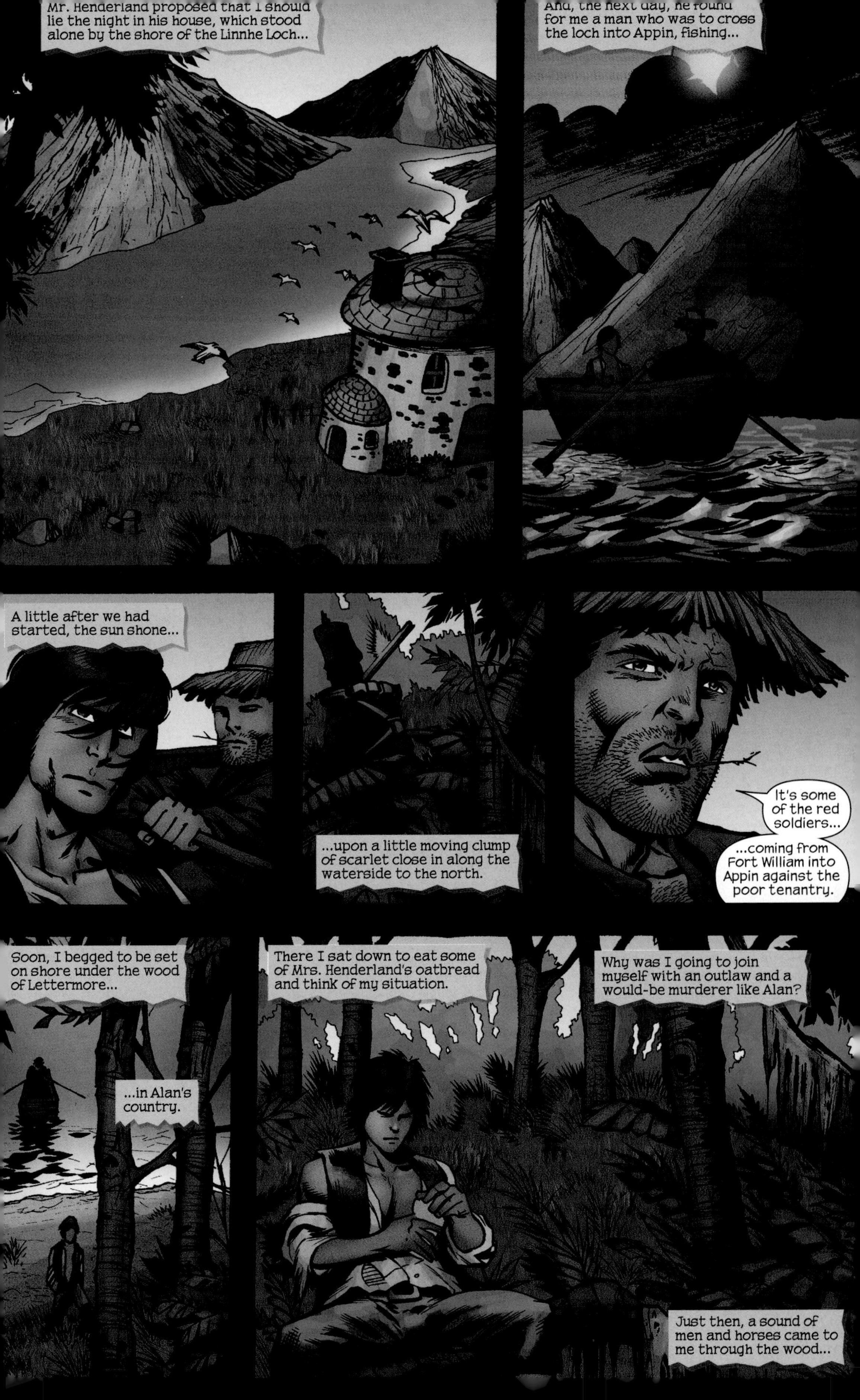

Mr. Henderland proposed that I should lie the night in his house, which stood alone by the shore of the Linnhe Loch...
And, the next day, he found for me a man who was to cross the loch into Appin, fishing...
A little after we had started, the sun shone...
...upon a little moving clump of scarlet close in along the waterside to the north.
It's some of the red soldiers...
...coming from Fort William into Appin against the poor tenantry.
Soon, I begged to be set on shore under the wood of Lettermore...
...in Alan's country.
There I sat down to eat some of Mrs. Henderland's oatbread and think of my situation.
Why was I going to join myself with an outlaw and a would-be murderer like Alan?
Just then, a sound of men and horses came to me through the wood...

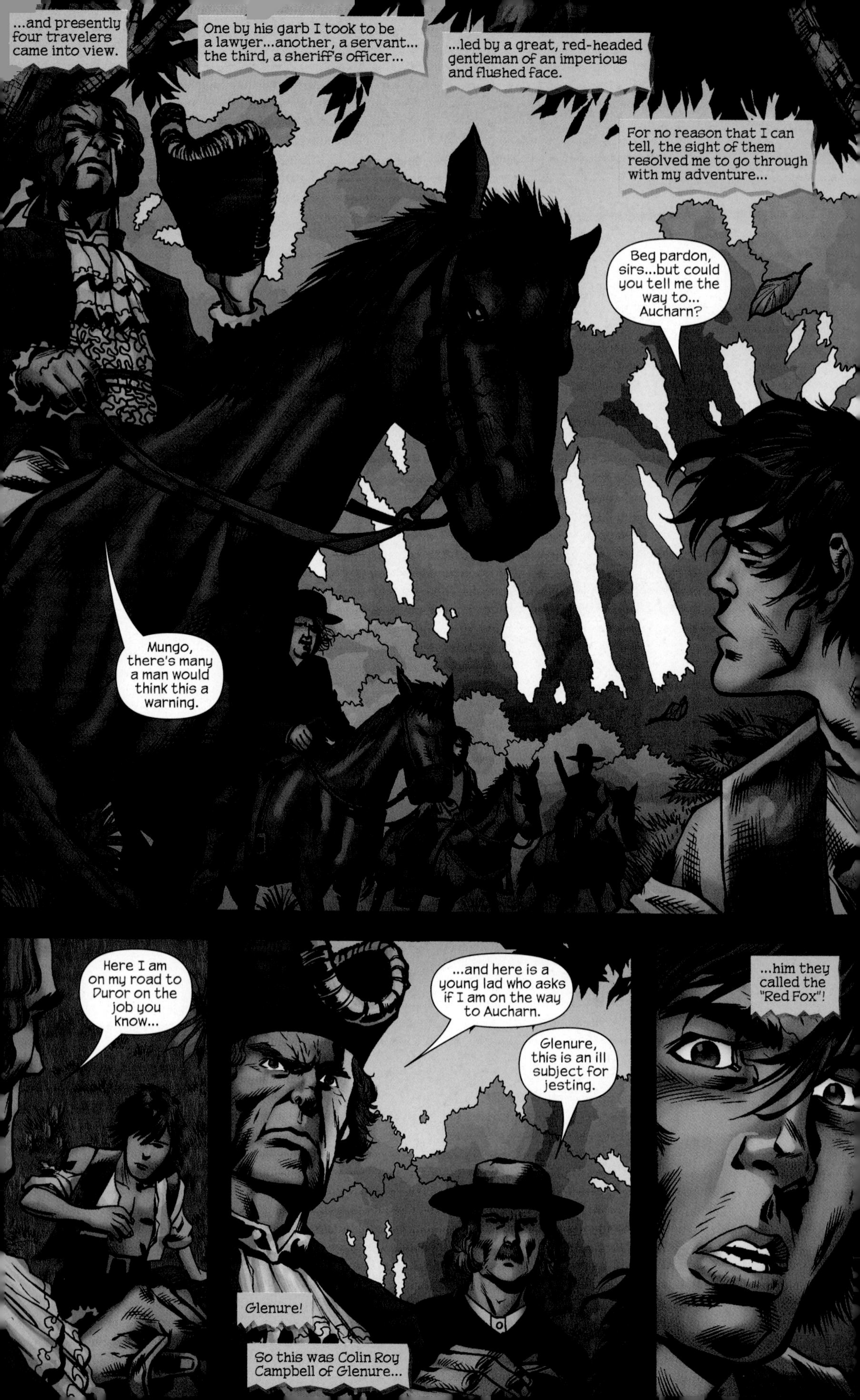
...and presently four travelers came into view.
One by his garb I took to be a lawyer...another, a servant... the third, a sheriff's officer...
...led by a great, red-headed gentleman of an imperious and flushed face.
For no reason that I can tell, the sight of them resolved me to go through with my adventure...
Beg pardon, sirs...but could you tell me the way to... Aucharn?
Mungo, there's many a man would think this a warning.
Here I am on my road to Duror on the job you know...
...and here is a young lad who asks if I am on the way to Aucharn.
Glenure, this is an ill subject for jesting.
Glenure!
So this was Colin Roy Campbell of Glenure...
...him they called the "Red Fox"!

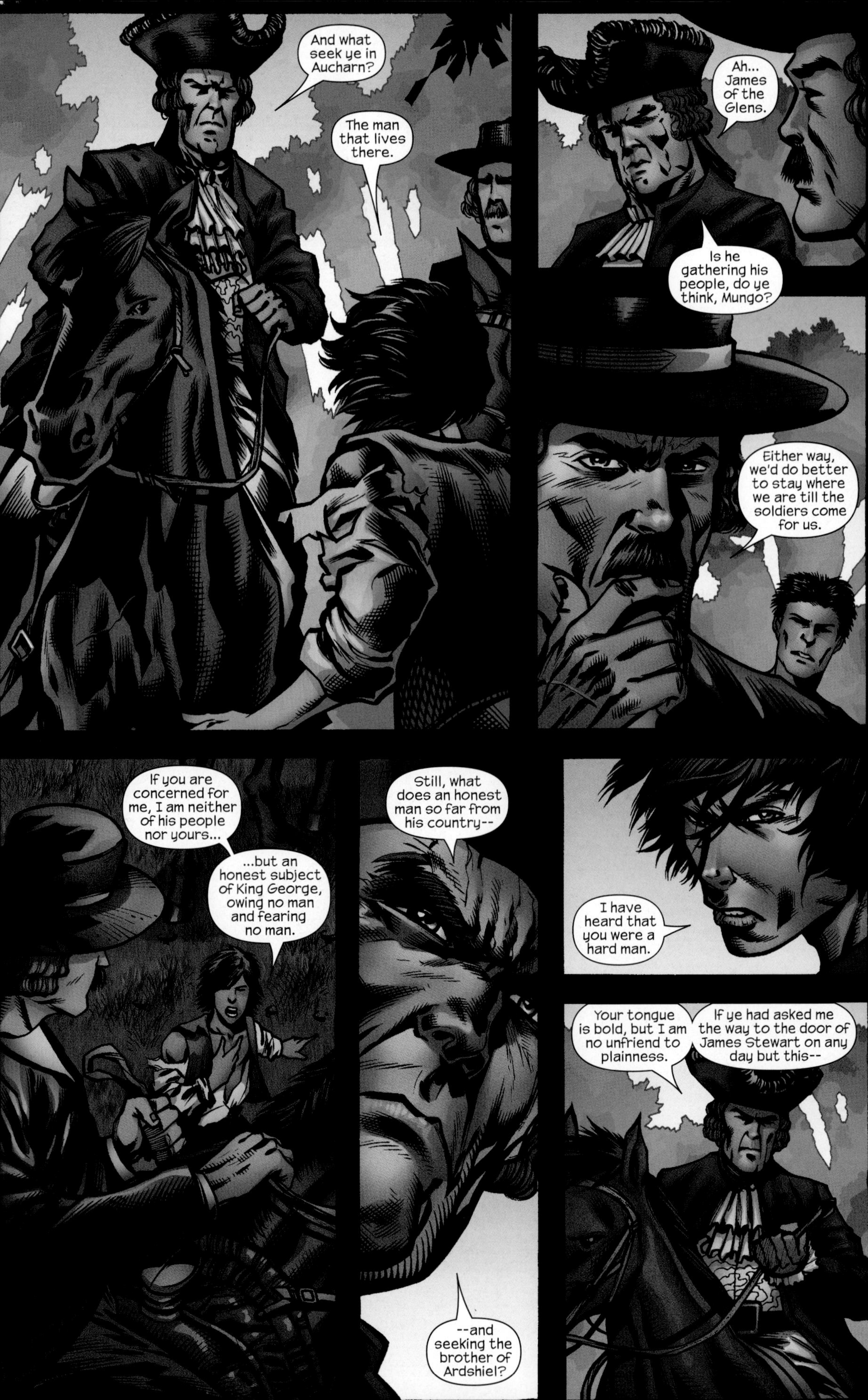
And what seek ye in Aucharn?
The man that lives there.
Ah... James of the Glens.
Is he gathering his people, do ye think, Mungo?
Either way, we'd do better to stay where we are till the soldiers come for us.
If you are concerned for me, I am neither of his people nor yours...
...but an honest subject of King George, owing no man and fearing no man.
Still, what does an honest man so far from his country--
--and seeking the brother of Ardshiel?
I have heard that you were a hard man.
Your tongue is bold, but I am no unfriend to plainness.
If ye had asked me the way to the door of James Stewart on any day but this--

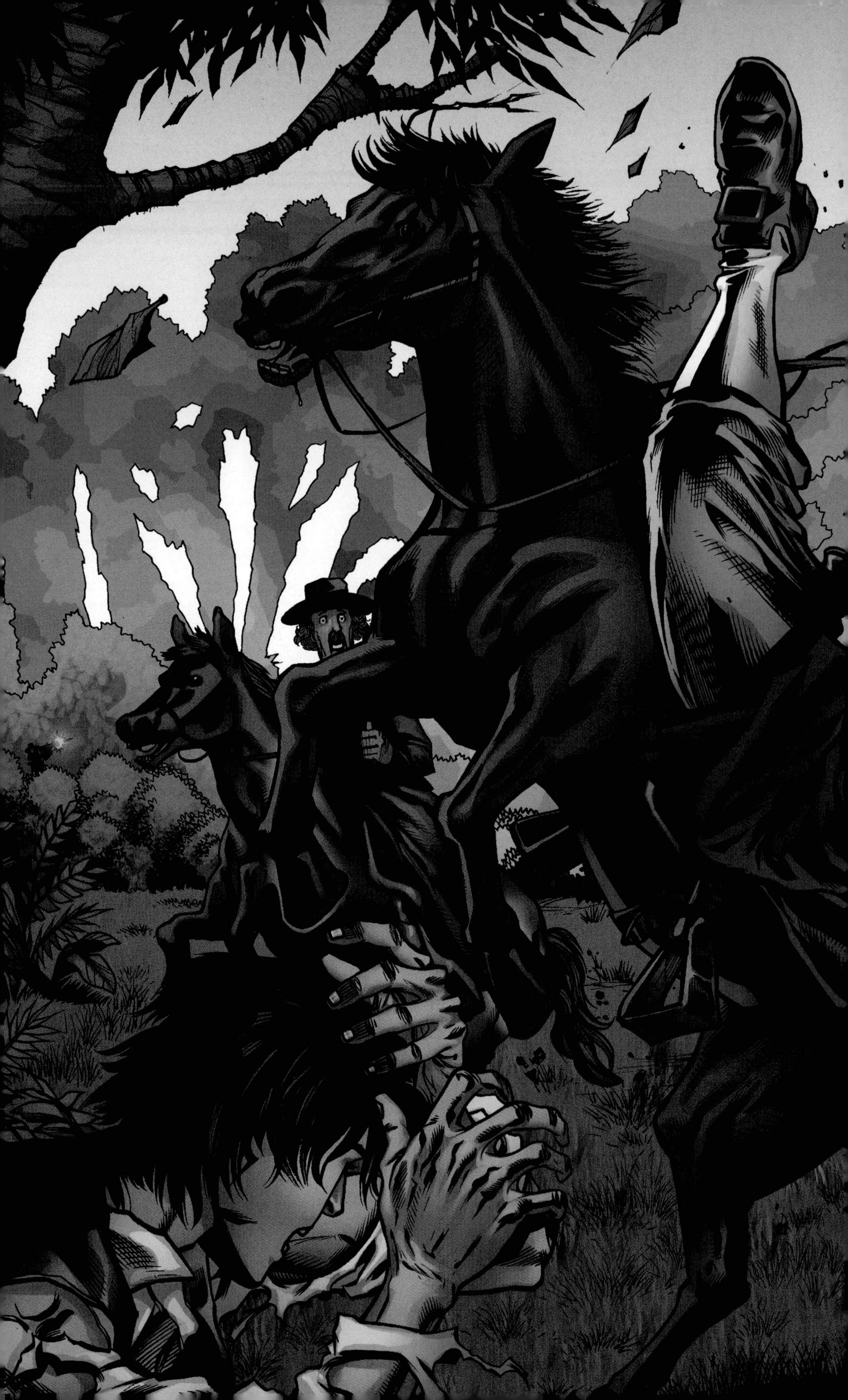

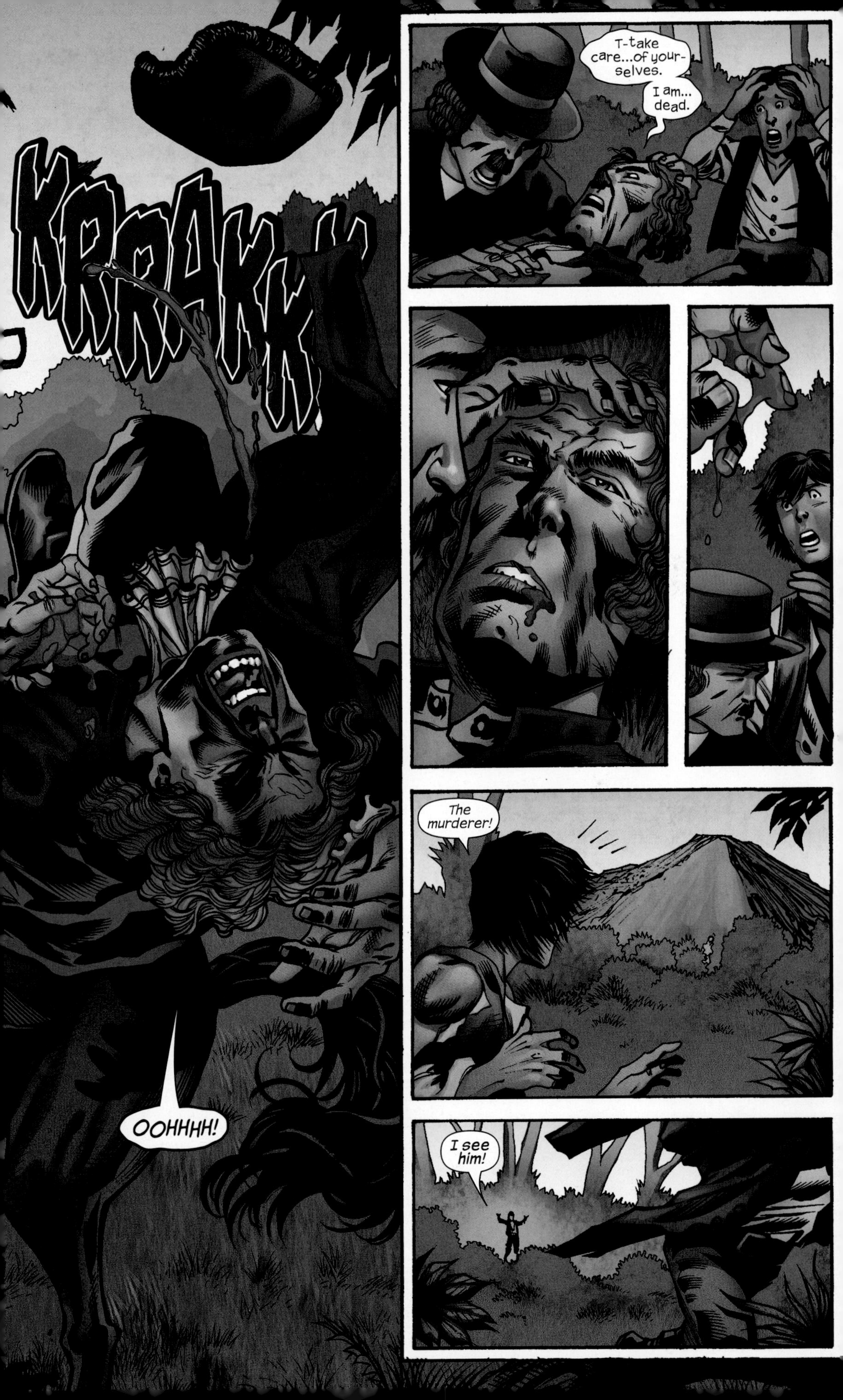
KRRAKK!
OOHHHH!
T-take care...of your-selves.
I am... dead.
The murderer!
I see him!

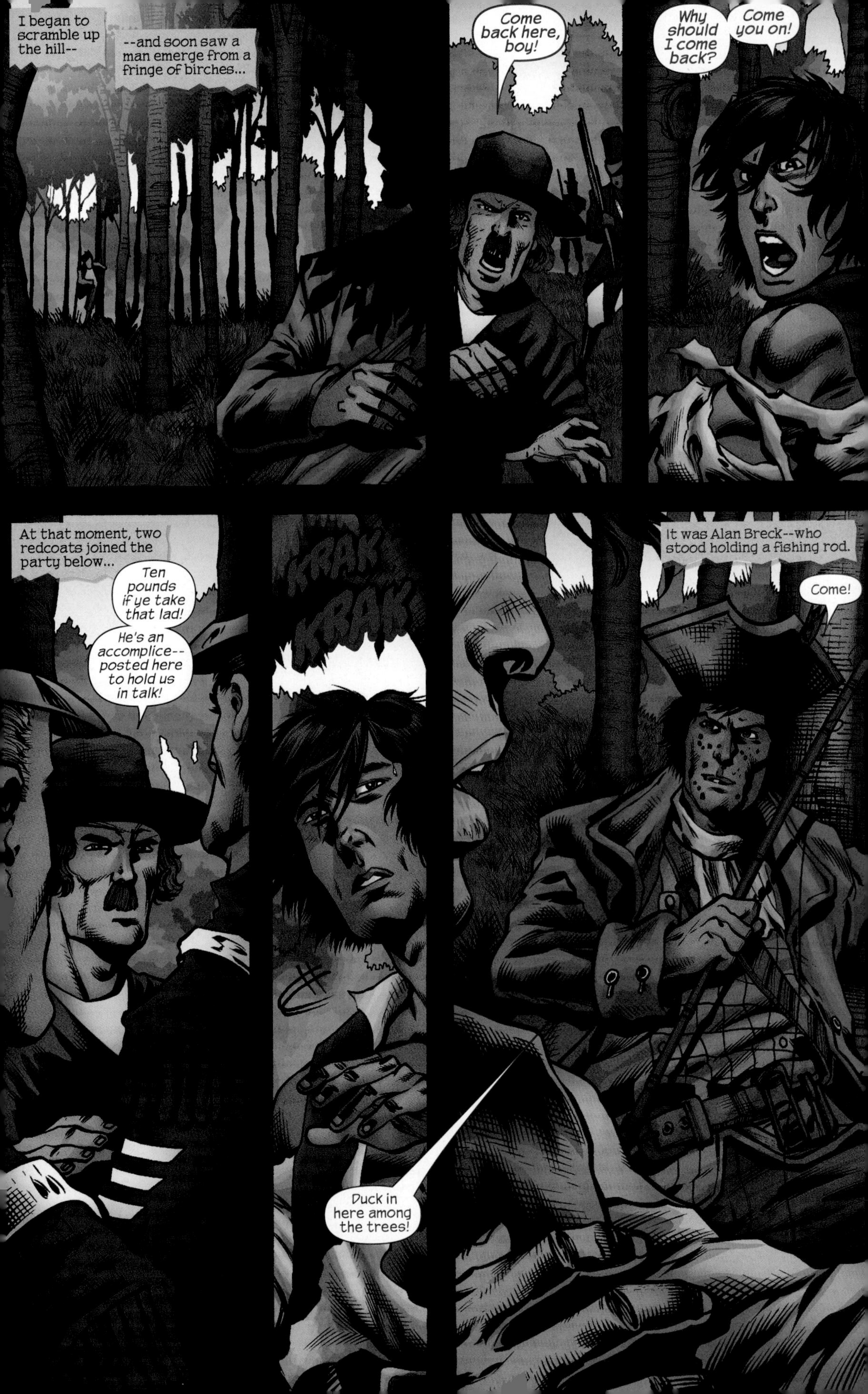
I began to scramble up the hill--
--and soon saw a man emerge from a fringe of birches...
Come back here, boy!
Why should I come back?
Come you on!
At that moment, two redcoats joined the party below...
Ten pounds if ye take that lad!
He's an accomplice--posted here to hold us in talk!
KRAK
KRAK
It was Alan Breck--who stood holding a fishing rod.
Come!
Duck in here among the trees!

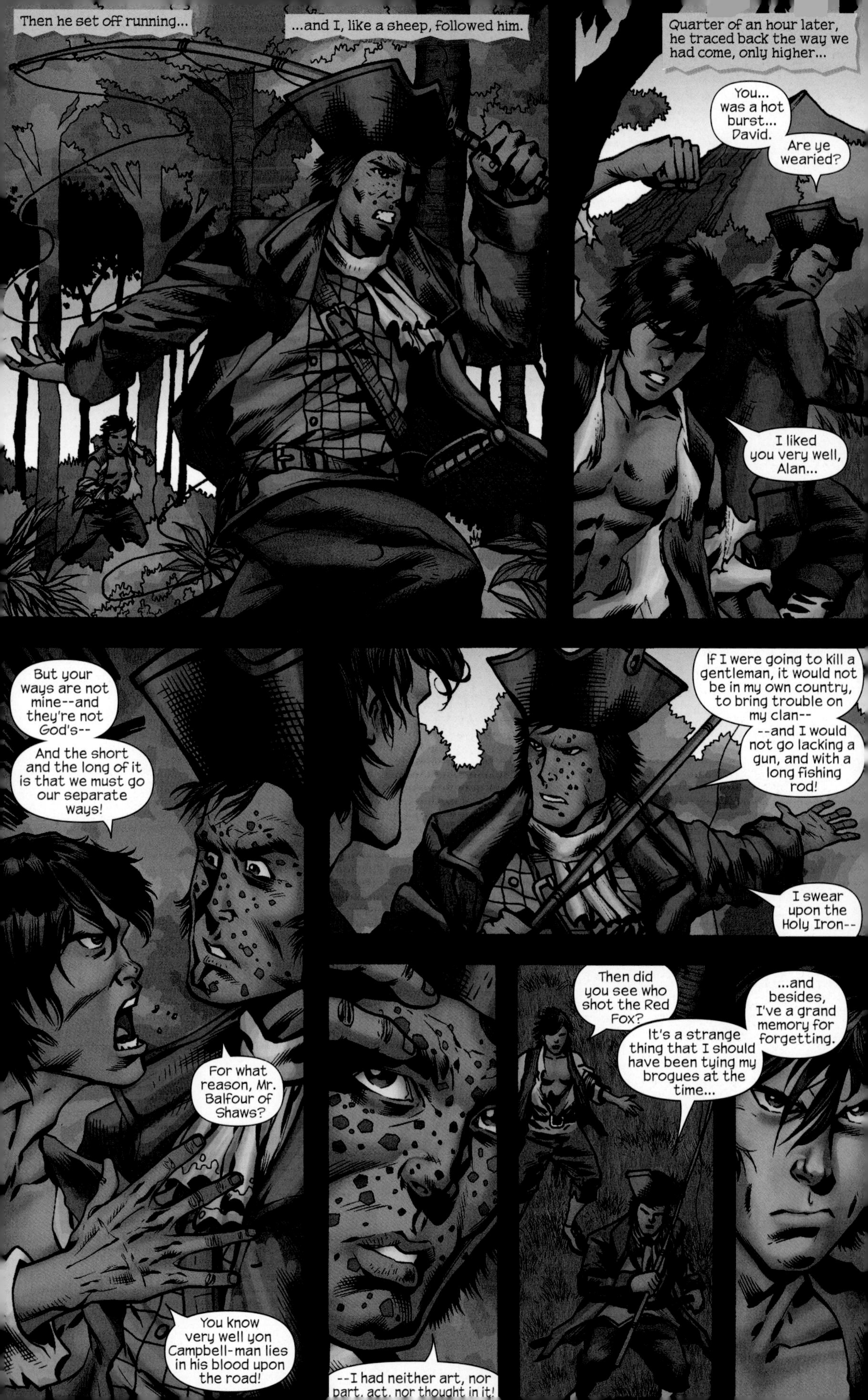
Then he set off running...
...and I, like a sheep, followed him.
Quarter of an hour later, he traced back the way we had come, only higher...
You... was a hot burst... David.
Are ye wearied?
I liked you very well, Alan...
But your ways are not mine--and they're not God's--
And the short and the long of it is that we must go our separate ways!
For what reason, Mr. Balfour of Shaws?
You know very well yon Campbell-man lies in his blood upon the road!
If I were going to kill a gentleman, it would not be in my own country, to bring trouble on my clan--
--and I would not go lacking a gun, and with a long fishing rod!
I swear upon the Holy Iron--
--I had neither art, nor part, act, nor thought in it!
Then did you see who shot the Red Fox?
It's a strange thing that I should have been tying my brogues at the time...
...and besides, I've a grand memory for forgetting.

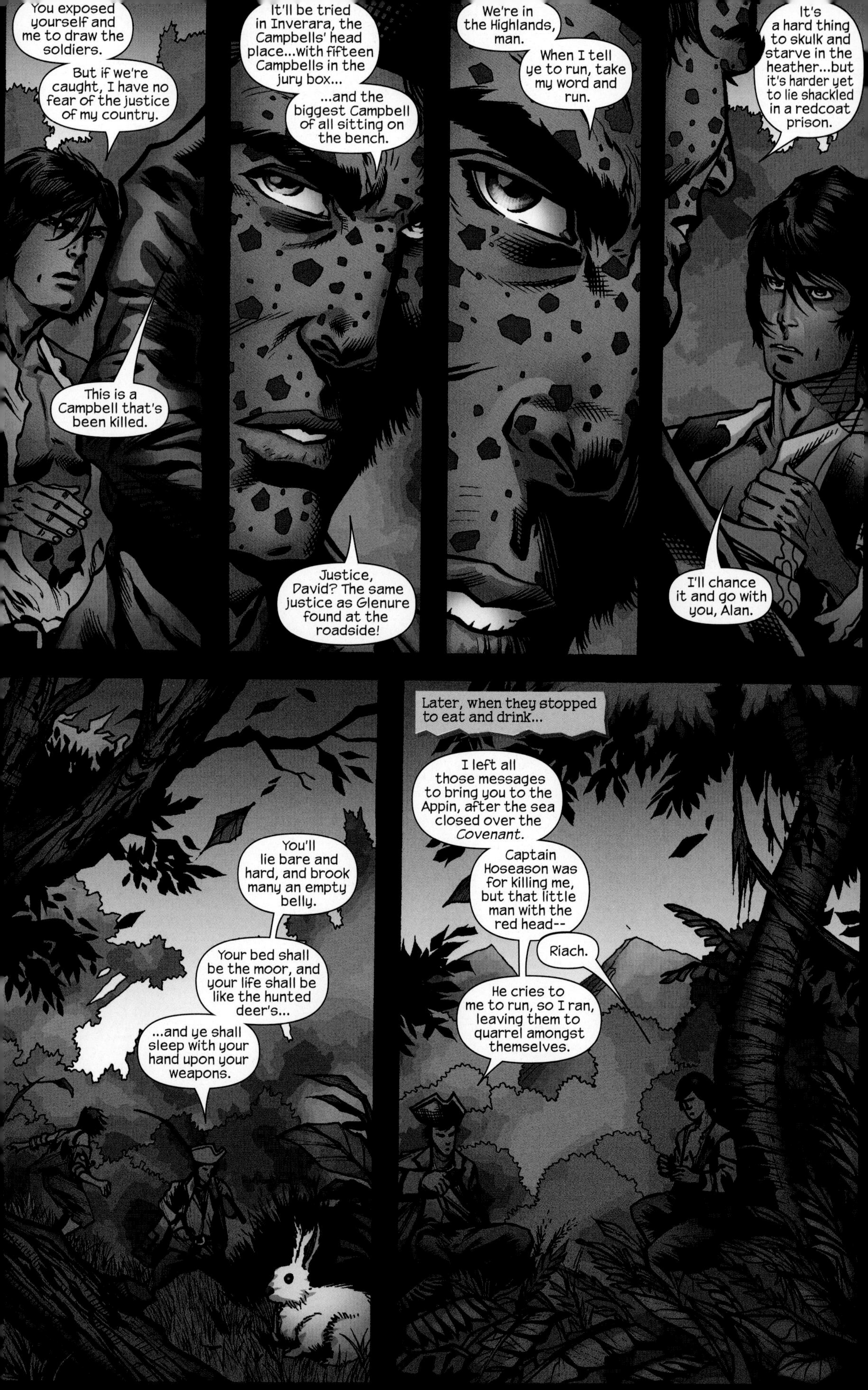

You exposed yourself and me to draw the soldiers.
But if we're caught, I have no fear of the justice of my country.
This is a Campbell that's been killed.
It'll be tried in Inverara, the Campbells' head place...with fifteen Campbells in the jury box...
...and the biggest Campbell of all sitting on the bench.
Justice, David? The same justice as Glenure found at the roadside!
We're in the Highlands, man.
When I tell ye to run, take my word and run.
It's a hard thing to skulk and starve in the heather...but it's harder yet to lie shackled in a redcoat prison.
I'll chance it and go with you, Alan.
You'll lie bare and hard, and brook many an empty belly.
Your bed shall be the moor, and your life shall be like the hunted deer's...
...and ye shall sleep with your hand upon your weapons.
Later, when they stopped to eat and drink...
I left all those messages to bring you to the Appin, after the sea closed over the *Covenant*.
Captain Hoseason was for killing me, but that little man with the red head--
Riach.
He cries to me to run, so I ran, leaving them to quarrel amongst themselves.

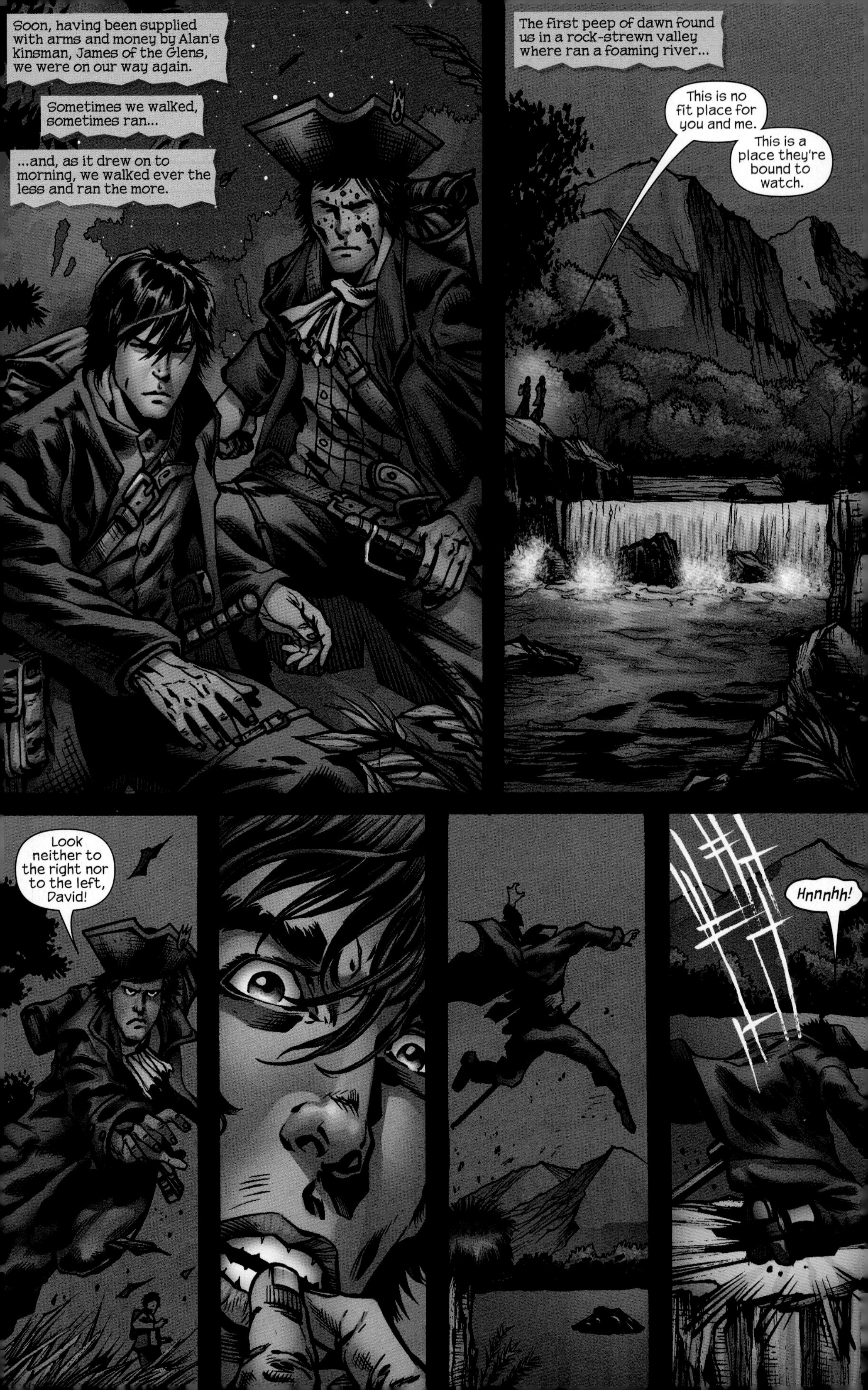
Soon, having been supplied with arms and money by Alan's Kinsman, James of the Glens, we were on our way again.
Sometimes we walked, sometimes ran...
...and, as it drew on to morning, we walked ever the less and ran the more.
The first peep of dawn found us in a rock-strewn valley where ran a foaming river...
This is no fit place for you and me.
This is a place they're bound to watch.
Look neither to the right nor to the left, David!
Hnnnhh!

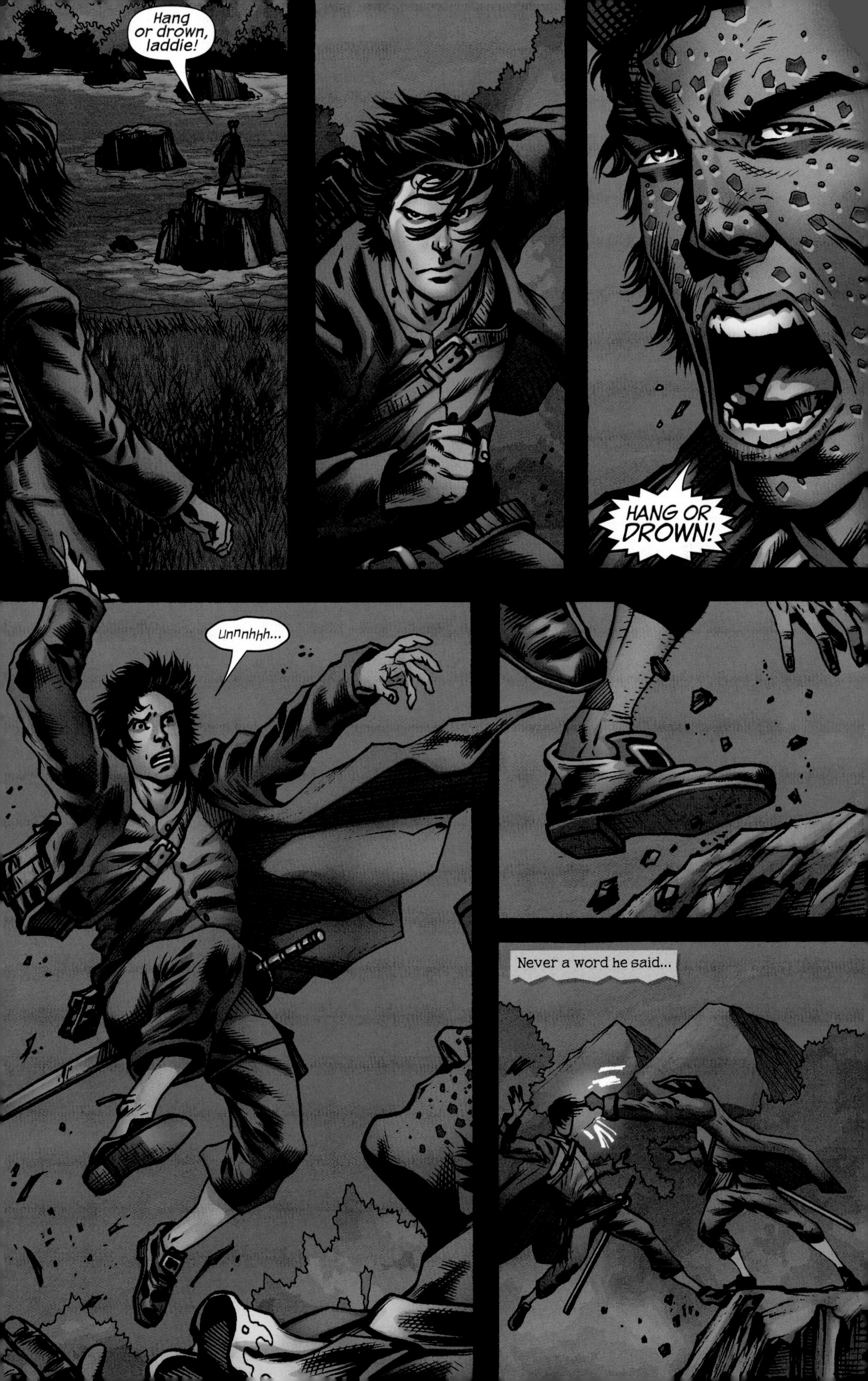
Hang or drown, laddie!
HANG OR DROWN!
Unnnhhh...
Never a word he said...

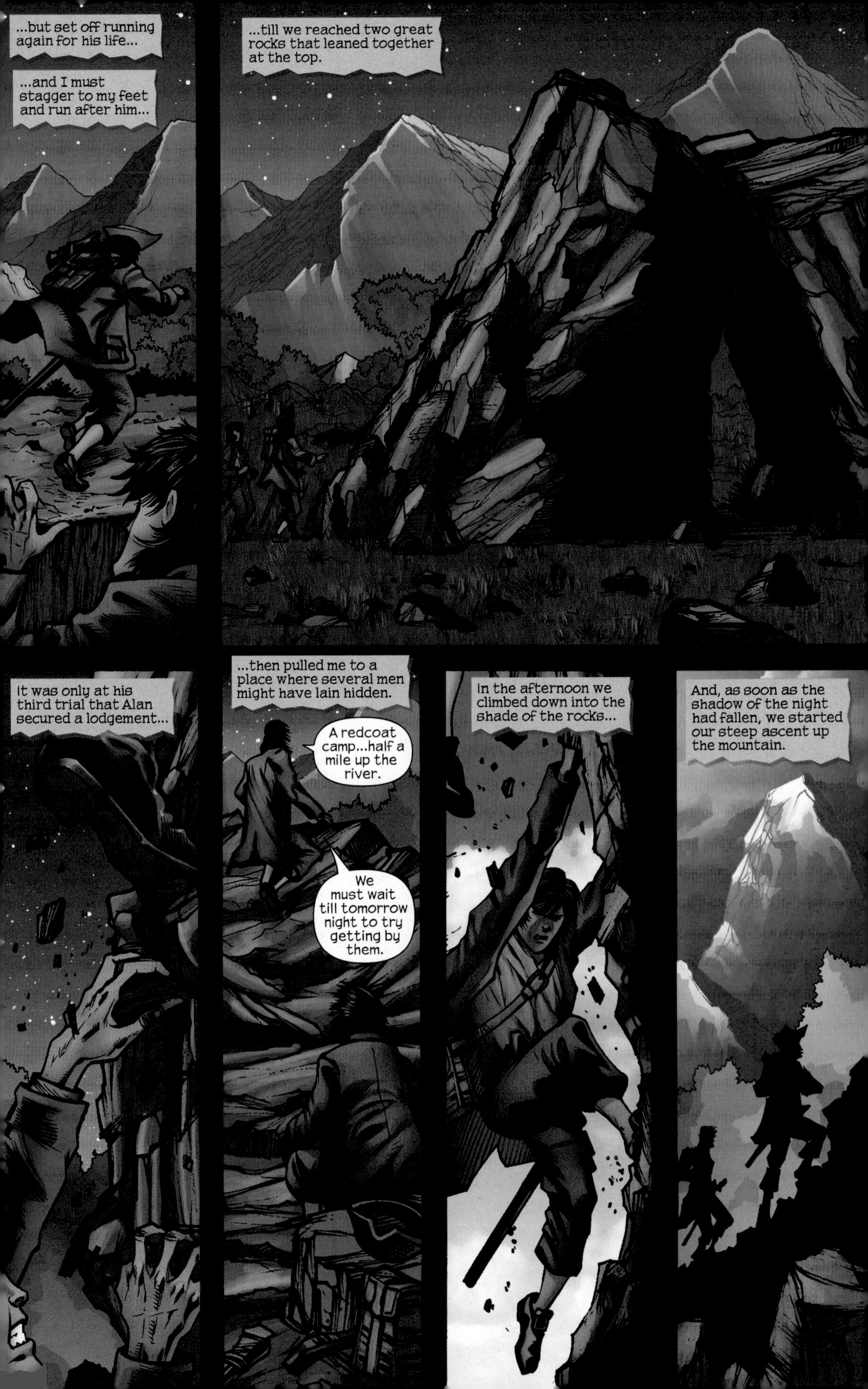
...but set off running again for his life...
...and I must stagger to my feet and run after him...
...till we reached two great rocks that leaned together at the top.
It was only at his third trial that Alan secured a lodgement...
...then pulled me to a place where several men might have lain hidden.
A redcoat camp...half a mile up the river.
We must wait till tomorrow night to try getting by them.
In the afternoon we climbed down into the shade of the rocks...
And, as soon as the shadow of the night had fallen, we started our steep ascent up the mountain.

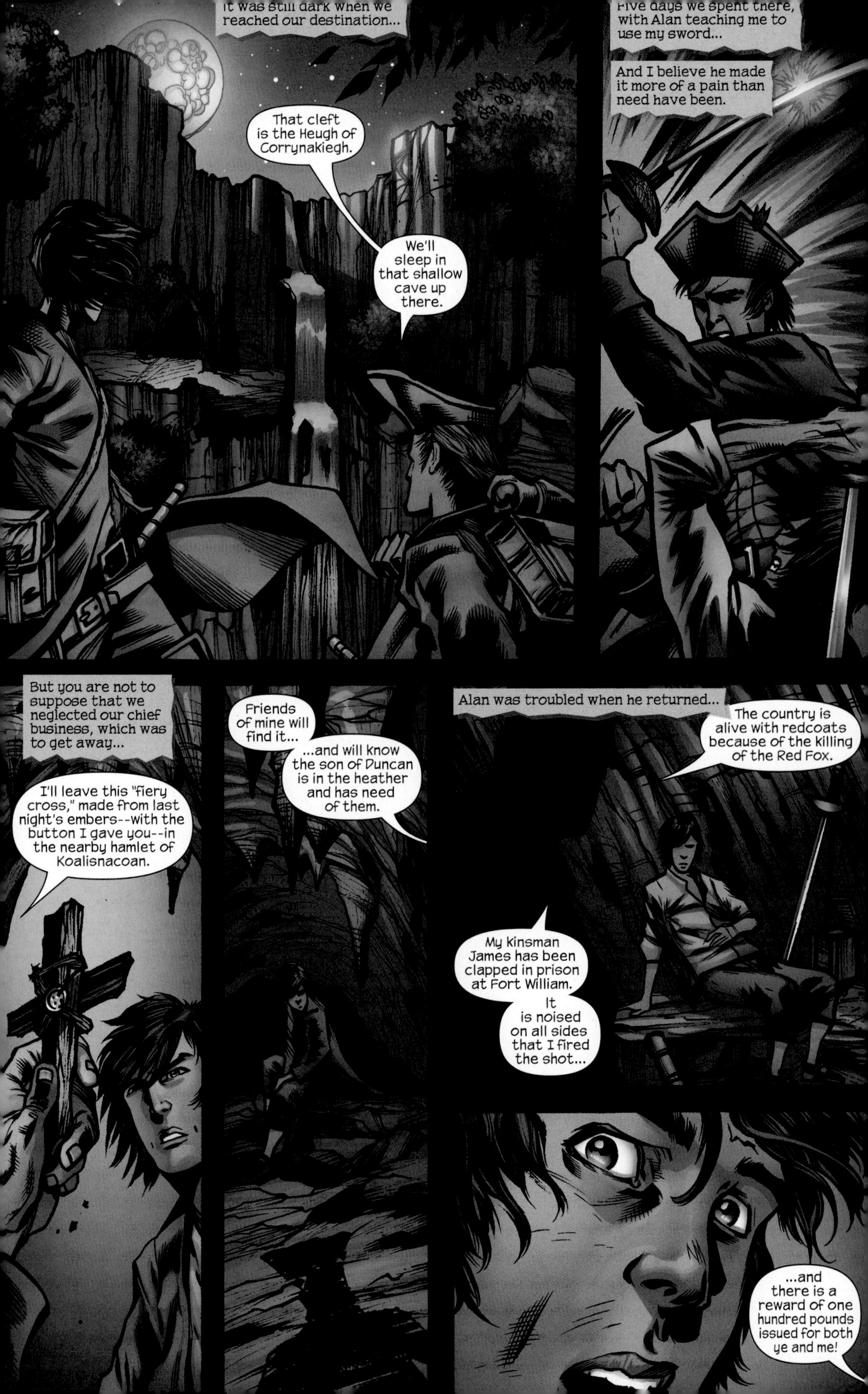
It was still dark when we reached our destination...
That cleft is the Heugh of Corrynakiegh.
We'll sleep in that shallow cave up there.
Five days we spent there, with Alan teaching me to use my sword...
And I believe he made it more of a pain than need have been.
But you are not to suppose that we neglected our chief business, which was to get away...
I'll leave this "fiery cross," made from last night's embers--with the button I gave you--in the nearby hamlet of Koalisnacoan.
Friends of mine will find it...
...and will know the son of Duncan is in the heather and has need of them.
Alan was troubled when he returned...
The country is alive with redcoats because of the killing of the Red Fox.
My kinsman James has been clapped in prison at Fort William.
It is noised on all sides that I fired the shot...
...and there is a reward of one hundred pounds issued for both ye and me!

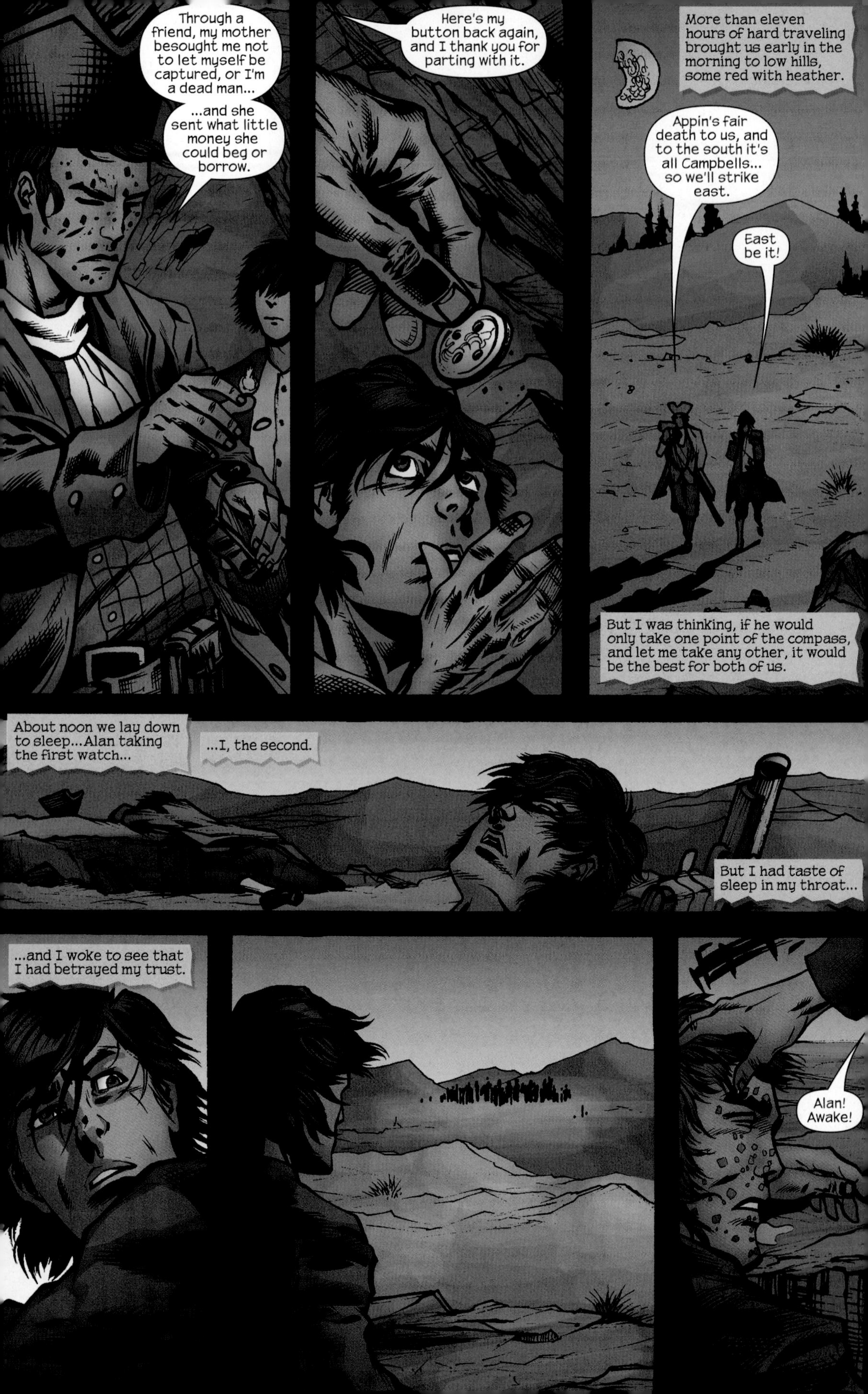
Through a friend, my mother besought me not to let myself be captured, or I'm a dead man...
...and she sent what little money she could beg or borrow.
Here's my button back again, and I thank you for parting with it.
More than eleven hours of hard traveling brought us early in the morning to low hills, some red with heather.
Appin's fair death to us, and to the south it's all Campbells... so we'll strike east.
East be it!
But I was thinking, if he would only take one point of the compass, and let me take any other, it would be the best for both of us.
About noon we lay down to sleep...Alan taking the first watch...
...I, the second.
But I had taste of sleep in my throat...
...and I woke to see that I had betrayed my trust.
Alan! Awake!

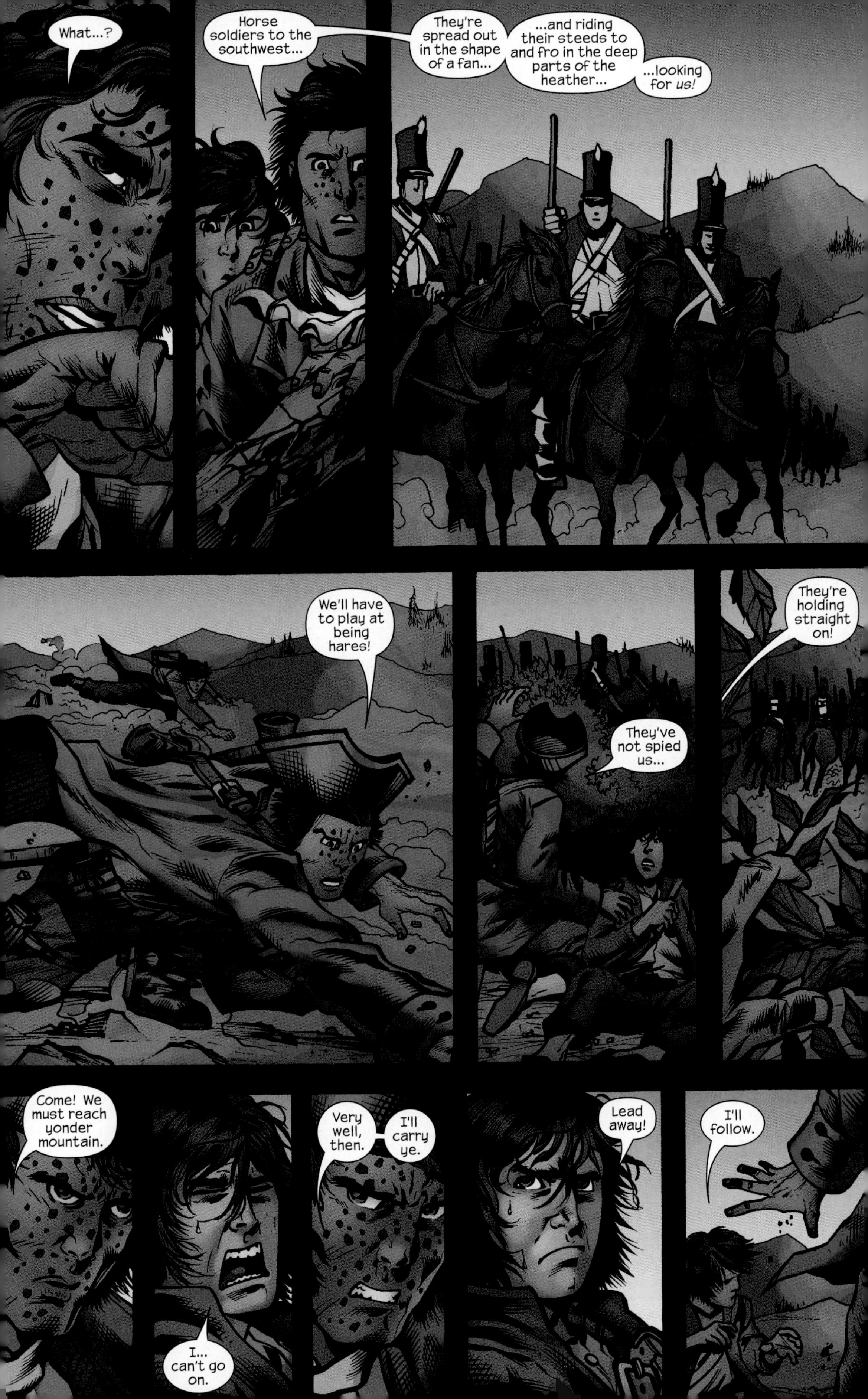
What...?
Horse soldiers to the southwest...
They're spread out in the shape of a fan...
...and riding their steeds to and fro in the deep parts of the heather...
...looking for us!
We'll have to play at being hares!
They've not spied us...
They're holding straight on!
Come! We must reach yonder mountain.
I... can't go on.
Very well, then.
I'll carry ye.
Lead away!
I'll follow.

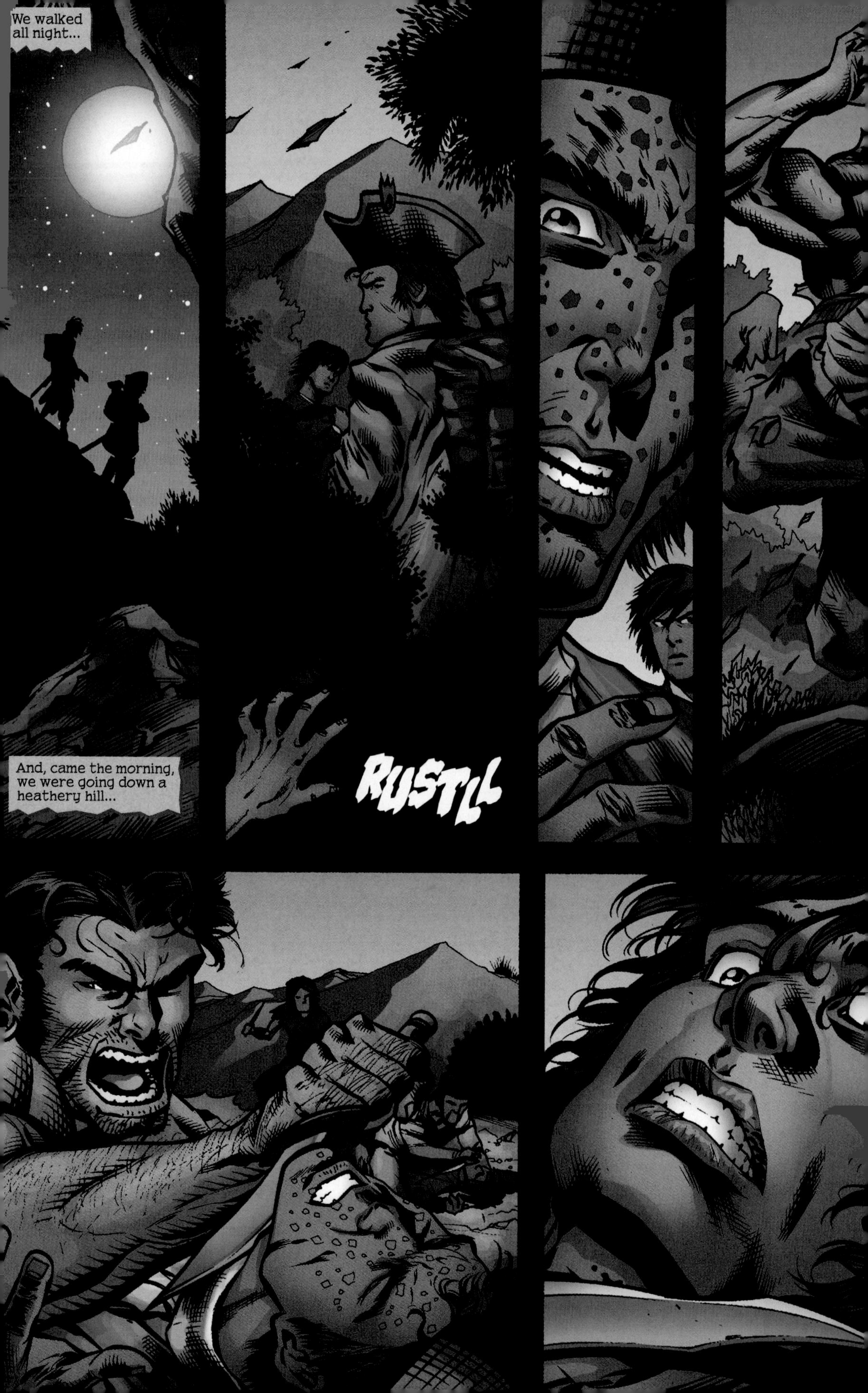
We walked all night...
And, came the morning, we were going down a heathery hill...
RUSTLL

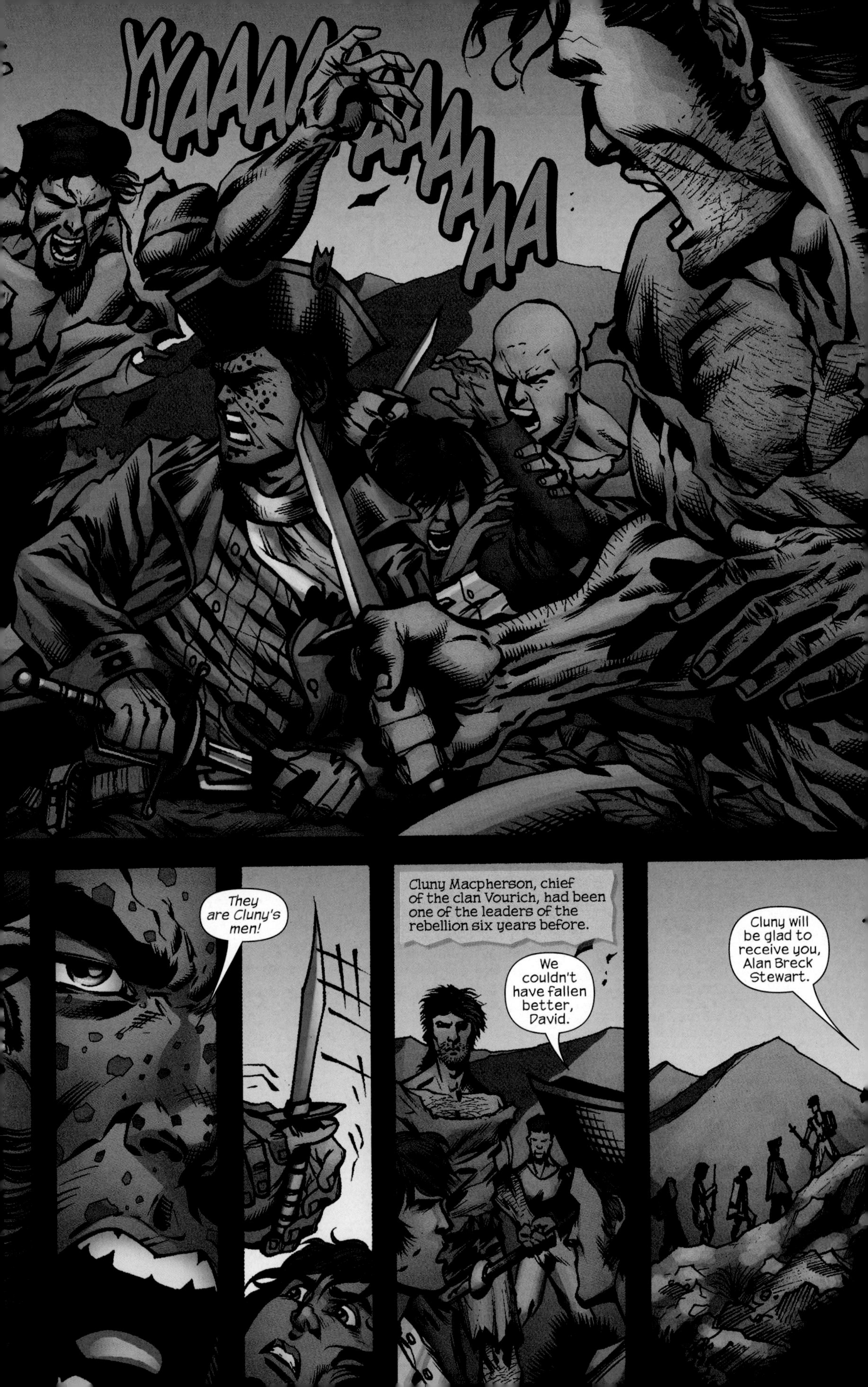
YYAAAAAAAAAAA
They are Cluny's men!
Cluny Macpherson, chief of the clan Vourich, had been one of the leaders of the rebellion six years before.
We couldn't have fallen better, David.
Cluny will be glad to receive you, Alan Breck Stewart.

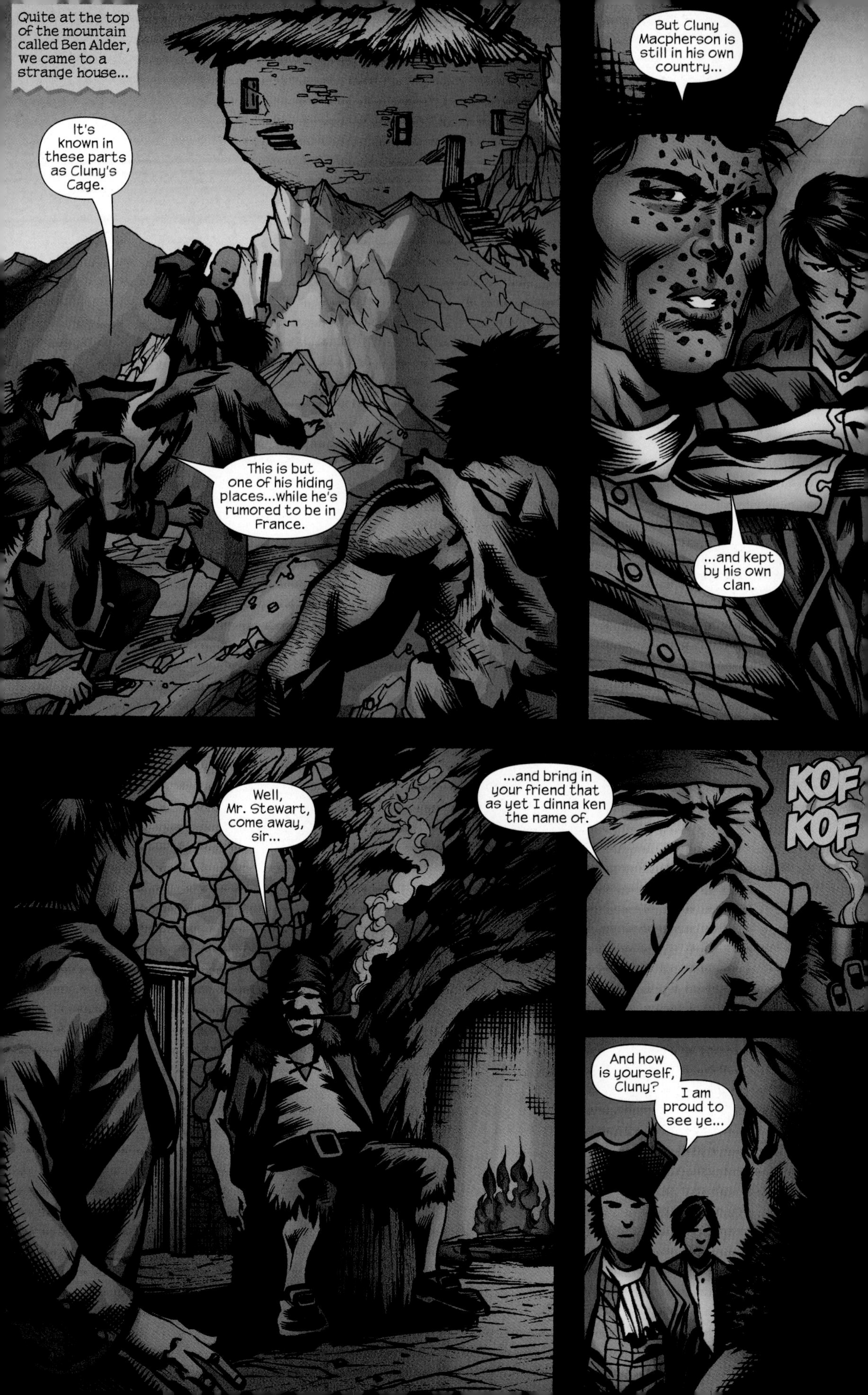
Quite at the top of the mountain called Ben Alder, we came to a strange house...
It's known in these parts as Cluny's Cage.
This is but one of his hiding places...while he's rumored to be in France.
But Cluny Macpherson is still in his own country...
...and kept by his own clan.
Well, Mr. Stewart, come away, sir...
...and bring in your friend that as yet I dinna ken the name of.
KOF KOF
And how is yourself, Cluny?
I am proud to see ye...

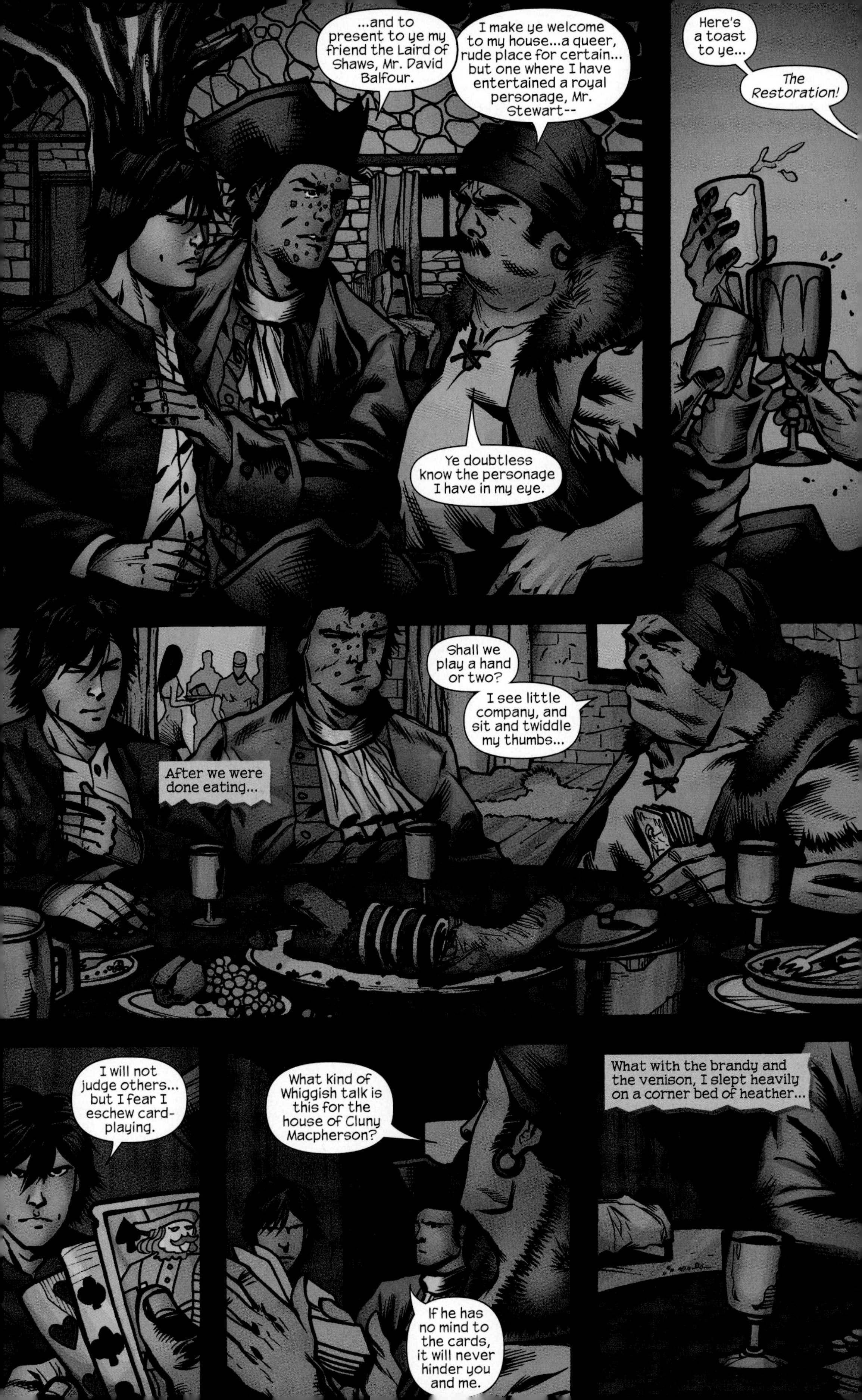
...and to present to ye my friend the Laird of Shaws, Mr. David Balfour.
I make ye welcome to my house...a queer, rude place for certain... but one where I have entertained a royal personage, Mr. Stewart--
Ye doubtless know the personage I have in my eye.
Here's a toast to ye...
The Restoration!
After we were done eating...
Shall we play a hand or two?
I see little company, and sit and twiddle my thumbs...
I will not judge others... but I fear I eschew card-playing.
What kind of Whiggish talk is this for the house of Cluny Macpherson?
If he has no mind to the cards, it will never hinder you and me.
What with the brandy and the venison, I slept heavily on a corner bed of heather...

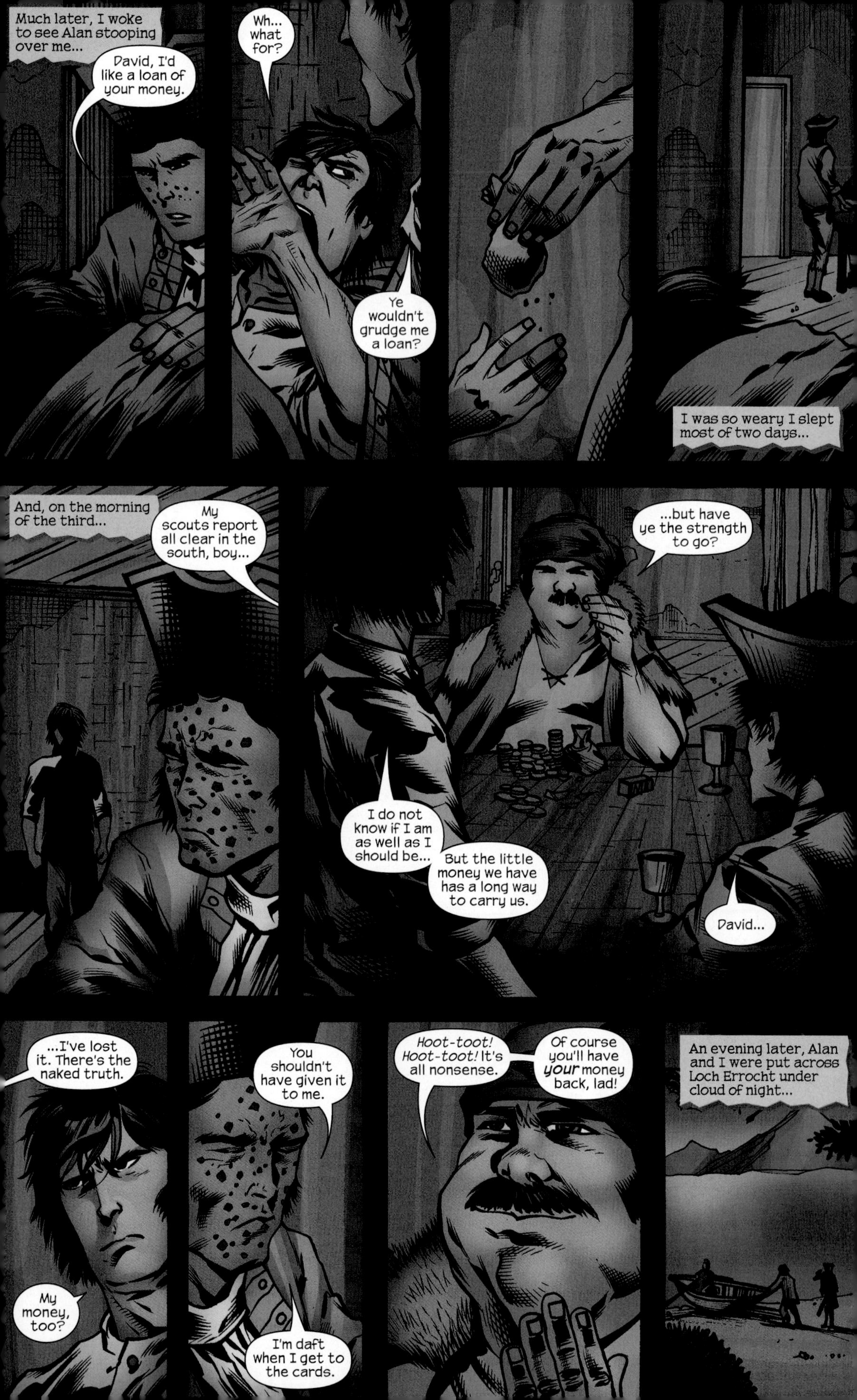
Much later, I woke to see Alan stooping over me...
David, I'd like a loan of your money.
Wh... what for?
Ye wouldn't grudge me a loan?
I was so weary I slept most of two days...
And, on the morning of the third...
My scouts report all clear in the south, boy...
...but have ye the strength to go?
I do not know if I am as well as I should be...
But the little money we have has a long way to carry us.
David...
...I've lost it. There's the naked truth.
My money, too?
You shouldn't have given it to me.
I'm daft when I get to the cards.
Hoot-toot! Hoot-toot! It's all nonsense.
Of course you'll have *your* money back, lad!
An evening later, Alan and I were put across Loch Errocht under cloud of night...

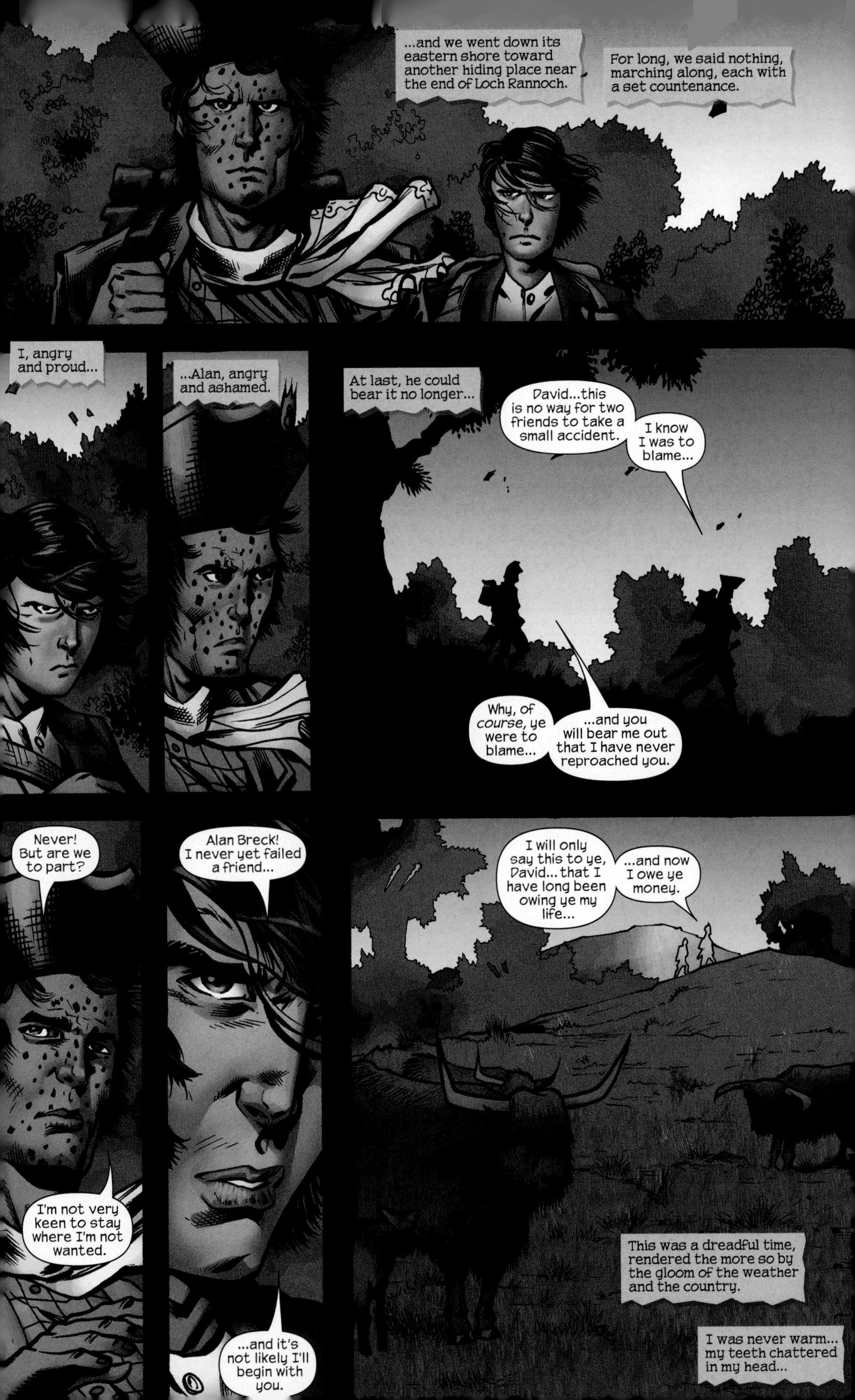
...and we went down its eastern shore toward another hiding place near the end of Loch Rannoch.
For long, we said nothing, marching along, each with a set countenance.
I, angry and proud...
...Alan, angry and ashamed.
At last, he could bear it no longer...
David...this is no way for two friends to take a small accident.
I know I was to blame...
Why, of course, ye were to blame...
...and you will bear me out that I have never reproached you.
Never! But are we to part?
Alan Breck! I never yet failed a friend...
I'm not very keen to stay where I'm not wanted.
...and it's not likely I'll begin with you.
I will only say this to ye, David...that I have long been owing ye my life...
...and now I owe ye money.
This was a dreadful time, rendered the more so by the gloom of the weather and the country.
I was never warm... my teeth chattered in my head...

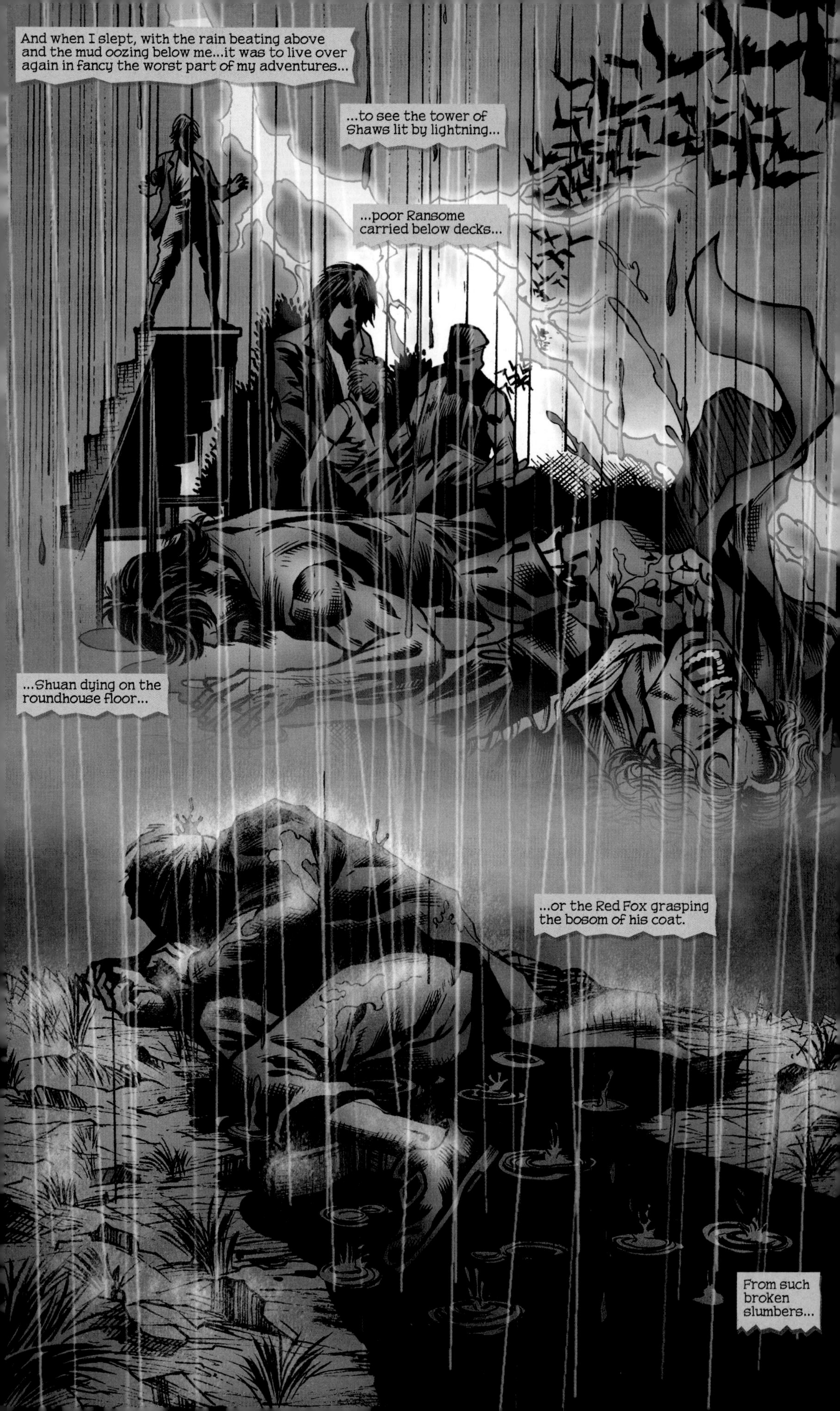
And when I slept, with the rain beating above and the mud oozing below me...it was to live over again in fancy the worst part of my adventures...
...to see the tower of Shaws lit by lightning...
...poor Ransome carried below decks...
...Shuan dying on the roundhouse floor...
...or the Red Fox grasping the bosom of his coat.
From such broken slumbers...

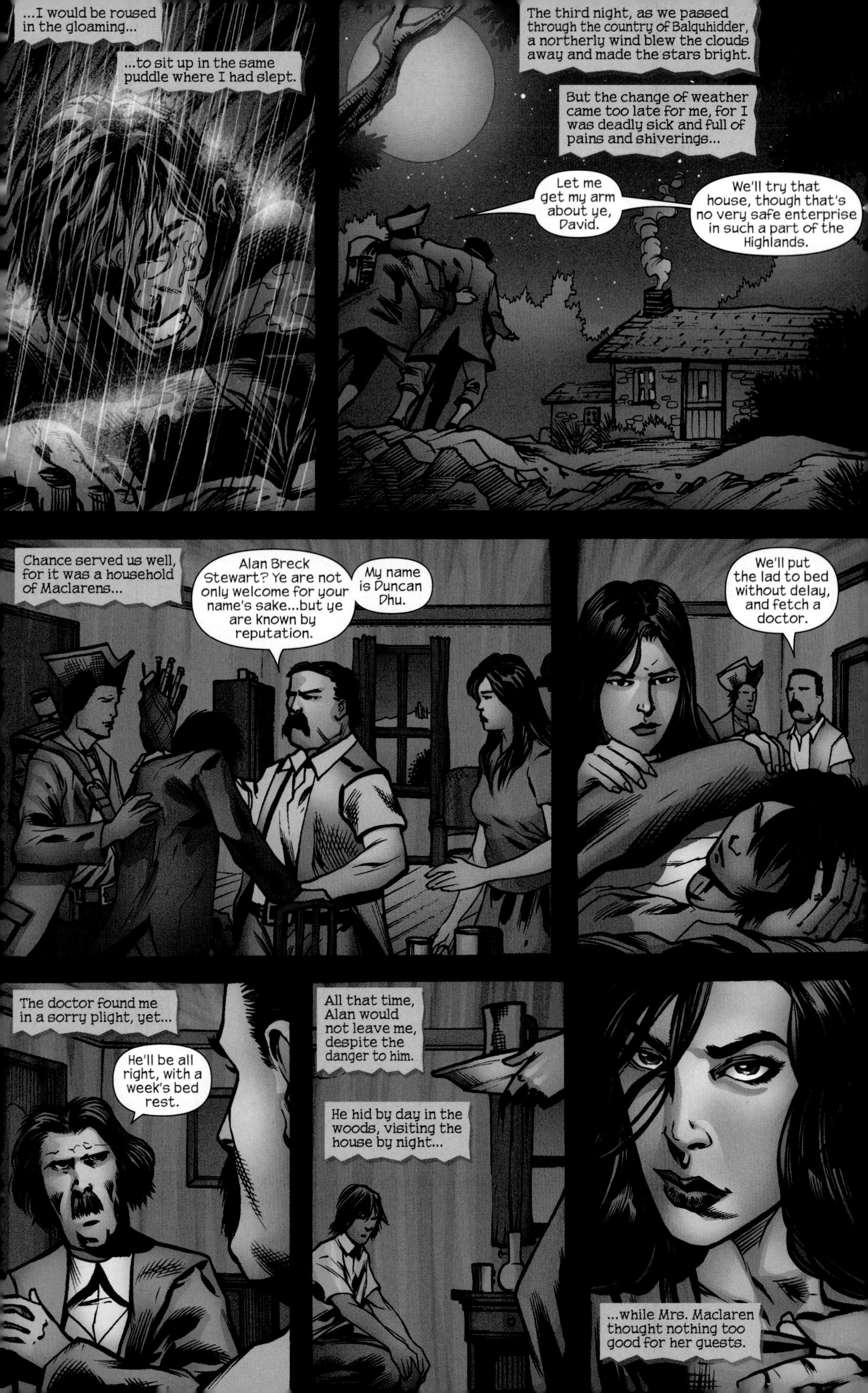
...I would be roused in the gloaming...
...to sit up in the same puddle where I had slept.
The third night, as we passed through the country of Balquhidder, a northerly wind blew the clouds away and made the stars bright.
But the change of weather came too late for me, for I was deadly sick and full of pains and shiverings...
Let me get my arm about ye, David.
We'll try that house, though that's no very safe enterprise in such a part of the Highlands.
Chance served us well, for it was a household of Maclarens...
Alan Breck Stewart? Ye are not only welcome for your name's sake...but ye are known by reputation.
My name is Duncan Dhu.
We'll put the lad to bed without delay, and fetch a doctor.
The doctor found me in a sorry plight, yet...
He'll be all right, with a week's bed rest.
All that time, Alan would not leave me, despite the danger to him.
He hid by day in the woods, visiting the house by night...
...while Mrs. Maclaren thought nothing too good for her guests.

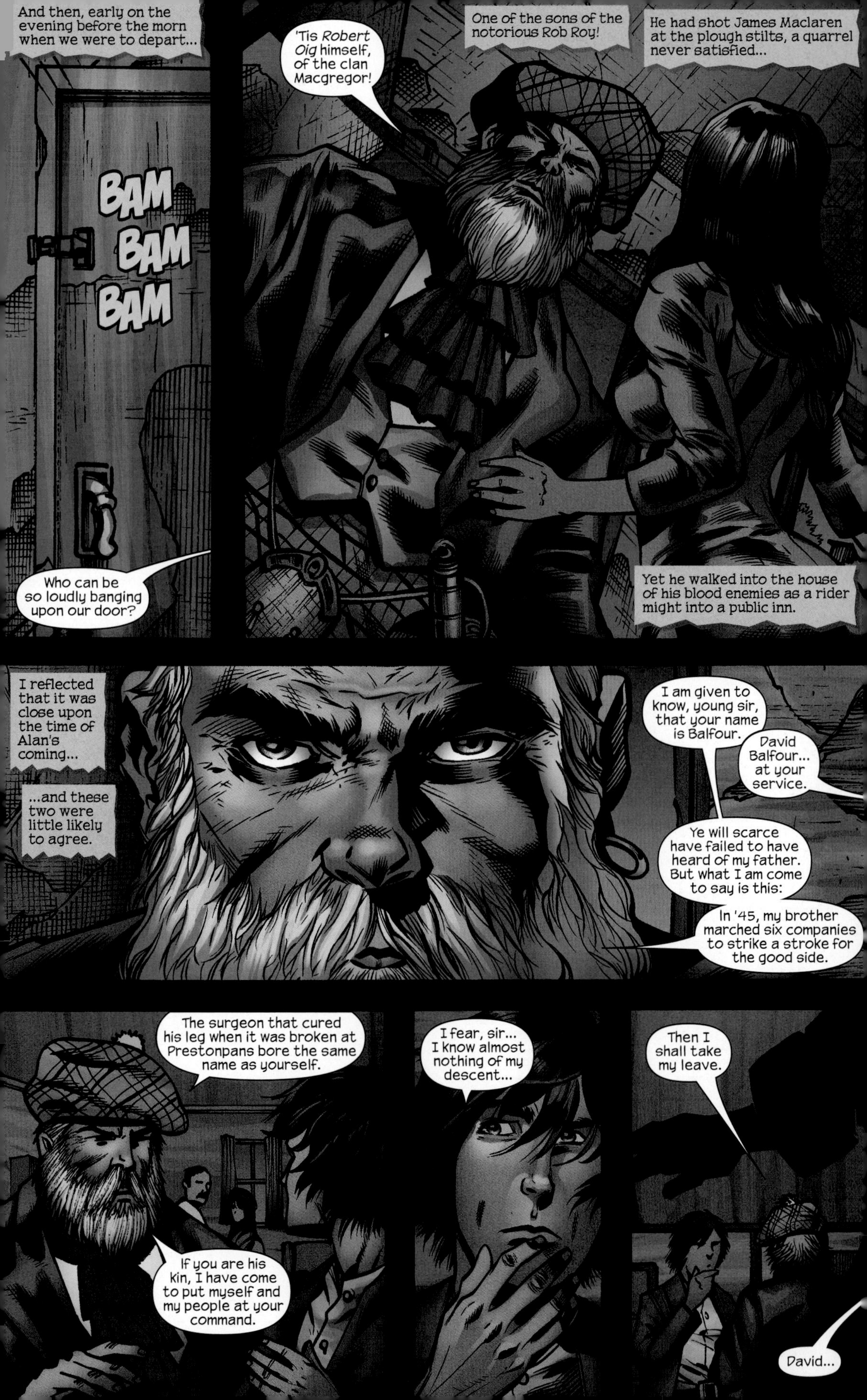
And then, early on the evening before the morn when we were to depart...
BAM BAM BAM
Who can be so loudly banging upon our door?
'Tis *Robert Oig* himself, of the clan Macgregor!
One of the sons of the notorious Rob Roy!
He had shot James Maclaren at the plough stilts, a quarrel never satisfied...
Yet he walked into the house of his blood enemies as a rider might into a public inn.
I reflected that it was close upon the time of Alan's coming...
...and these two were little likely to agree.
I am given to know, young sir, that your name is Balfour.
David Balfour... at your service.
Ye will scarce have failed to have heard of my father. But what I am come to say is this:
In '45, my brother marched six companies to strike a stroke for the good side.
The surgeon that cured his leg when it was broken at Prestonpans bore the same name as yourself.
If you are his kin, I have come to put myself and my people at your command.
I fear, sir... I know almost nothing of my descent...
Then I shall take my leave.
David...

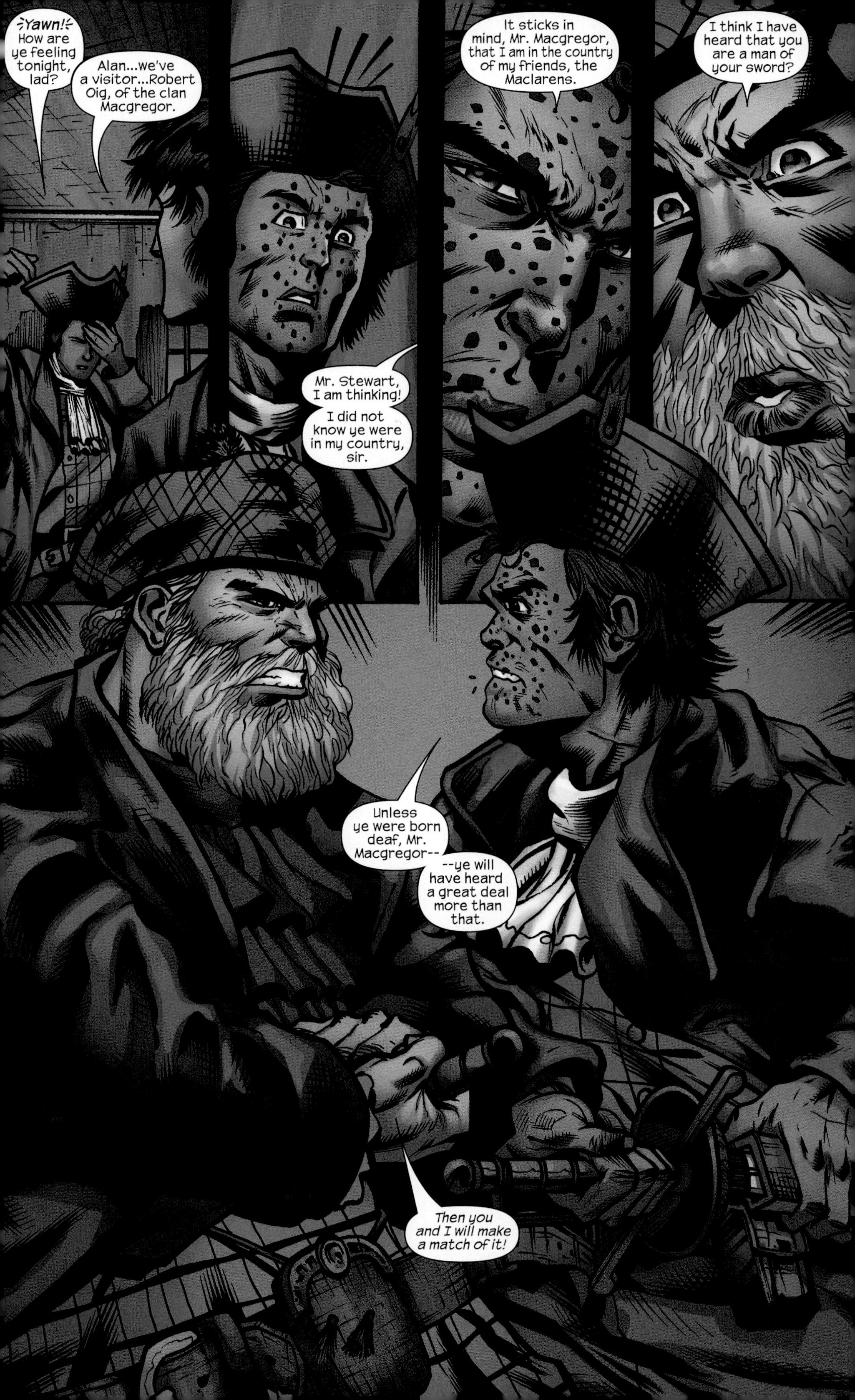

Yawn!
How are ye feeling tonight, lad?
Alan...we've a visitor...Robert Oig, of the clan Macgregor.
It sticks in mind, Mr. Macgregor, that I am in the country of my friends, the Maclarens.
I think I have heard that you are a man of your sword?
Mr. Stewart, I am thinking!
I did not know ye were in my country, sir.
Unless ye were born deaf, Mr. Macgregor--
--ye will have heard a great deal more than that.
Then you and I will make a match of it!

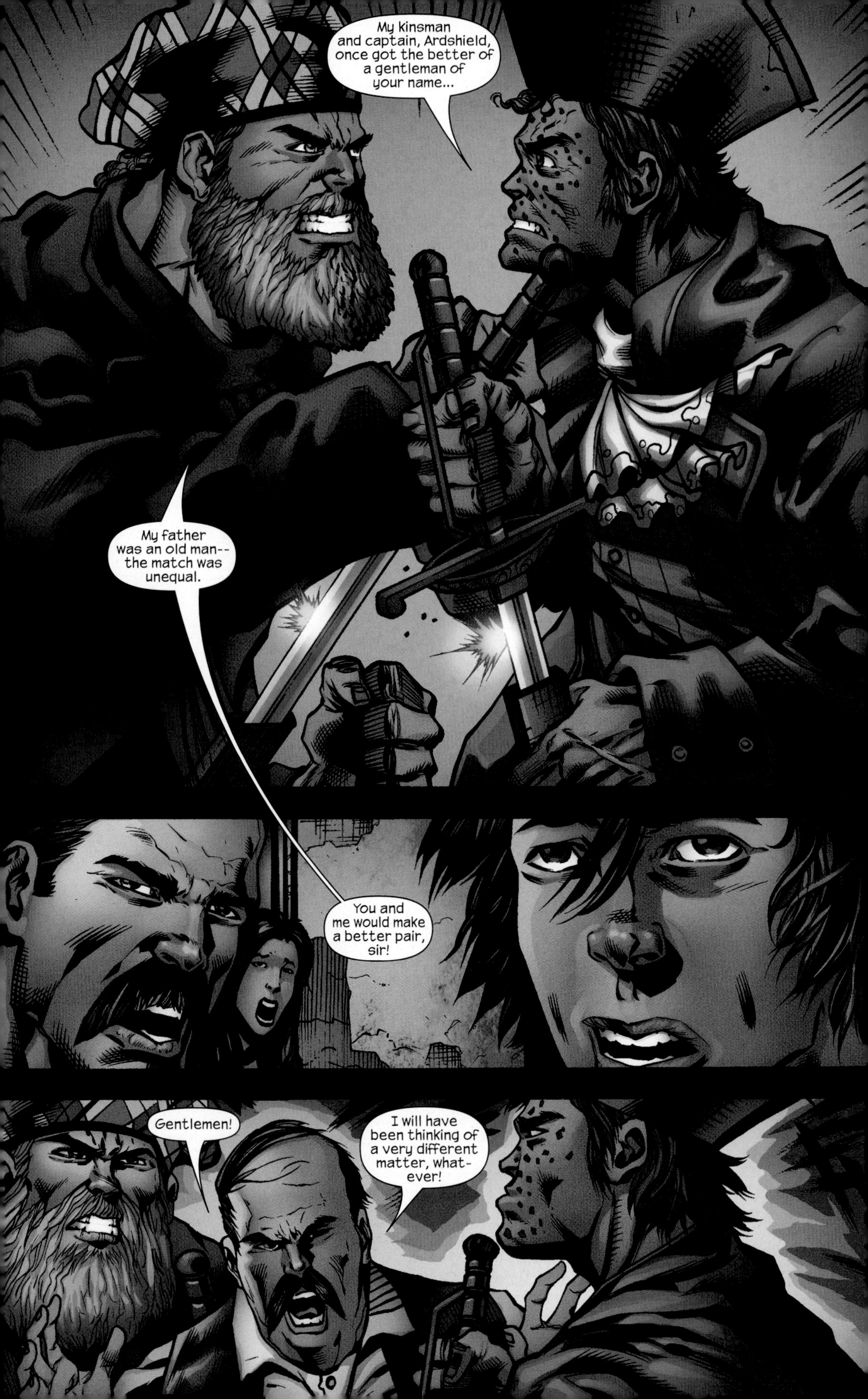
My kinsman and captain, Ardshield, once got the better of a gentleman of your name...
My father was an old man-- the match was unequal.
You and me would make a better pair, sir!
Gentlemen!
I will have been thinking of a very different matter, what-ever!

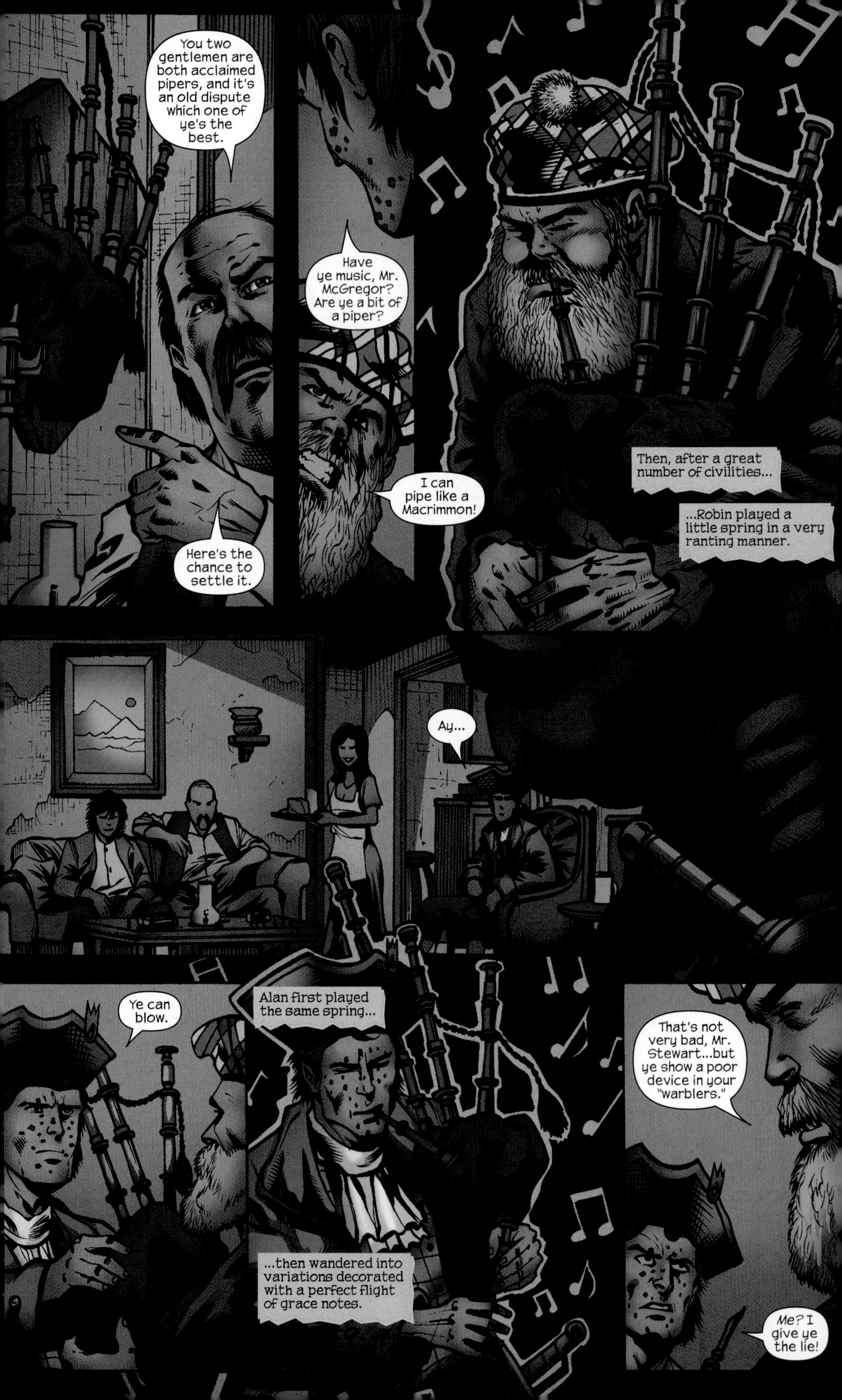
You two gentlemen are both acclaimed pipers, and it's an old dispute which one of ye's the best.
Here's the chance to settle it.
Have ye music, Mr. McGregor? Are ye a bit of a piper?
I can pipe like a Macrimmon!
Then, after a great number of civilities...
...Robin played a little spring in a very ranting manner.
Ay...
Ye can blow.
Alan first played the same spring...
...then wandered into variations decorated with a perfect flight of grace notes.
That's not very bad, Mr. Stewart...but ye show a poor device in your "warblers."
Me? I give ye the lie!

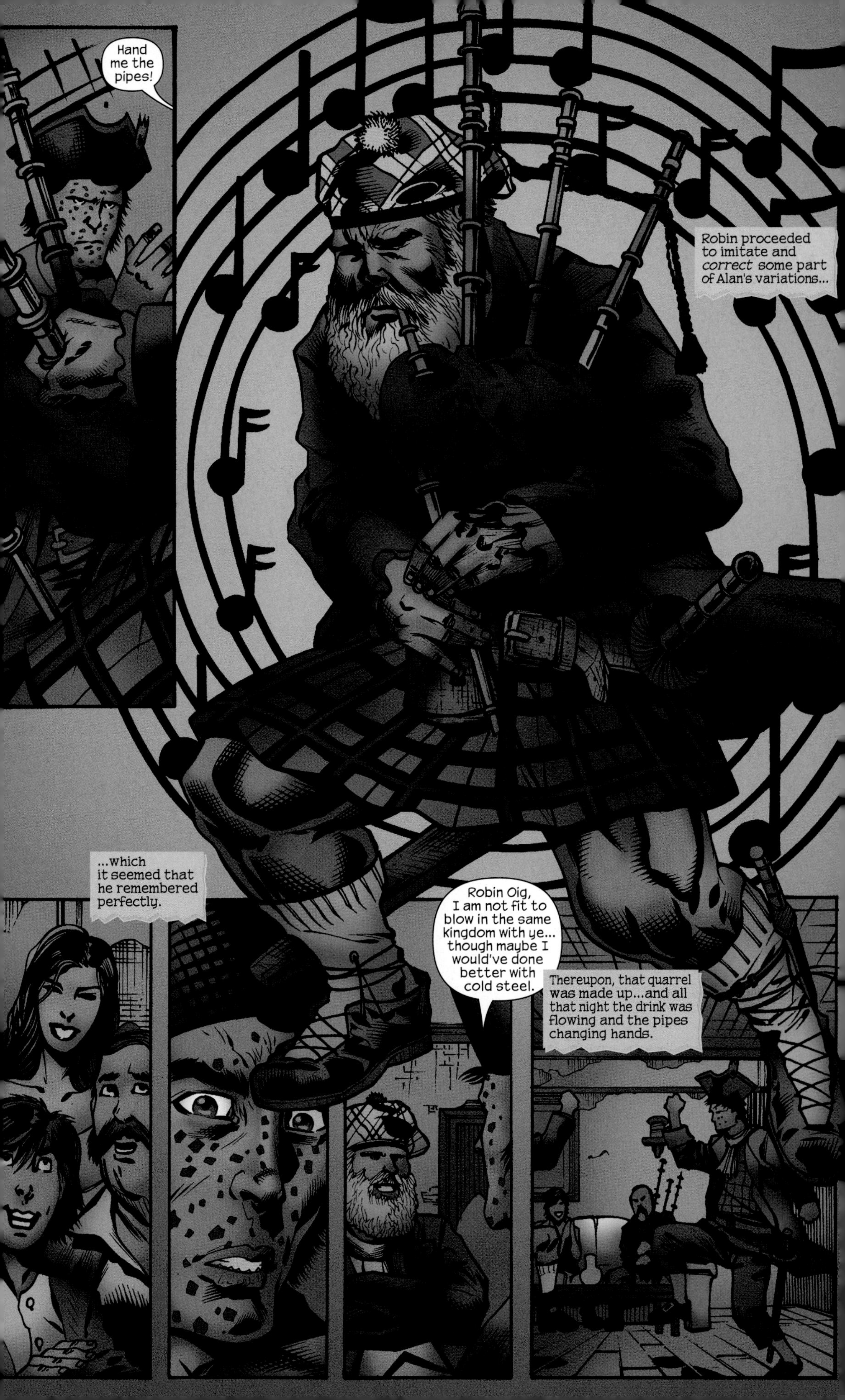

Hand me the pipes!
Robin proceeded to imitate and *correct* some part of Alan's variations...
...which it seemed that he remembered perfectly.
Robin Oig, I am not fit to blow in the same kingdom with ye... though maybe I would've done better with cold steel.
Thereupon, that quarrel was made up...and all that night the drink was flowing and the pipes changing hands.

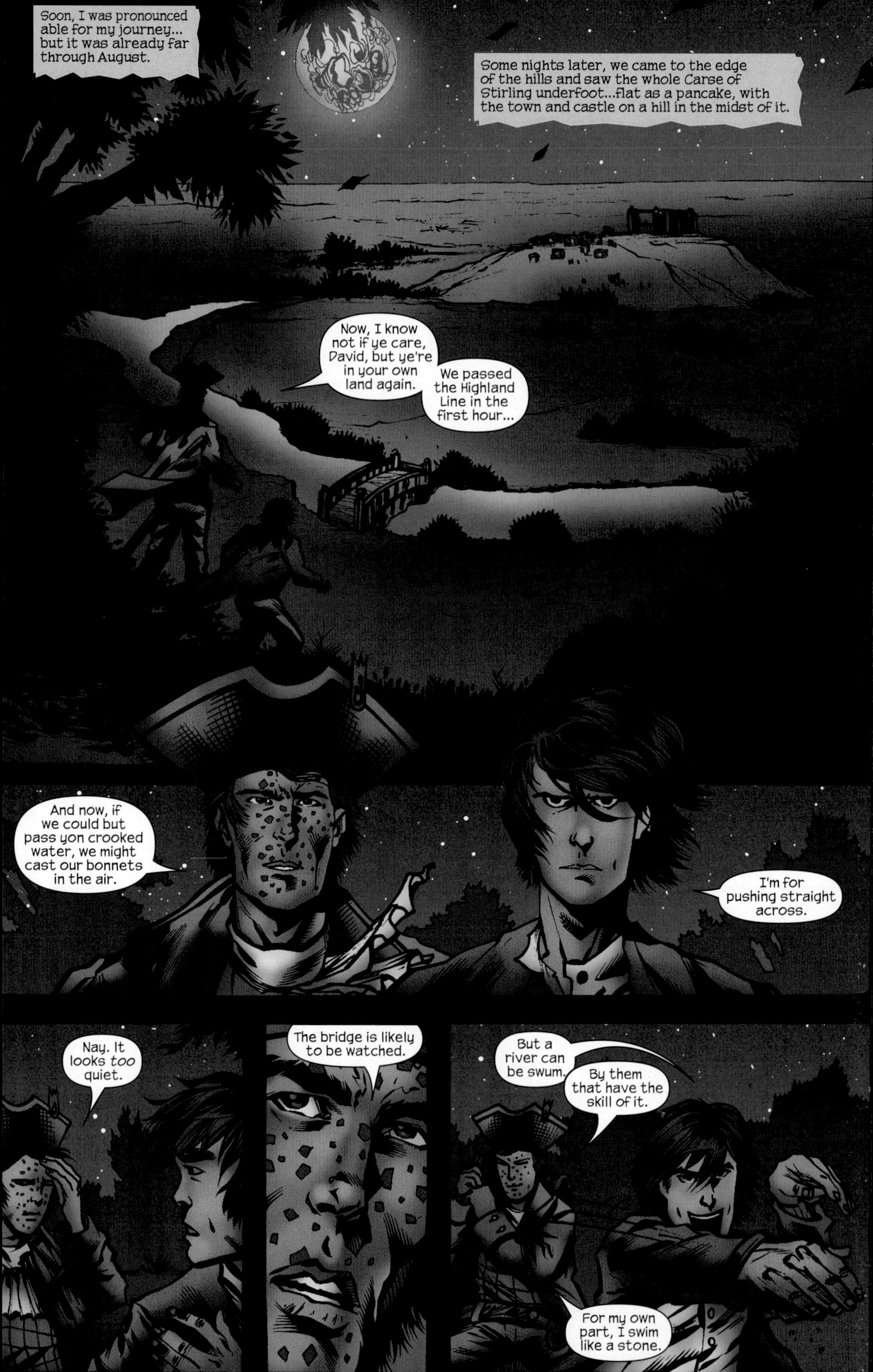
Soon, I was pronounced able for my journey... but it was already far through August.
Some nights later, we came to the edge of the hills and saw the whole Carse of Stirling underfoot...flat as a pancake, with the town and castle on a hill in the midst of it.
Now, I know not if ye care, David, but ye're in your own land again.
We passed the Highland Line in the first hour...
And now, if we could but pass yon crooked water, we might cast our bonnets in the air.
I'm for pushing straight across.
Nay. It looks *too* quiet.
The bridge is likely to be watched.
But a river can be swum.
By them that have the skill of it.
For my own part, I swim like a stone.

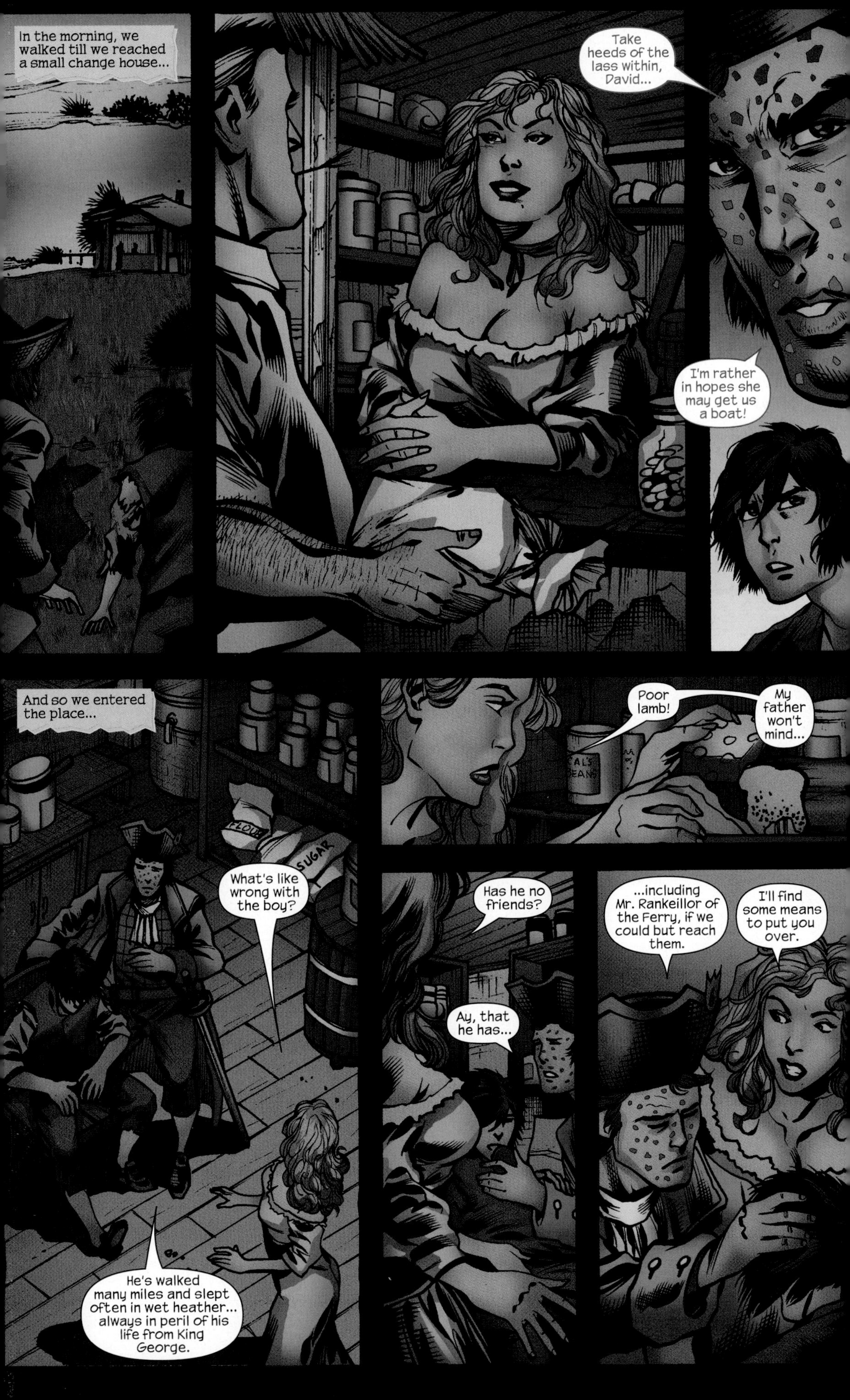
In the morning, we walked till we reached a small change house...
Take heeds of the lass within, David...
I'm rather in hopes she may get us a boat!
And so we entered the place...
What's like wrong with the boy?
He's walked many miles and slept often in wet heather... always in peril of his life from King George.
Poor lamb!
My father won't mind...
Has he no friends?
Ay, that he has...
...including Mr. Rankeillor of the Ferry, if we could but reach them.
I'll find some means to put you over.

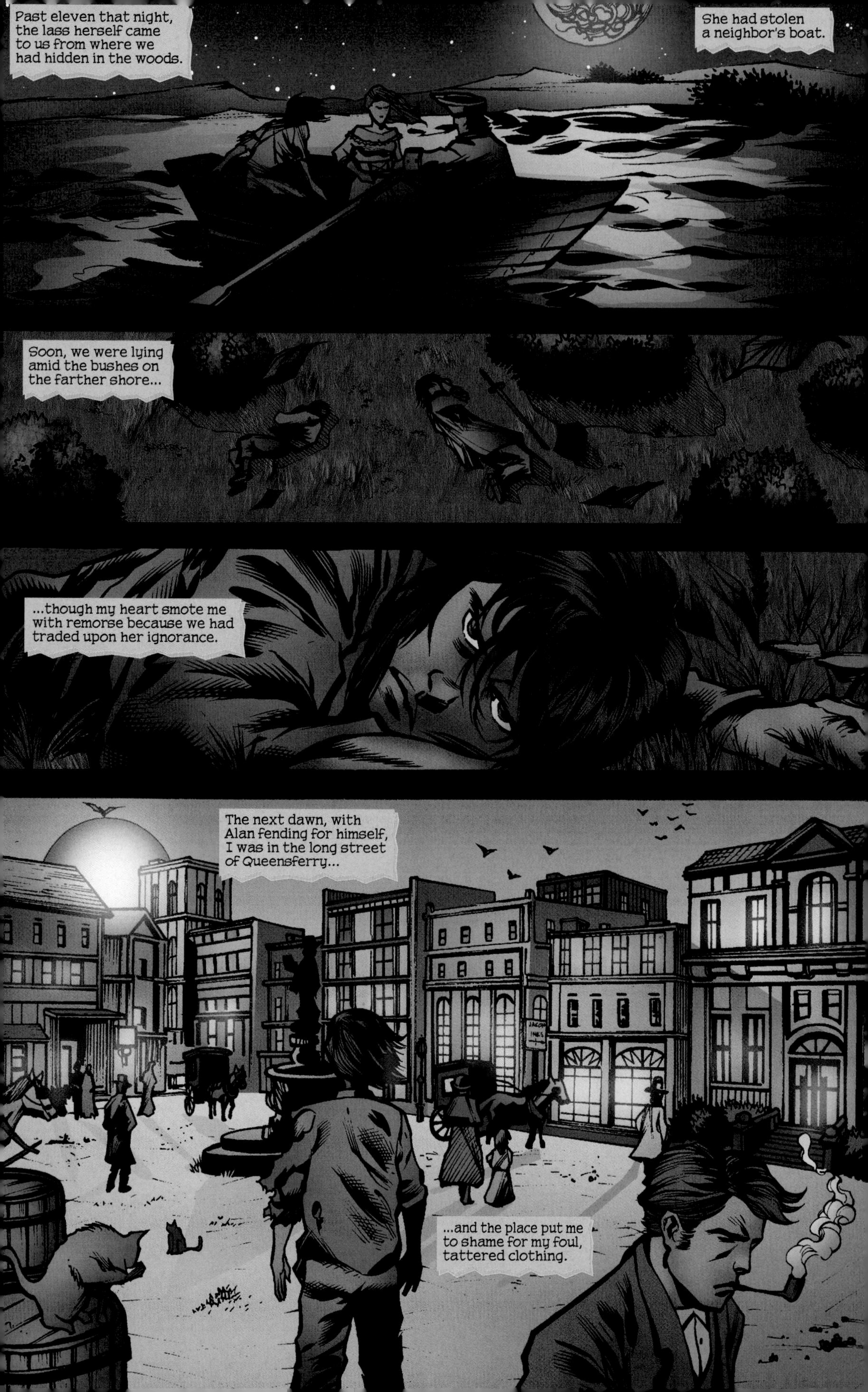
Past eleven that night, the lass herself came to us from where we had hidden in the woods.
She had stolen a neighbor's boat.
Soon, we were lying amid the bushes on the farther shore...
...though my heart smote me with remorse because we had traded upon her ignorance.
The next dawn, with Alan fending for himself, I was in the long street of Queensferry...
...and the place put me to shame for my foul, tattered clothing.

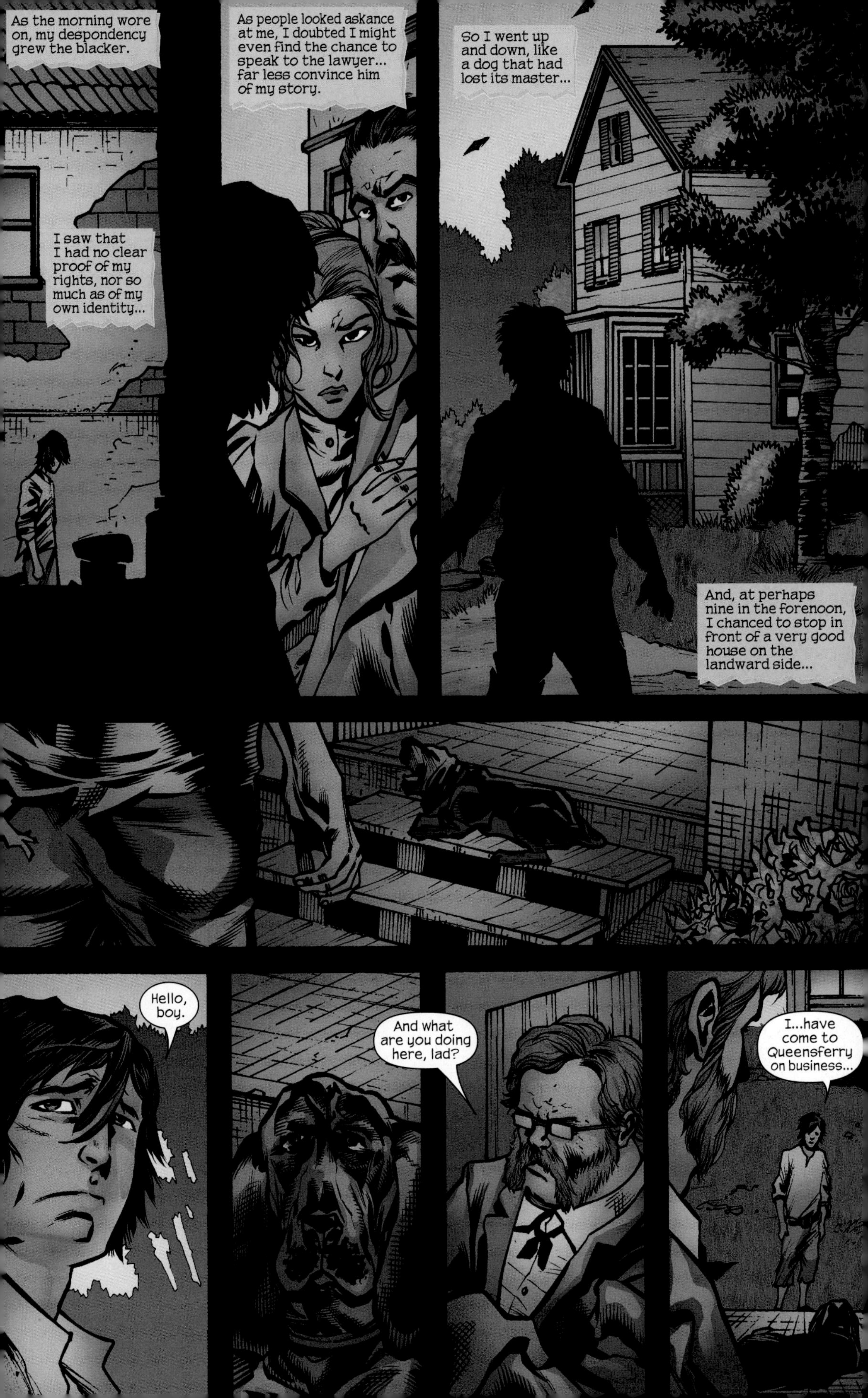
As the morning wore on, my despondency grew the blacker.
I saw that I had no clear proof of my rights, nor so much as of my own identity...
As people looked askance at me, I doubted I might even find the chance to speak to the lawyer... far less convince him of my story.
So I went up and down, like a dog that had lost its master...
And, at perhaps nine in the forenoon, I chanced to stop in front of a very good house on the landward side...
Hello, boy.
And what are you doing here, lad?
I...have come to Queensferry on business...

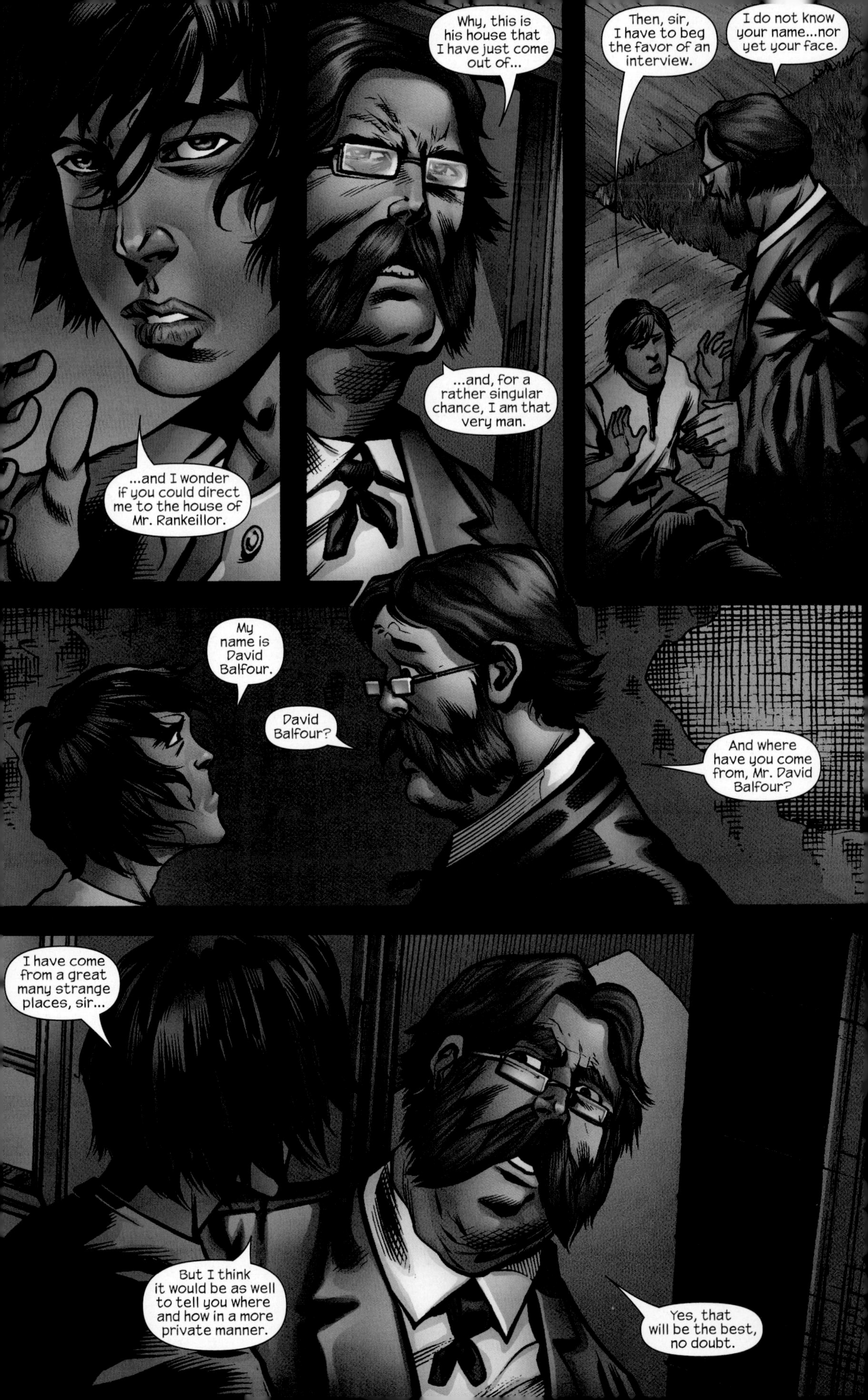
...and I wonder if you could direct me to the house of Mr. Rankeillor.
Why, this is his house that I have just come out of...
...and, for a rather singular chance, I am that very man.
Then, sir, I have to beg the favor of an interview.
I do not know your name...nor yet your face.
My name is David Balfour.
David Balfour?
And where have you come from, Mr. David Balfour?
I have come from a great many strange places, sir...
But I think it would be as well to tell you where and how in a more private manner.
Yes, that will be the best, no doubt.

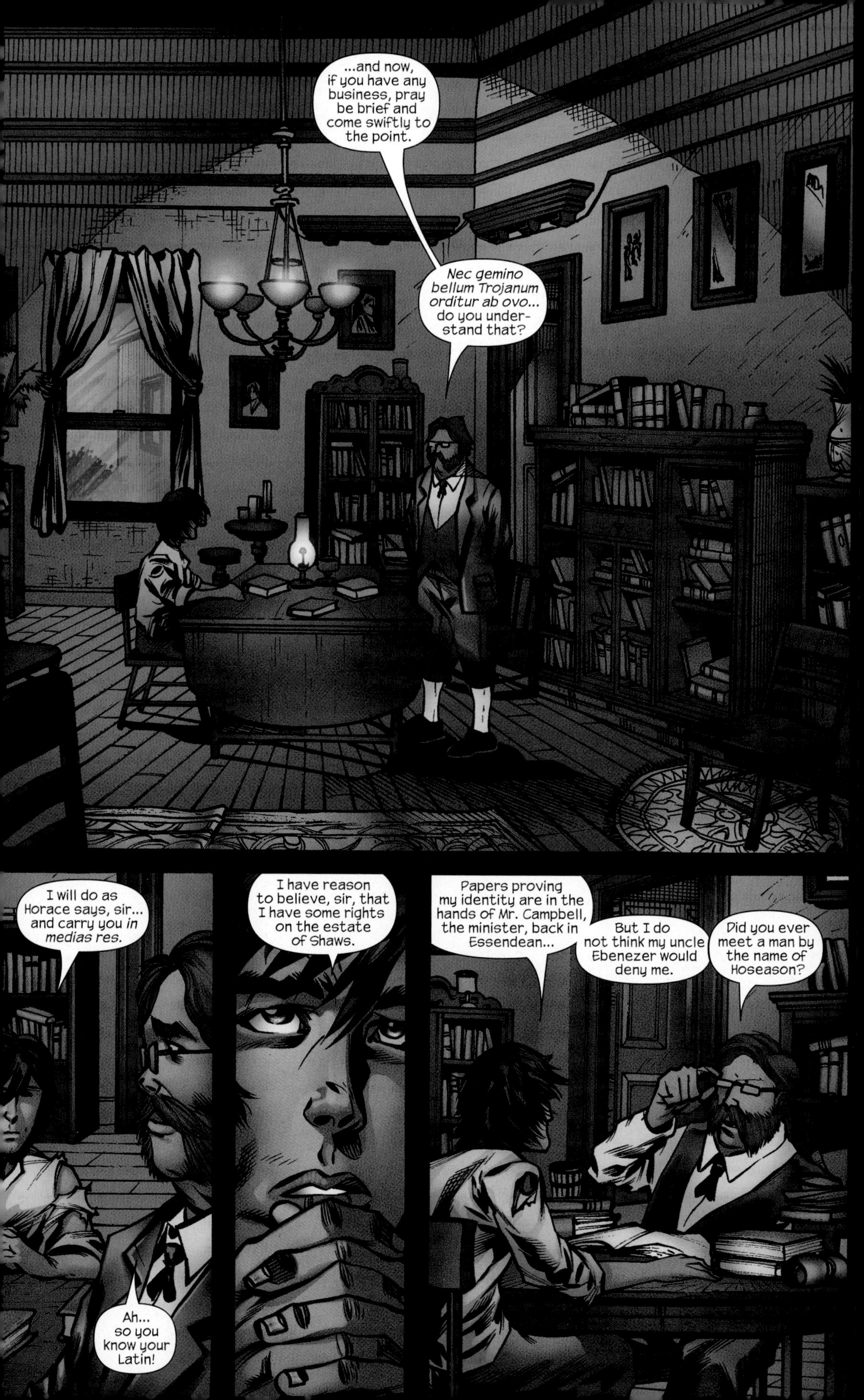
...and now, if you have any business, pray be brief and come swiftly to the point.
Nec gemino bellum Trojanum orditur ab ovo... do you understand that?
I will do as Horace says, sir... and carry you *in medias res.*
Ah... so you know your Latin!
I have reason to believe, sir, that I have some rights on the estate of Shaws.
Papers proving my identity are in the hands of Mr. Campbell, the minister, back in Essendean...
But I do not think my uncle Ebenezer would deny me.
Did you ever meet a man by the name of Hoseason?

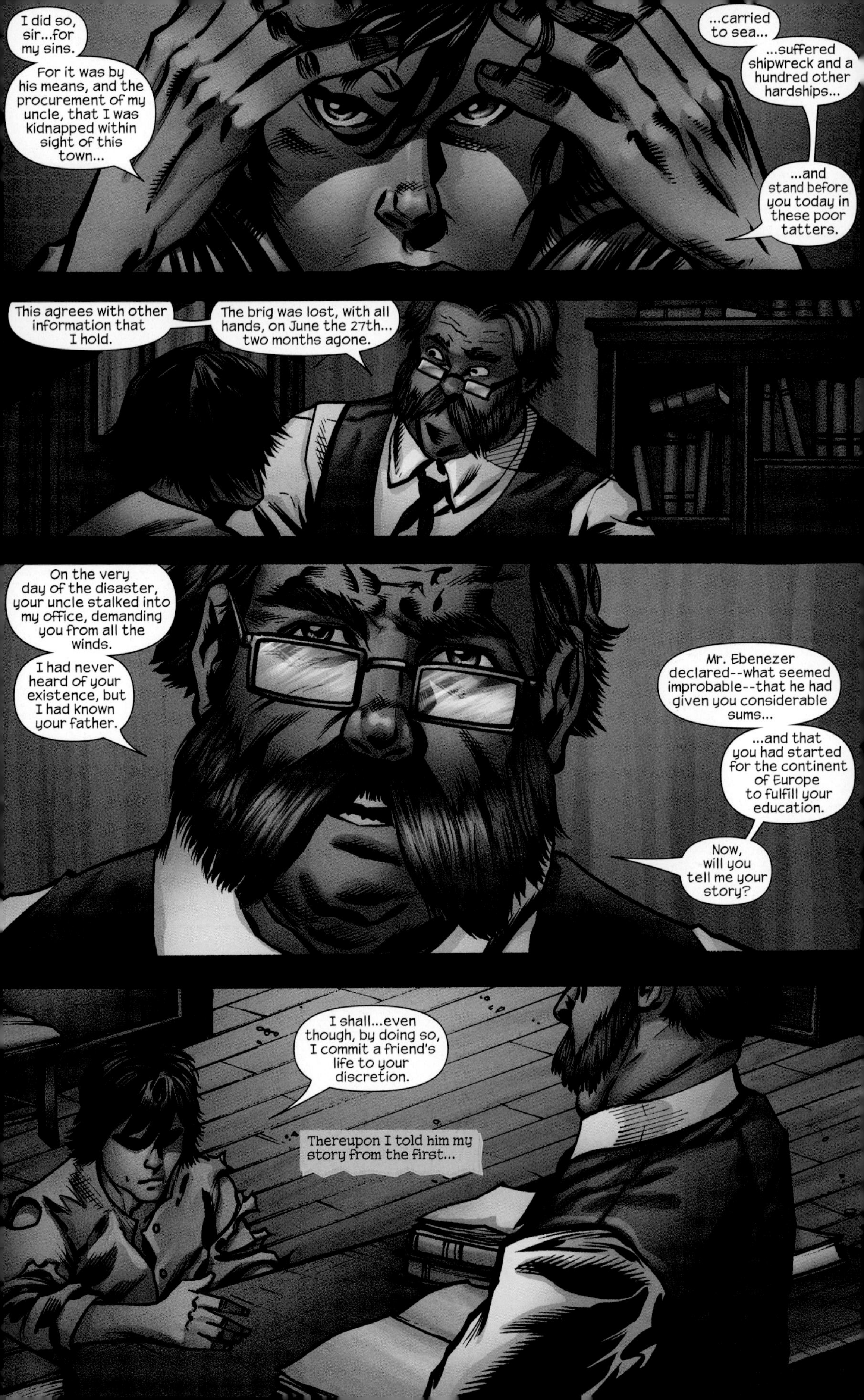
I did so, sir...for my sins.
For it was by his means, and the procurement of my uncle, that I was kidnapped within sight of this town...
...carried to sea...
...suffered shipwreck and a hundred other hardships...
...and stand before you today in these poor tatters.
This agrees with other information that I hold.
The brig was lost, with all hands, on June the 27th... two months agone.
On the very day of the disaster, your uncle stalked into my office, demanding you from all the winds.
I had never heard of your existence, but I had known your father.
Mr. Ebenezer declared--what seemed improbable--that he had given you considerable sums...
...and that you had started for the continent of Europe to fulfill your education.
Now, will you tell me your story?
I shall...even though, by doing so, I commit a friend's life to your discretion.
Thereupon I told him my story from the first...

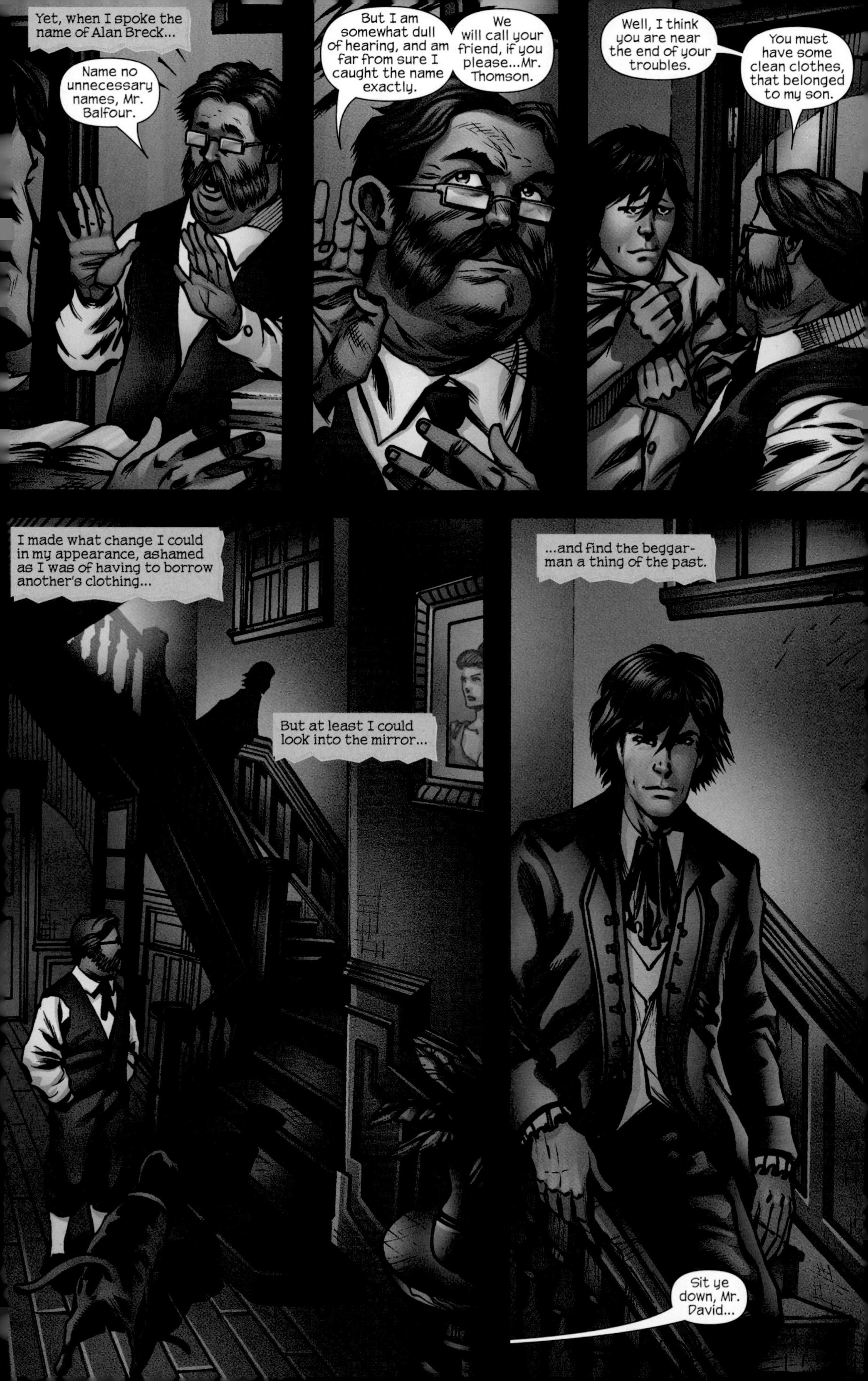
Yet, when I spoke the name of Alan Breck...
Name no unnecessary names, Mr. Balfour.
But I am somewhat dull of hearing, and am far from sure I caught the name exactly.
We will call your friend, if you please...Mr. Thomson.
Well, I think you are near the end of your troubles.
You must have some clean clothes, that belonged to my son.
I made what change I could in my appearance, ashamed as I was of having to borrow another's clothing...
But at least I could look into the mirror...
...and find the beggar-man a thing of the past.
Sit ye down, Mr. David...

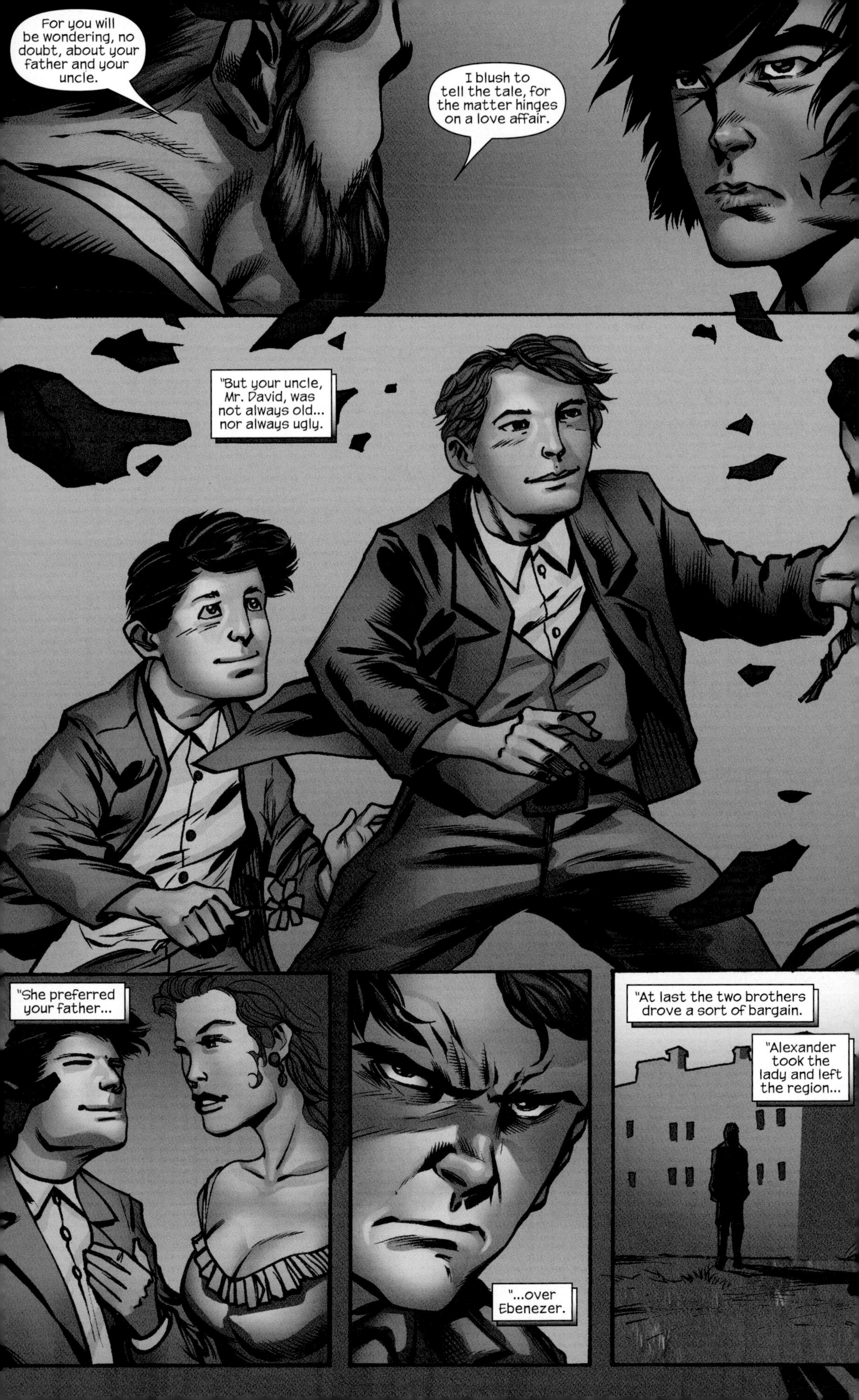
For you will be wondering, no doubt, about your father and your uncle.
I blush to tell the tale, for the matter hinges on a love affair.
"But your uncle, Mr. David, was not always old... nor always ugly.
"She preferred your father...
"...over Ebenezer.
"At last the two brothers drove a sort of bargain.
"Alexander took the lady and left the region...

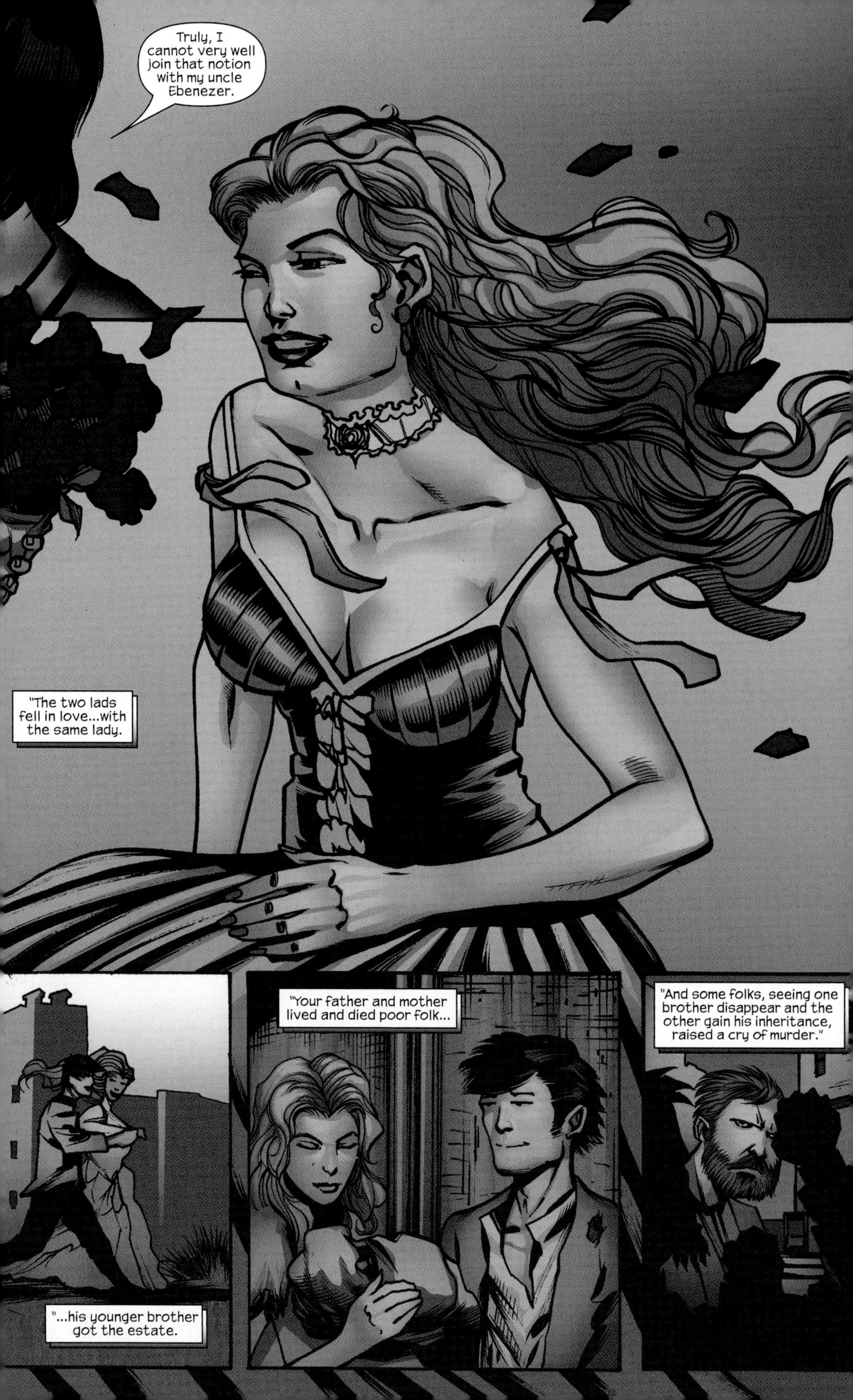
Truly, I cannot very well join that notion with my uncle Ebenezer.
"The two lads fell in love...with the same lady.
"...his younger brother got the estate.
"Your father and mother lived and died poor folk...
"And some folks, seeing one brother disappear and the other gain his inheritance, raised a cry of murder."

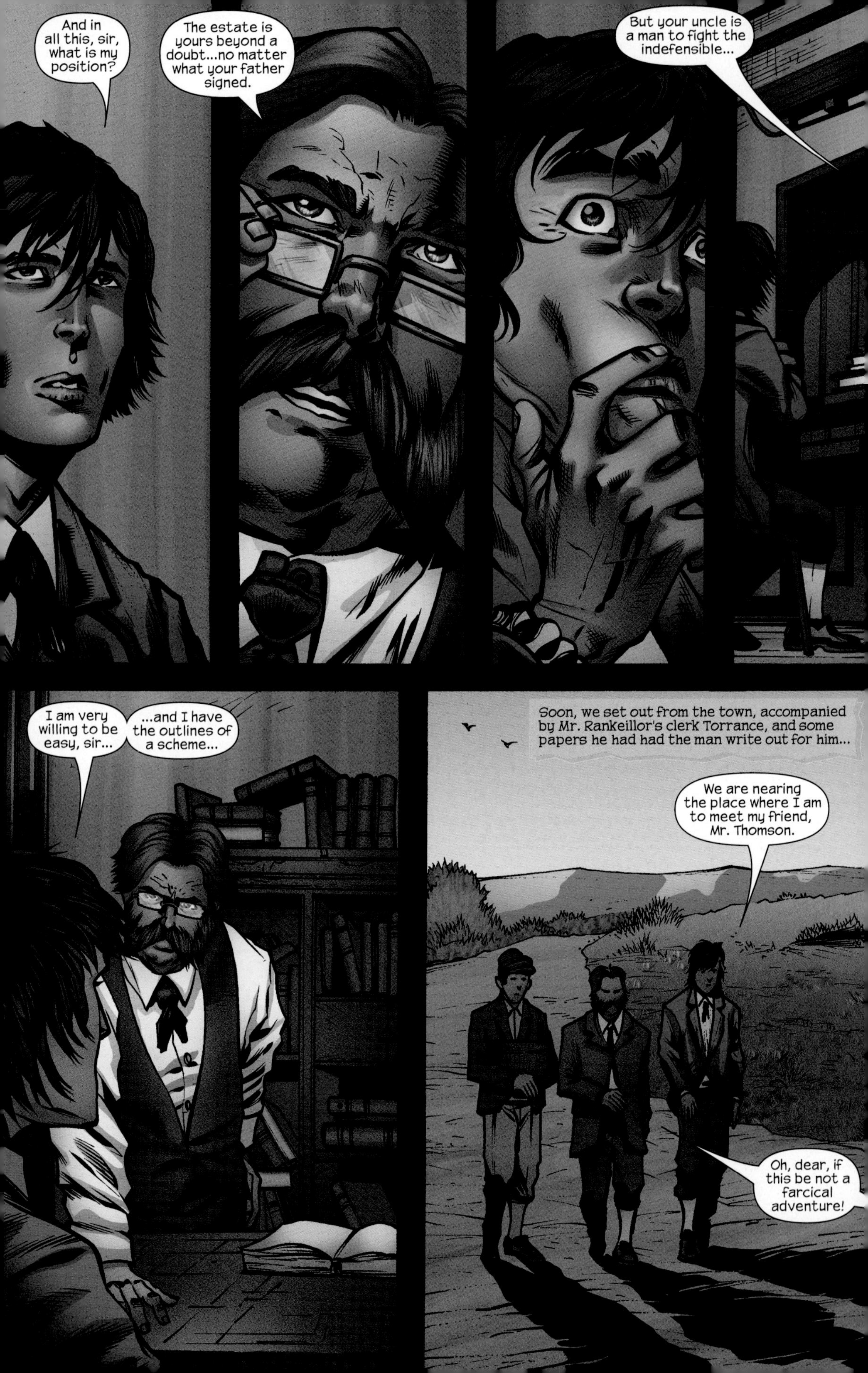
And in all this, sir, what is my position?
The estate is yours beyond a doubt...no matter what your father signed.
But your uncle is a man to fight the indefensible...
I am very willing to be easy, sir...
...and I have the outlines of a scheme...
Soon, we set out from the town, accompanied by Mr. Rankeillor's clerk Torrance, and some papers he had had the man write out for him...
We are nearing the place where I am to meet my friend, Mr. Thomson.
Oh, dear, if this be not a farcical adventure!

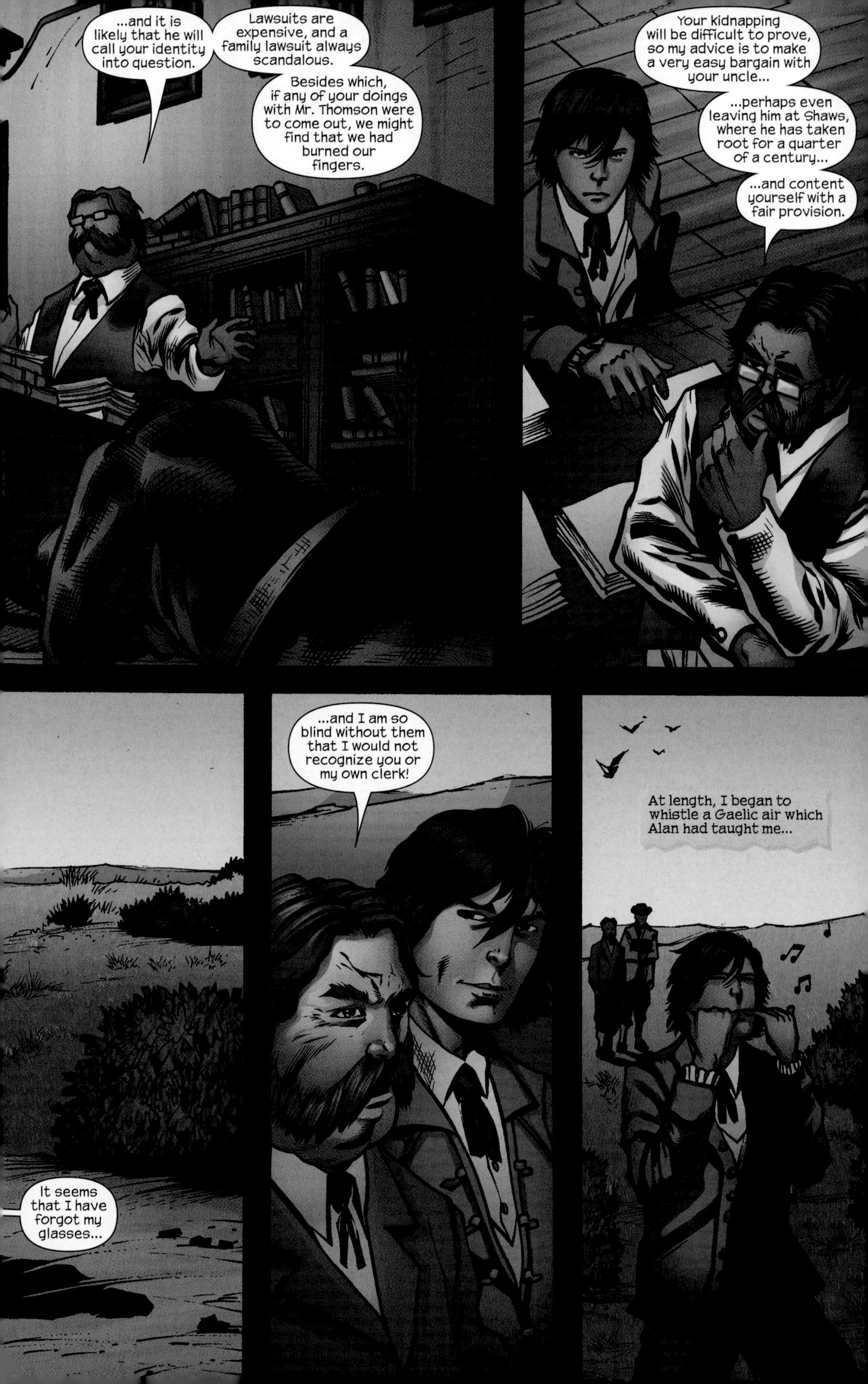

...and it is likely that he will call your identity into question.
Lawsuits are expensive, and a family lawsuit always scandalous.
Besides which, if any of your doings with Mr. Thomson were to come out, we might find that we had burned our fingers.
Your kidnapping will be difficult to prove, so my advice is to make a very easy bargain with your uncle...
...perhaps even leaving him at Shaws, where he has taken root for a quarter of a century...
...and content yourself with a fair provision.
It seems that I have forgot my glasses...
...and I am so blind without them that I would not recognize you or my own clerk!
At length, I began to whistle a Gaelic air which Alan had taught me...

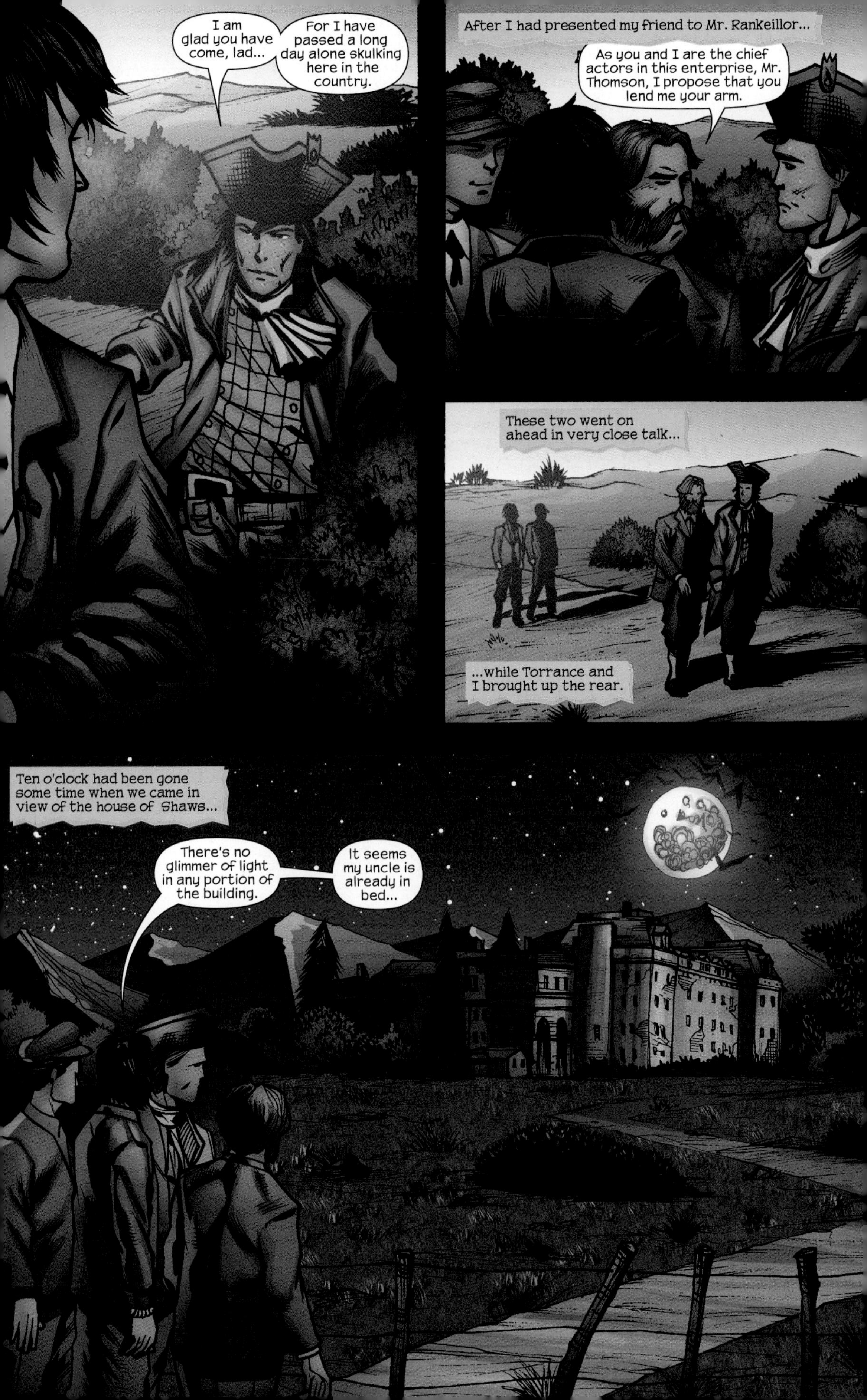
I am glad you have come, lad...
For I have passed a long day alone skulking here in the country.
After I had presented my friend to Mr. Rankeillor...
As you and I are the chief actors in this enterprise, Mr. Thomson, I propose that you lend me your arm.
These two went on ahead in very close talk...
...while Torrance and I brought up the rear.
Ten o'clock had been gone some time when we came in view of the house of Shaws...
There's no glimmer of light in any portion of the building.
It seems my uncle is already in bed...

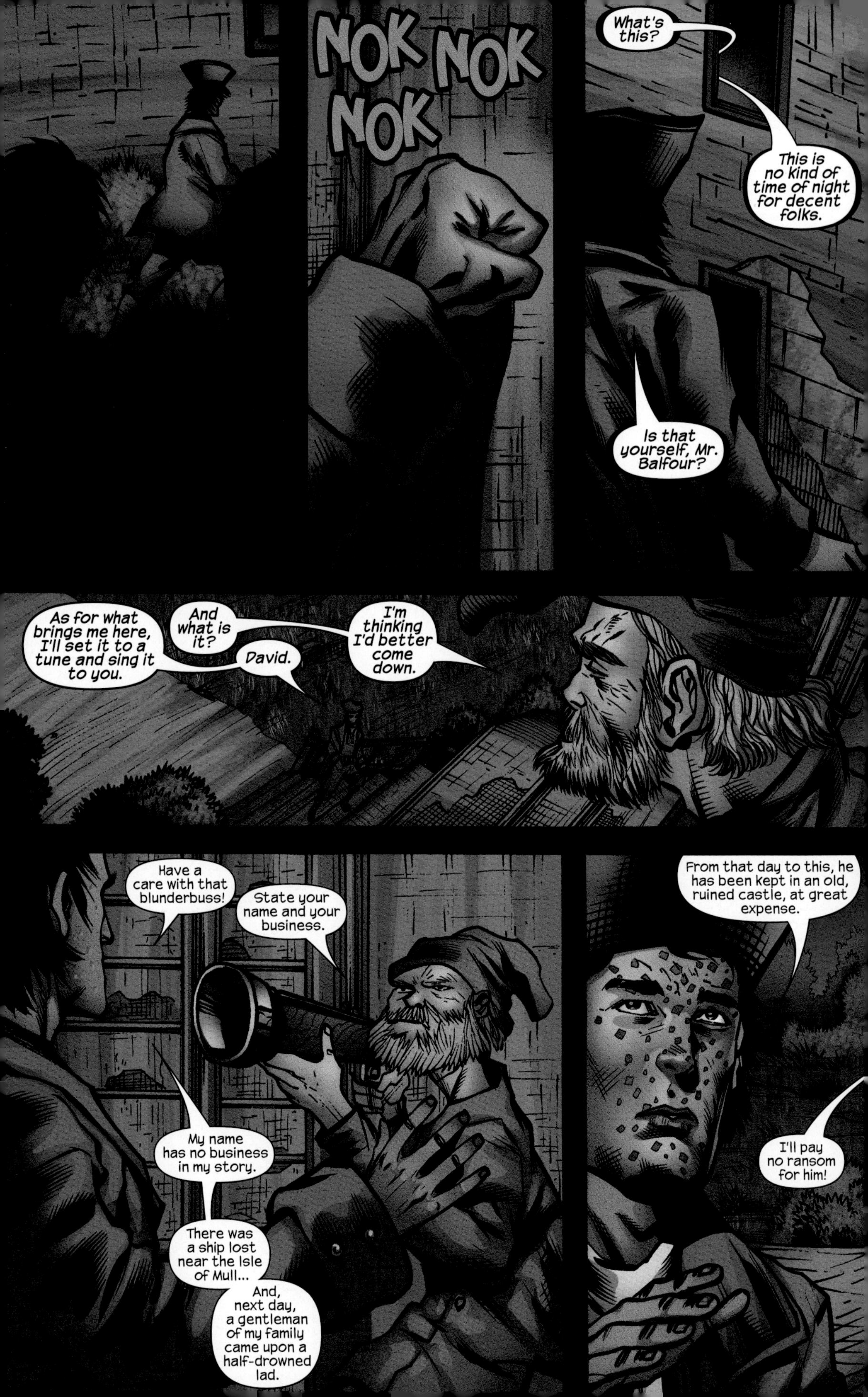
NOK NOK NOK
What's this?
This is no kind of time of night for decent folks.
Is that yourself, Mr. Balfour?
As for what brings me here, I'll set it to a tune and sing it to you.
And what is it?
David.
I'm thinking I'd better come down.
Have a care with that blunderbuss!
State your name and your business.
My name has no business in my story.
There was a ship lost near the Isle of Mull...
And, next day, a gentleman of my family came upon a half-drowned lad.
From that day to this, he has been kept in an old, ruined castle, at great expense.
I'll pay no ransom for him!

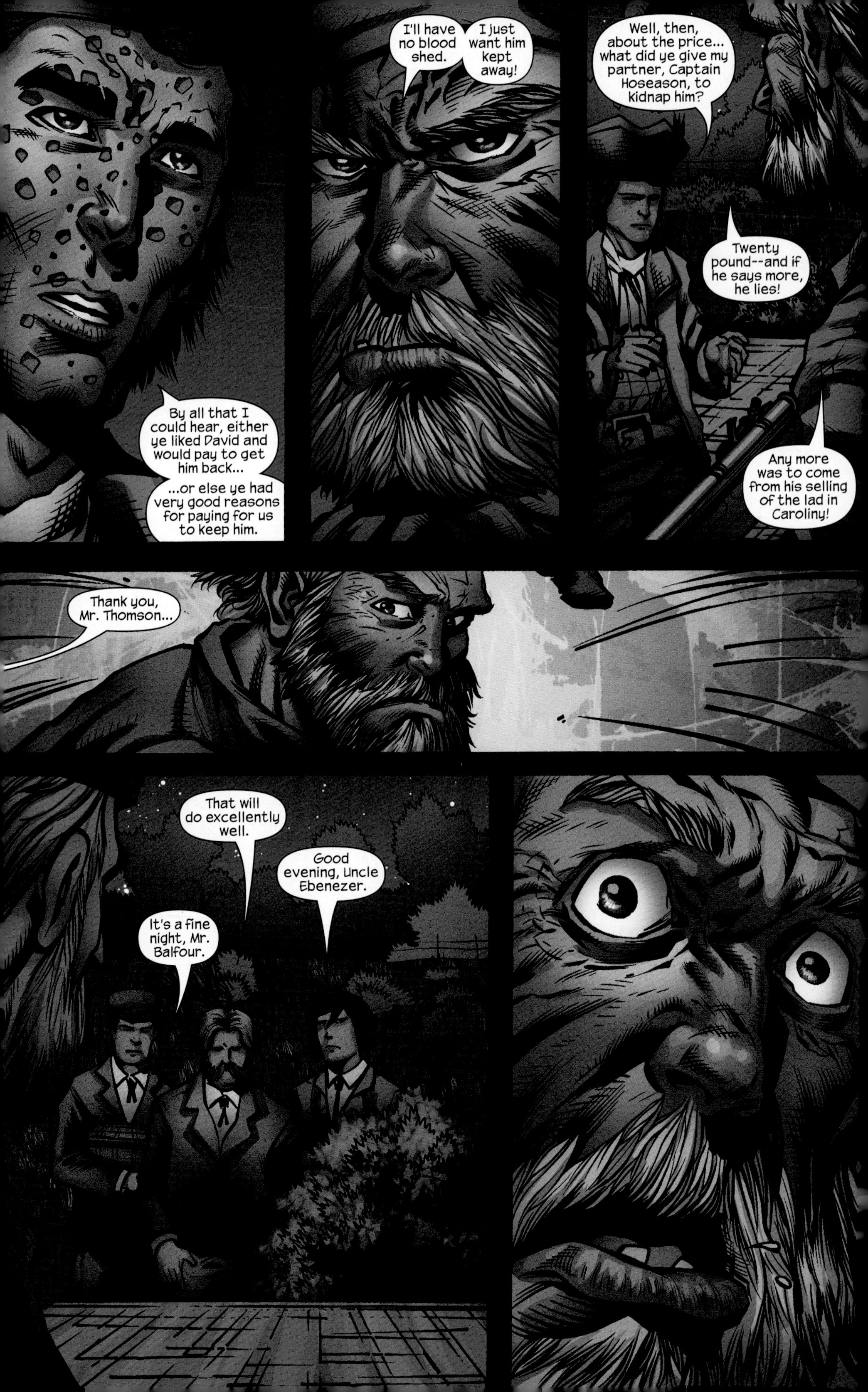
By all that I could hear, either ye liked David and would pay to get him back...
...or else ye had very good reasons for paying for us to keep him.
I'll have no blood shed.
I just want him kept away!
Well, then, about the price... what did ye give my partner, Captain Hoseason, to kidnap him?
Twenty pound--and if he says more, he lies!
Any more was to come from his selling of the lad in Caroliny!
Thank you, Mr. Thomson...
That will do excellently well.
It's a fine night, Mr. Balfour.
Good evening, Uncle Ebenezer.

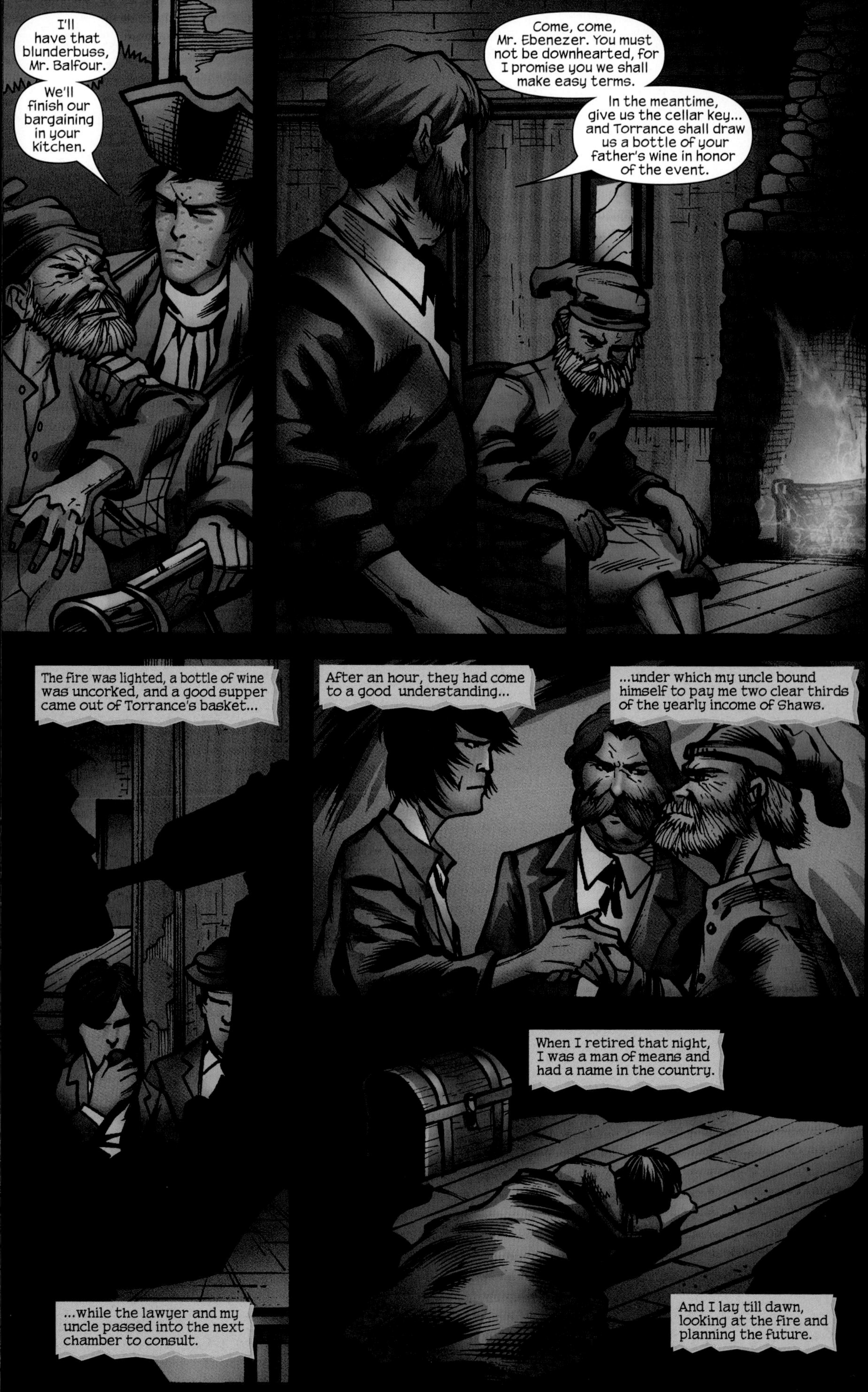

I'll have that blunderbuss, Mr. Balfour.
We'll finish our bargaining in your kitchen.
Come, come, Mr. Ebenezer. You must not be downhearted, for I promise you we shall make easy terms.
In the meantime, give us the cellar key... and Torrance shall draw us a bottle of your father's wine in honor of the event.
The fire was lighted, a bottle of wine was uncorked, and a good supper came out of Torrance's basket...
...while the lawyer and my uncle passed into the next chamber to consult.
After an hour, they had come to a good understanding...
...under which my uncle bound himself to pay me two clear thirds of the yearly income of Shaws.
When I retired that night, I was a man of means and had a name in the country.
And I lay till dawn, looking at the fire and planning the future.

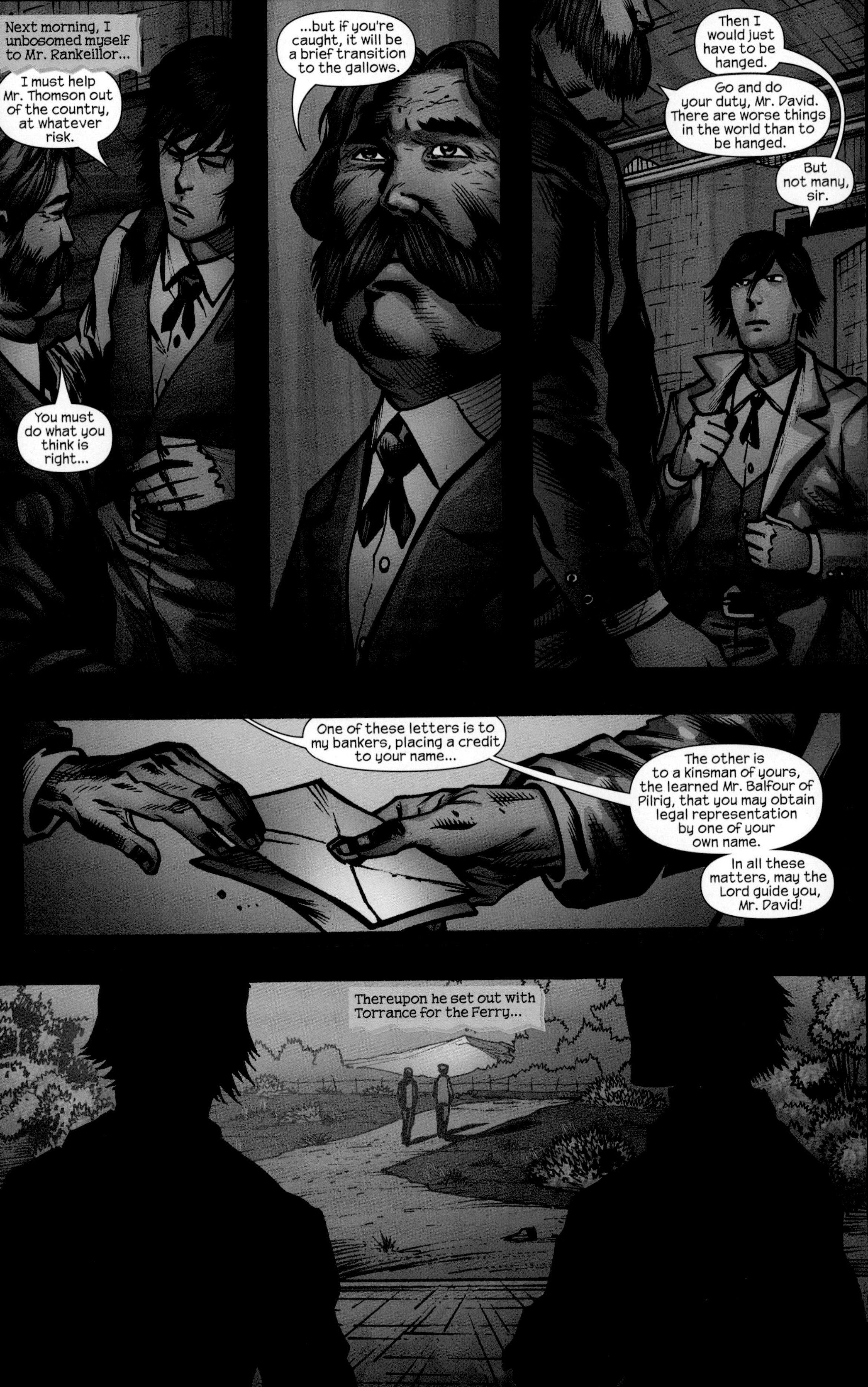
Next morning, I unbosomed myself to Mr. Rankeillor...
I must help Mr. Thomson out of the country, at whatever risk.
You must do what you think is right...
...but if you're caught, it will be a brief transition to the gallows.
Then I would just have to be hanged.
Go and do your duty, Mr. David. There are worse things in the world than to be hanged.
But not many, sir.
One of these letters is to my bankers, placing a credit to your name...
The other is to a kinsman of yours, the learned Mr. Balfour of Pilrig, that you may obtain legal representation by one of your own name.
In all these matters, may the Lord guide you, Mr. David!
Thereupon he set out with Torrance for the Ferry...

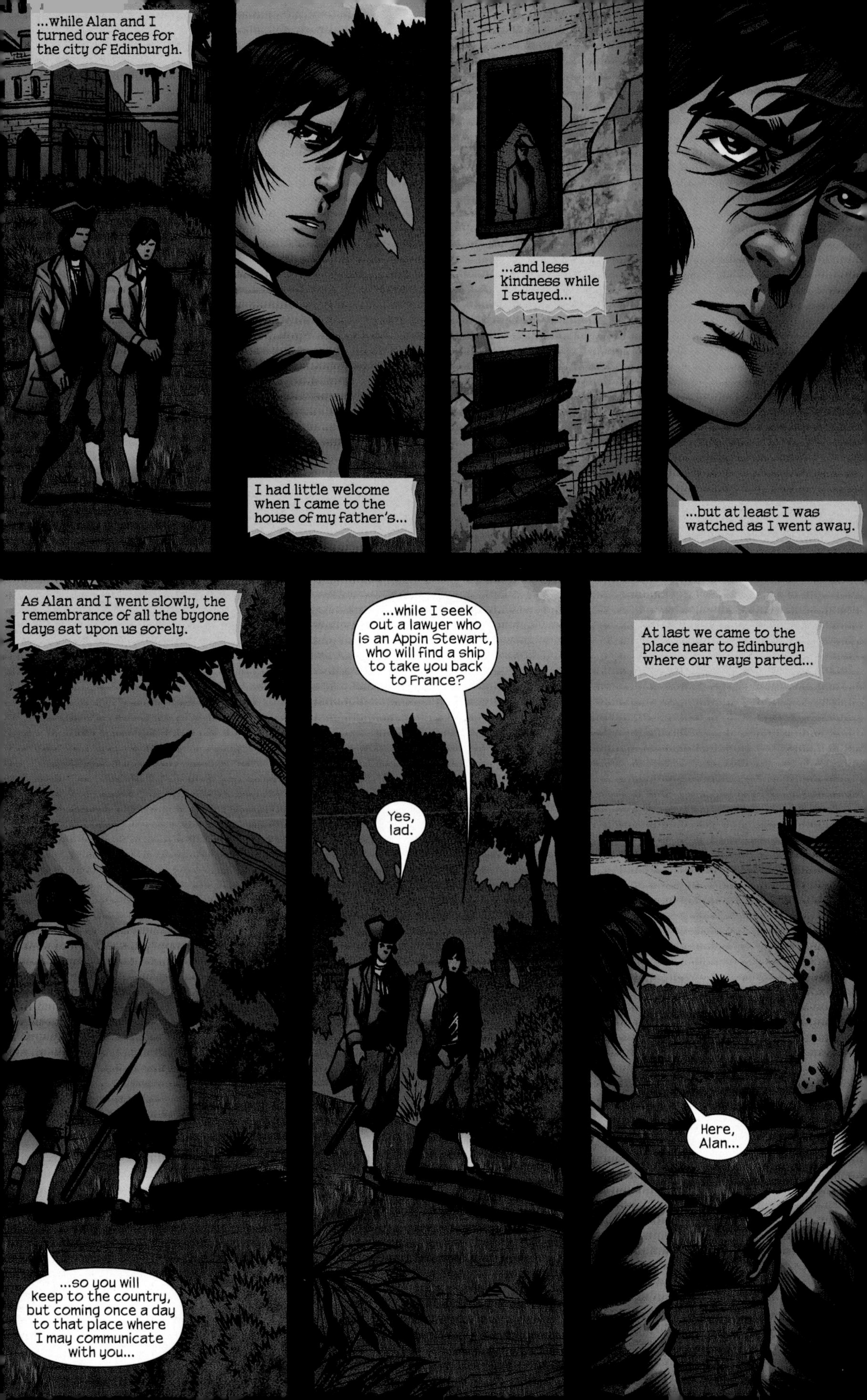
...while Alan and I turned our faces for the city of Edinburgh.
I had little welcome when I came to the house of my father's...
...and less kindness while I stayed...
...but at least I was watched as I went away.
As Alan and I went slowly, the remembrance of all the bygone days sat upon us sorely.
...so you will keep to the country, but coming once a day to that place where I may communicate with you...
...while I seek out a lawyer who is an Appin Stewart, who will find a ship to take you back to France?
Yes, lad.
At last we came to the place near to Edinburgh where our ways parted...
Here, Alan...

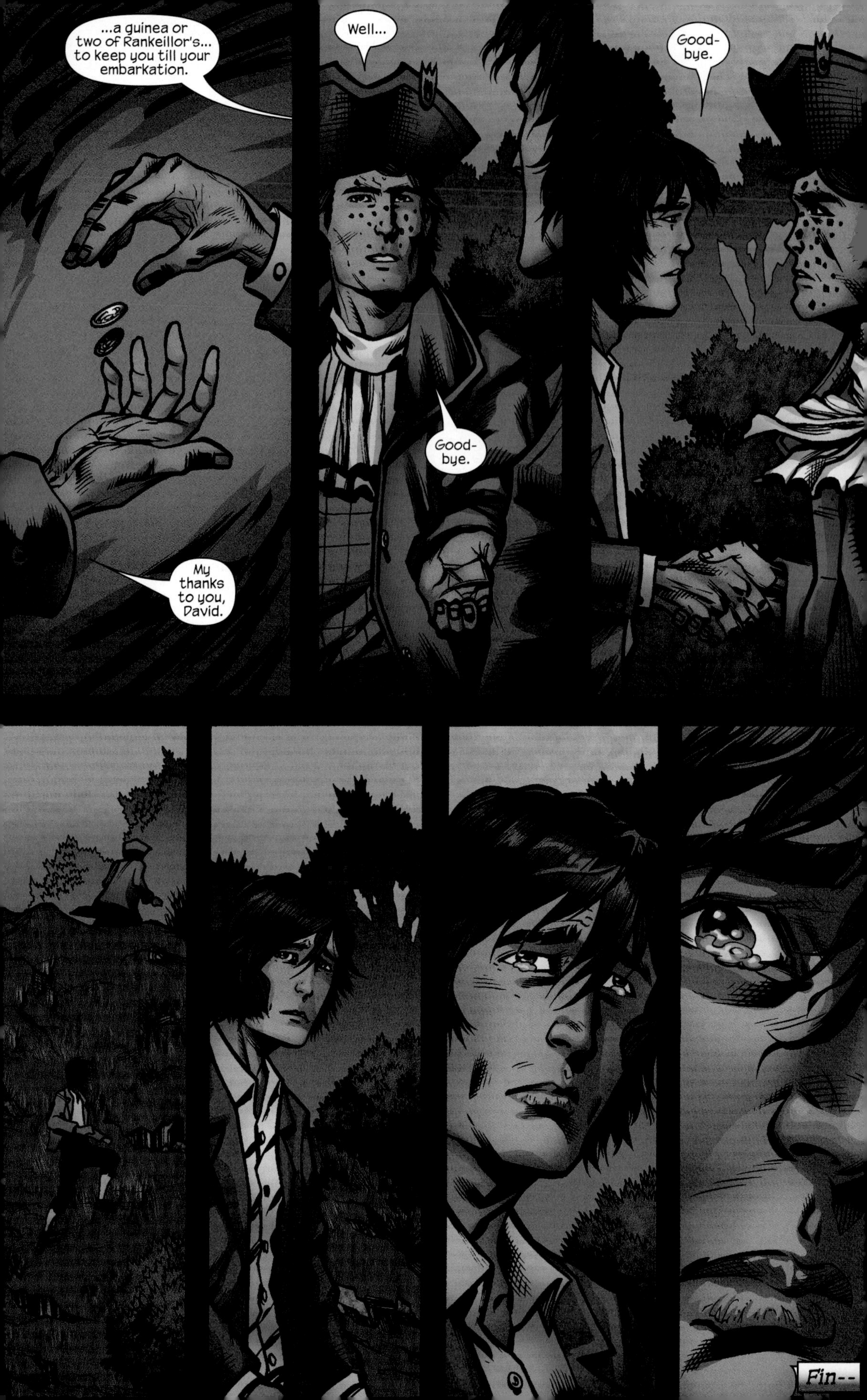

...a guinea or two of Rankeillor's... to keep you till your embarkation.
My thanks to you, David.
Well...
Good-bye.
Good-bye.
Fin--

Robert Louis Stevenson: His Life's Work
by Michael Hoskin

Born November 13, 1850 in Edinburgh, Scotland, Robert Louis Balfour Stevenson was the son of lighthouse engineer Thomas Stevenson and Margaret Balfour, a minister's daughter. Robert suffered from bouts of sickness in his childhood; sadly, he would grapple with maintaining his health for the rest of his life. Although his father intended for him to become an engineer, Robert chose to become a writer and began publishing essays in his 20s, with his first short stories published in 1877 and collected in 1882 as *New Arabian Nights*. His early short stories included the thriller *Sire De Maletroit's Door* (1877) and two adventures of Prince Florizel: *the Suicide Club* and *The Rajah's Diamond* (both 1878). In 1879 he published *Travels With a Donkey* a travelogue recounting his journeys in France. In 1880, Robert married US citizen Fanny Vandegrift Osbourne, who already had two children (Isobel and Lloyd) from a previous marriage.

It was with his new roles as a husband and a father that Robert's promise as a writer began to take shape. While fabricating a tale of pirates for Lloyd, Robert wound up penning his first novel, *Treasure Island*, published in 1883. This classic tale of young Jim Hawkins matching wits against Long John Silver remains one of his most famous works with more than fifty film adaptations. Additional works followed, notably including the historical adventure novel *Black Arrow* (1883) set in the War of the Roses, his short story recounting grave robbing entitled *The Body Snatcher* (1884), the political intrigue *Prince Otto* (1885), the tense short story thriller *Markheim* (1885) and his collection of poetry for children *A Child's Garden of Verses* (1885), which included the poem "My Shadow." In 1885 he collaborated with Fanny in *More New Arabian Nights* and with Lloyd wrote the novels *The Wrong Box* (1889), *The Wrecker* (1892) and *the Ebb-Tide* (1894).

However, it is the 1886 novella *the Strange Case of Dr. Jekyll and Mr. Hyde* which is Stevenson's best-known work. Inspired by a nightmare the author had experienced, it delved into the story of Dr. Jekyll and his mysterious friend Mr. Hyde, whose relationship to Jekyll is nearer than anyone surmises. Stevenson's tale of one man's inner wickedness has inspired more than one hundred film adaptations to this day.

Also in 1886, Stevenson published the novel *Kidnapped*, the adventure tale of David Balfour who escapes from near-slavery to clash with Jacobites in the 1750s.

In 1890, Stevenson moved his family to Upolu in the Samoan islands, establishing the estate of Vailima. In Samoa, Stevenson was beloved by the locals as Tusitala ("Story Writer"). His later works included the collections *The Merry Men* (1887) and *Island Nights Entertainments* (1893), which included *The Bottle Imp*, a tale of the miseries inflicted by magical wishes and *The Beach of Falesa*, a South Seas tale of competing store owners, one of whom uses superstitions to his advantage; the novels *the Master of Ballantrae* (1889), an adventure tale which drew on many of his interests, including pirates and the Jacobite, uprising and *Catriona* (1893), a sequel to *Kidnapped* which brought back its hero David Balfour; *Underwoods* (1887), *Ballads* (1891) and *Songs of Travel and Other Verses* (1896), each collections of verses; the essay collection *Memories and Portraits* (1887); and the travelogue *Silverado Squatters* (1883) which recounted his visits to the United States around the time of his wedding.

Stevenson died suddenly on December 3, 1894, only forty-four years old. He was buried on Upolu. His tomb included lines from his poem "Requiem:"

> "Here he lies where he longed to be;
> Home is the sailor, home from sea,
> And the hunter home from the hill."

On the very day of his death, Stevenson was in the midst of penning his novel *The Weir of Hermiston*; although it was later published in 1896 and was highly regarded for the strength of his story, it was left incomplete at the very mid-sentence where Stevenson broke off; it remains incomplete to this day. His other work-in-progress, *St. Ives,* was completed by Arthur Quiller-Couch and published in 1897.

Robert Louis Stevenson's works have made occasional forays into the medium of comic books. In addition to Roy Thomas and Mario Gully's adaptation of *Kidnapped*, Marvel has also adapted the tale to comics format as *Marvel Classics Comics #27* (1977) by Bill Mantlo and Dino Castrillo. *Treasure Island* was adapted by Doug Moench and Peter Lijauco in *Marvel Classics Comics #15* (1976) and in Roy Thomas and Mario Gully's *Marvel Illustrated: Treasure Island* (2007-08). *The Strange Case of Dr. Jekyll and Mr. Hyde* inspired the Marvel Comics super-villain Mr. Hyde, created by Stan Lee and Don Heck and debuted in *Journey into Mystery #99* (1963); the story itself was adapted by Ron Goulart and Winslow Mortimer in *Supernatural Thrillers #4* (1973) and *Marvel Classics Comics #1* (1976) by Kin Platt and Nestor Redondo and inspired a parody by Bill Everett in *Wild #1* (1954). Jekyll and Hyde also figured into the inspiration of Stan Lee and Jack Kirby's monster hero the Hulk in *Incredible Hulk #1* (1963).

*University librarian **Michael Hoskin** is a contributing writer to Marvel Comics including the* Official Handbook of the Marvel Universe, Official Index of the Marvel Universe *and the* Marvel Atlas. *He is also a distant relation of Robert Louis Stevenson.*

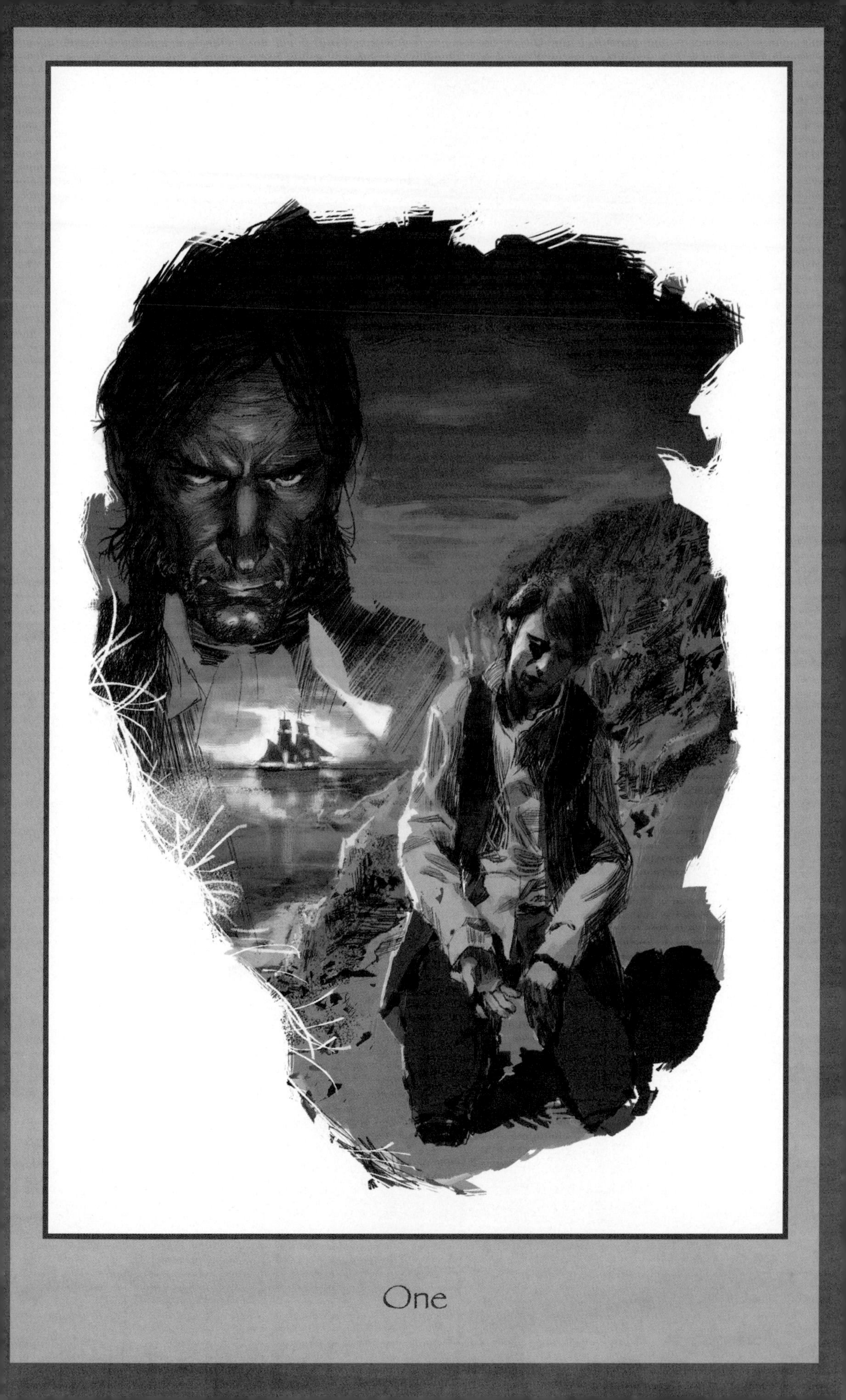

One

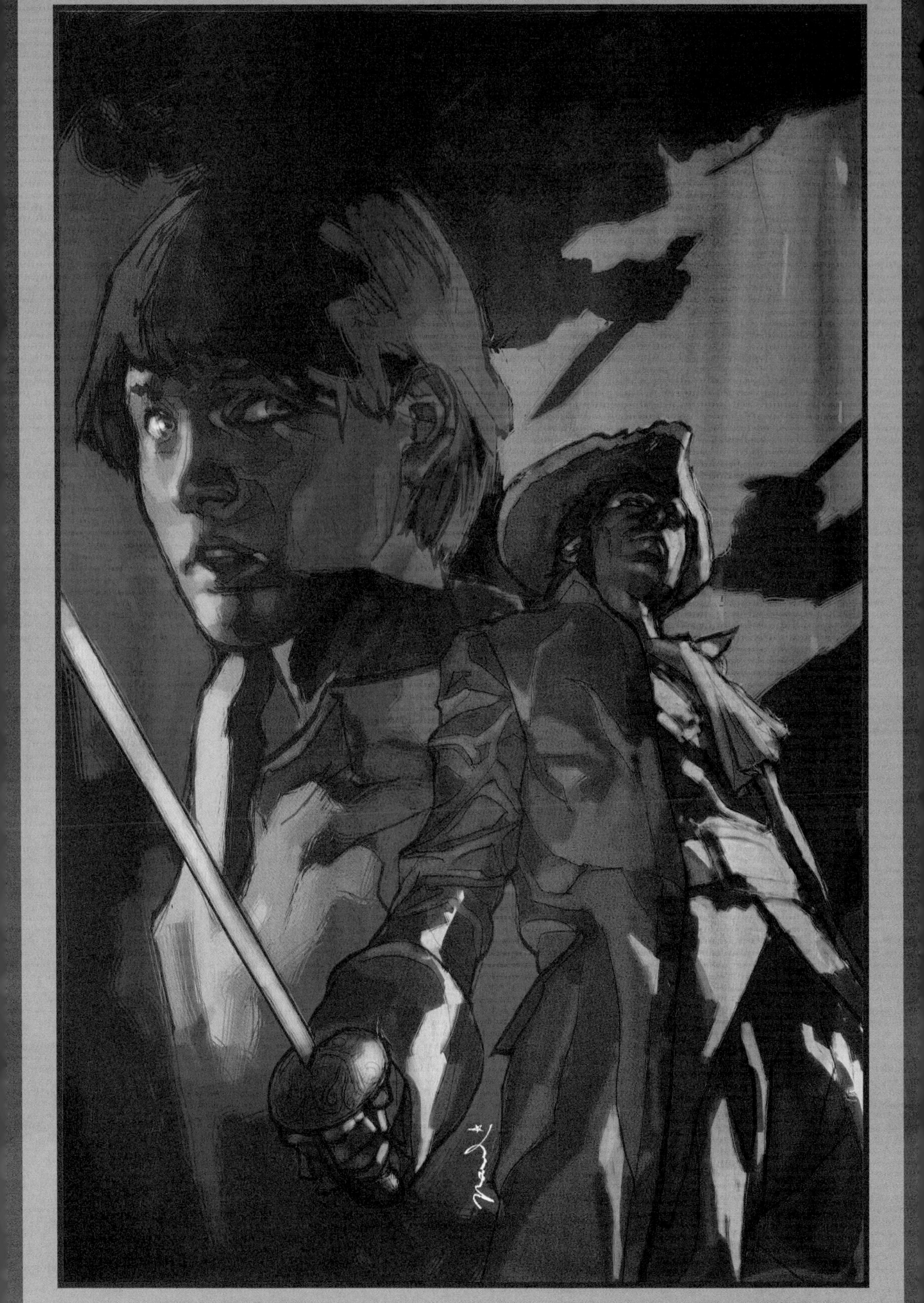

Two

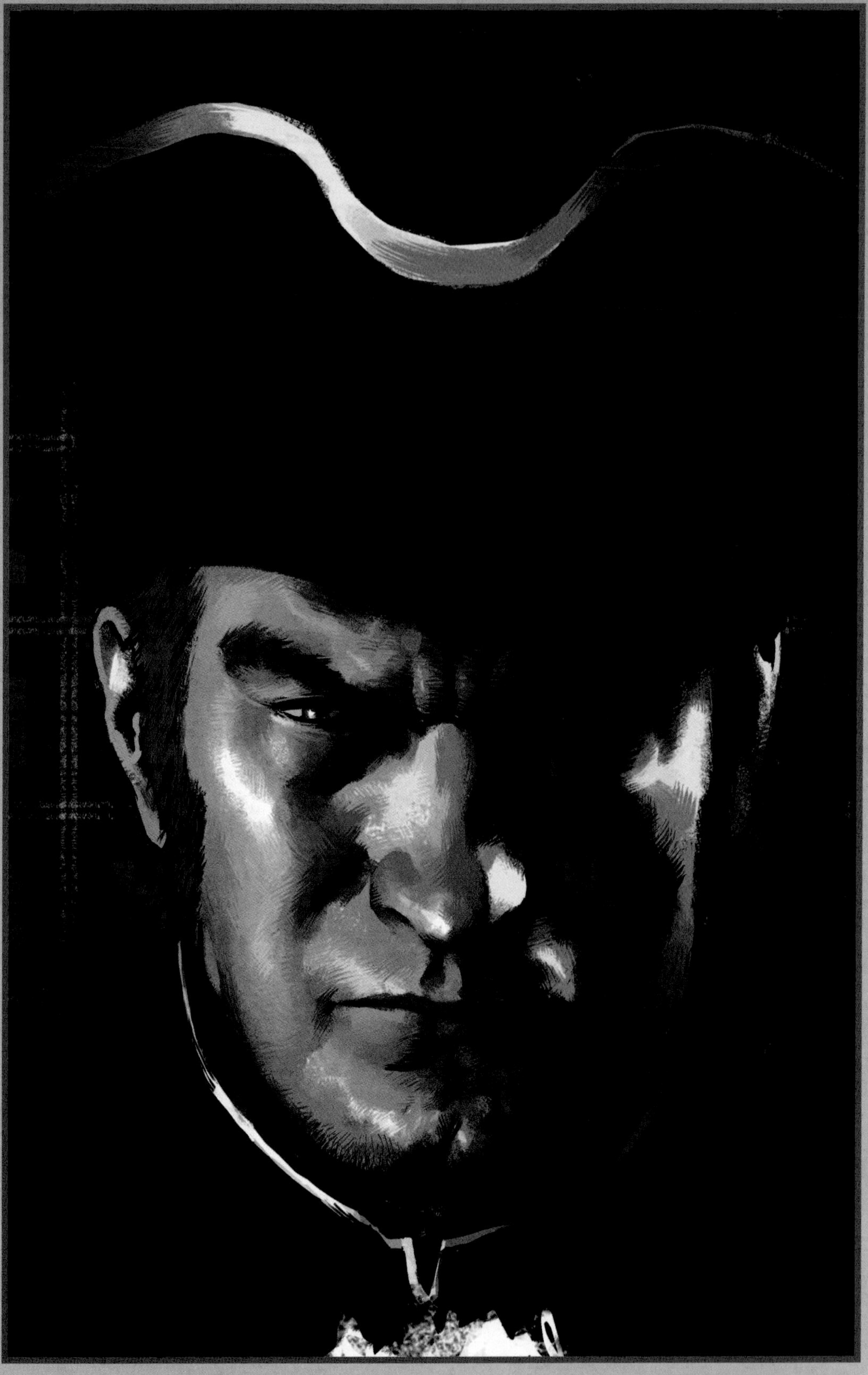

Three

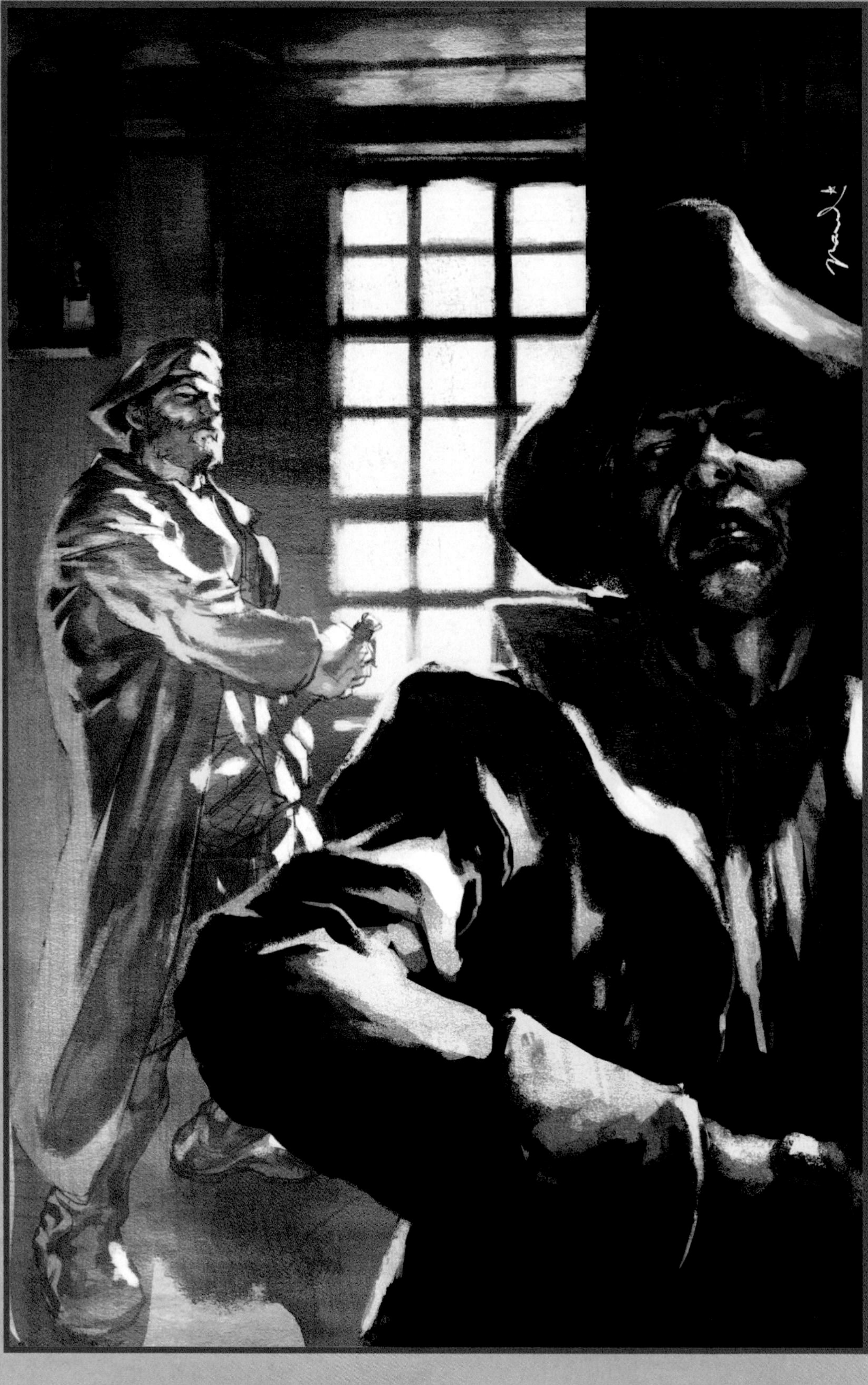

Four

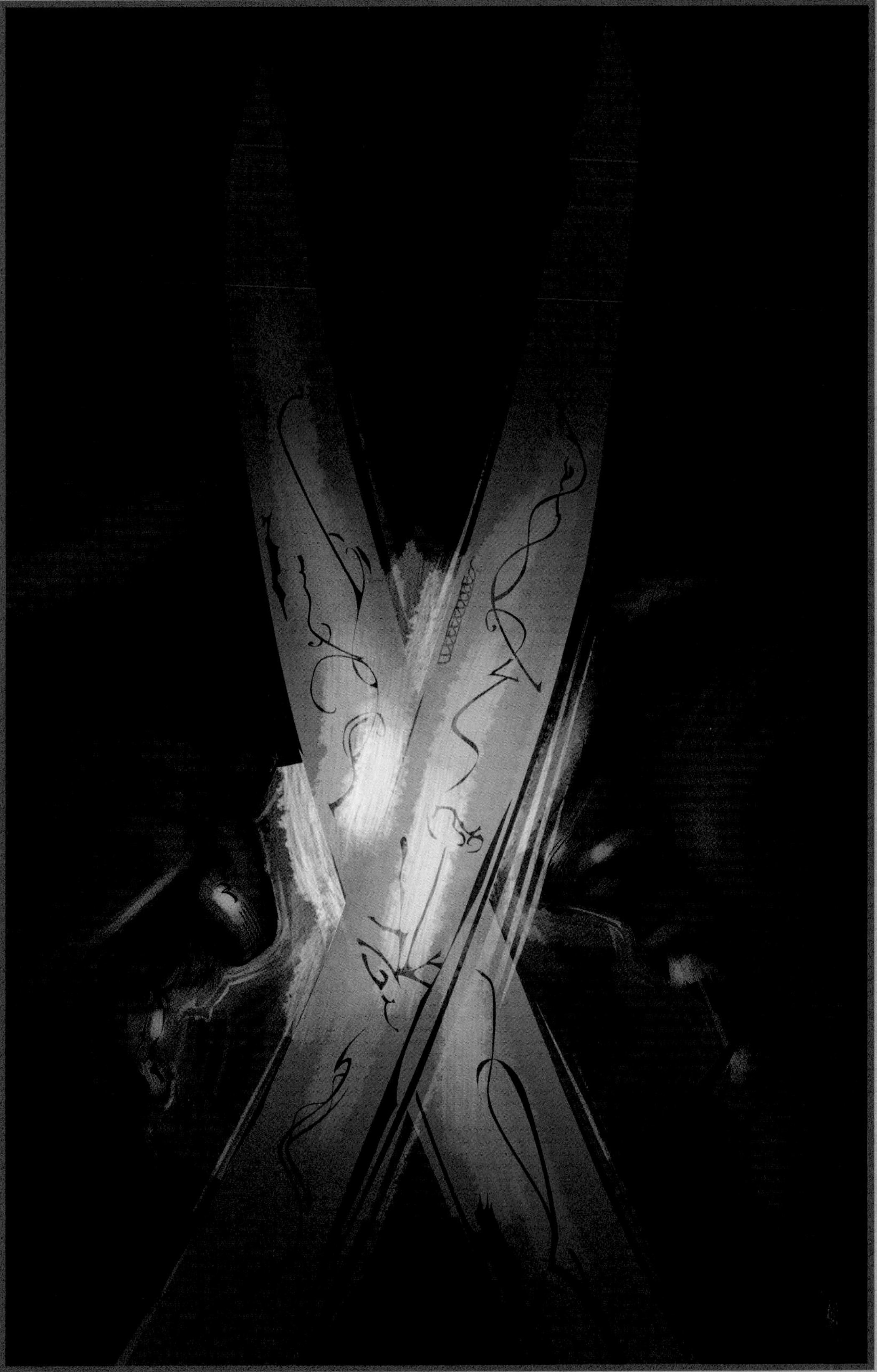

Five

The Glossary of Kidnapped!

anchorage – part of a harbor suitable for anchoring

ballad – any light, simple song expressing sentiment

bonnie – pleasing to the eye

brig – a two-masted vessel square-rigged on both masts

chapbook – a small book or pamphlet of popular tales

cutlass – a short, heavy, slightly curved sword with a single cutting edge

fife – a high-pitched flute

ford – the part of a river or other body of water that is shallow enough to walk through

hornpipe – a clarinet that uses one ox horn

indignation – displeasure toward anything offensive or insulting

inheritance – property or other form of wealth passing to an heir at the time of owner's death

jest – joke or a witty remark

harry – to harass, annoy, or prove a nuisance by repeated attacks

kiln – a furnace for baking (usually clay)

kinsfolk – people of the same family

laird – person who owns land

lassie – a young girl

manse – a house occupied by a landholder

miserly – behavior that lacks generosity

peat – vegetable matter that decays in marshy or damp regions

plaid – a long piece of cloth

pound – the basic monetary unit of the United Kingdom

reputable – considered with honor and respect

scabbard – a sheath for a dagger or sword

semblance – a likeness in outward aspect or appearance

skiff – a boat small enough for sailing or rowing by one person

trifle – a small quantity or amount

trudge – to walk laboriously or wearily

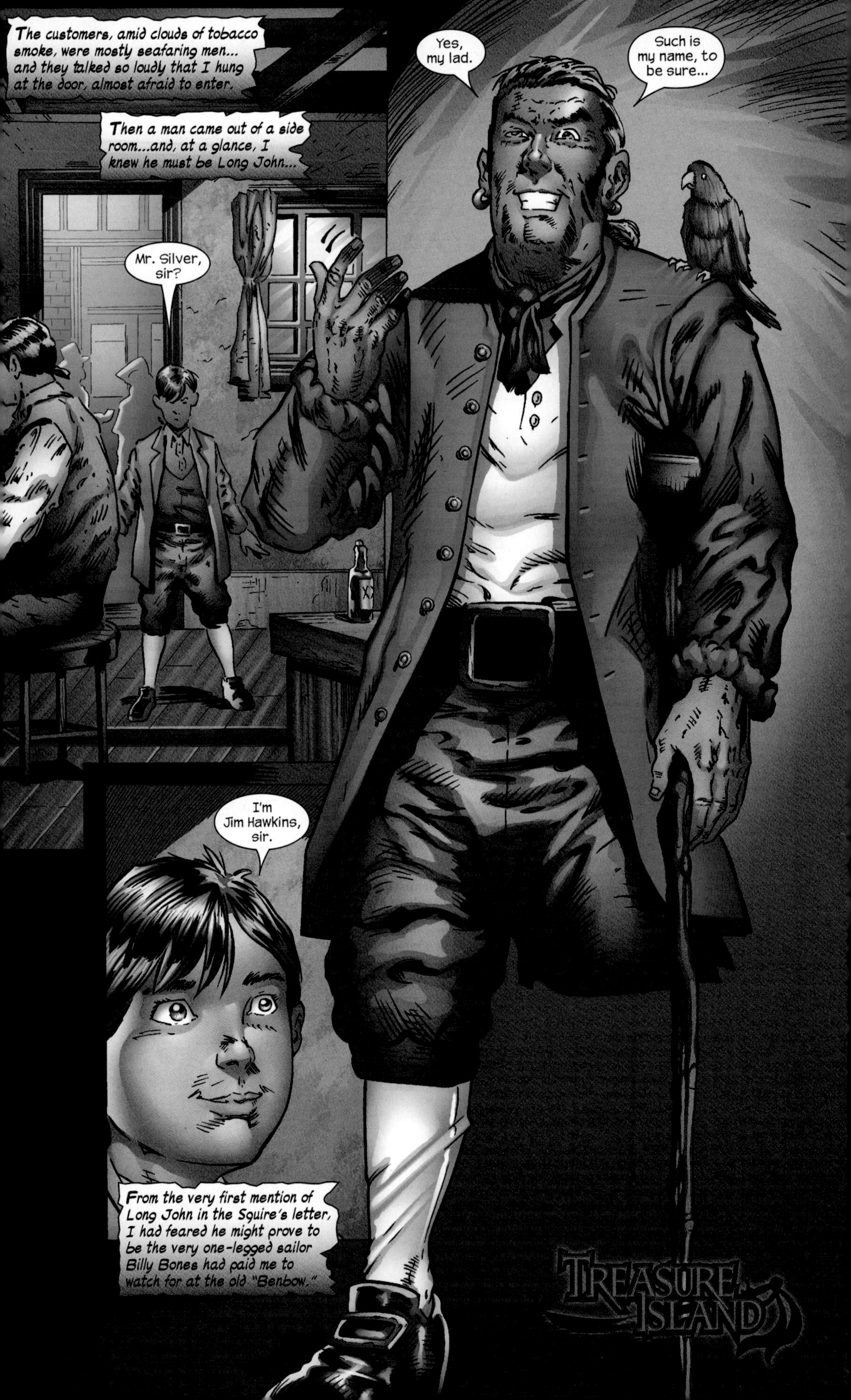
The customers, amid clouds of tobacco smoke, were mostly seafaring men... and they talked so loudly that I hung at the door, almost afraid to enter.
Then a man came out of a side room...and, at a glance, I knew he must be Long John...
Mr. Silver, sir?
Yes, my lad.
Such is my name, to be sure...
I'm Jim Hawkins, sir.
From the very first mention of Long John in the Squire's letter, I had feared he might prove to be the very one-legged sailor Billy Bones had paid me to watch for at the old "Benbow."
TREASURE ISLAND

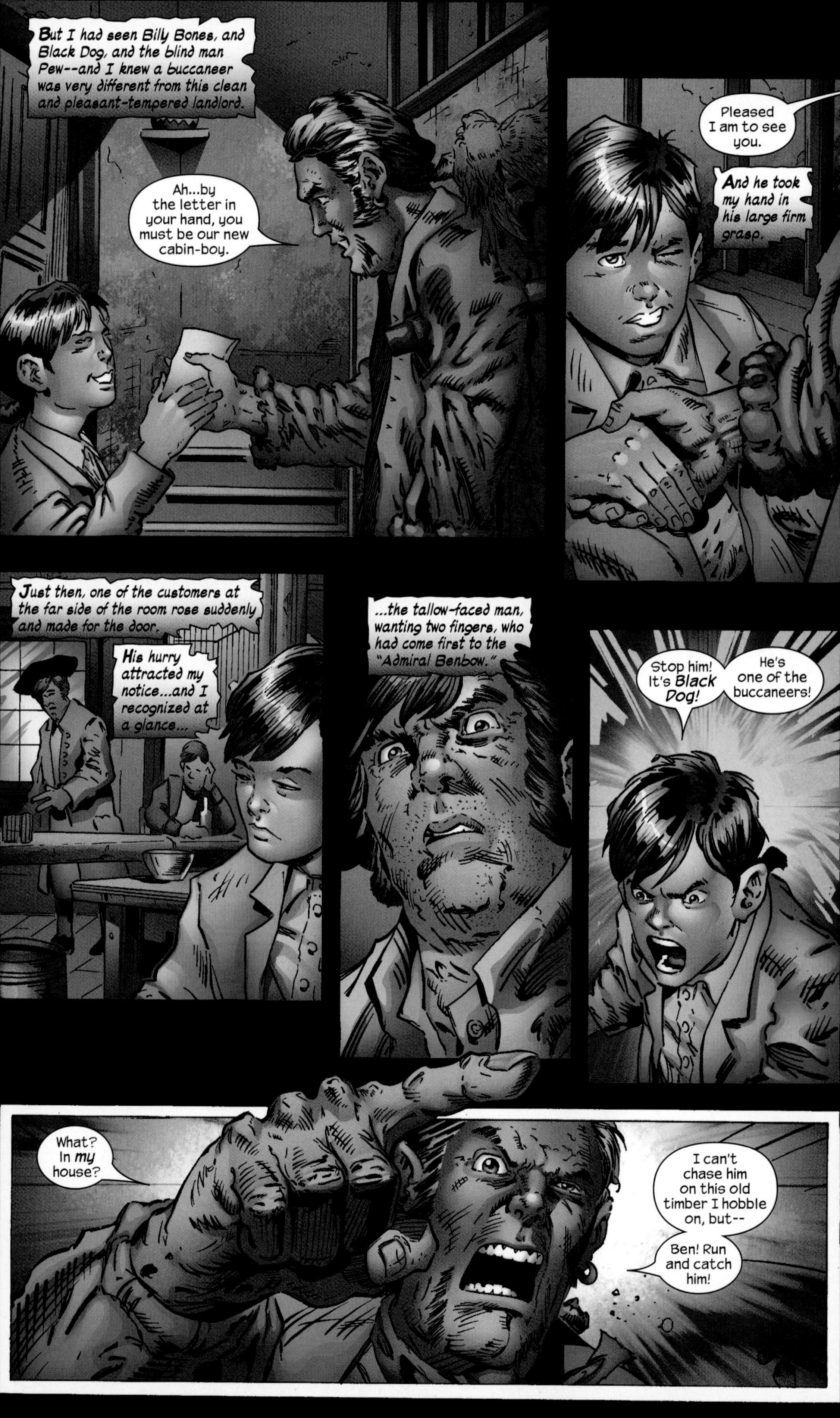
But I had seen Billy Bones, and Black Dog, and the blind man Pew--and I knew a buccaneer was very different from this clean and pleasant-tempered landlord.
Ah...by the letter in your hand, you must be our new cabin-boy.
Pleased I am to see you.
And he took my hand in his large firm grasp.
Just then, one of the customers at the far side of the room rose suddenly and made for the door.
His hurry attracted my notice...and I recognized at a glance...
...the tallow-faced man, wanting two fingers, who had come first to the "Admiral Benbow."
Stop him! It's Black Dog!
He's one of the buccaneers!
What? In my house?
I can't chase him on this old timber I hobble on, but--
Ben! Run and catch him!

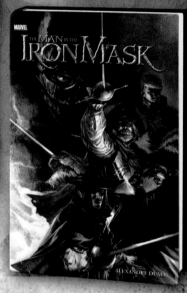